Self-guided Salzburg &
The Sound of Music

Written and researched by BRETT HARRIMAN

2017

Brett Harriman — Travel Publishing, April 2017.

Copyright © 2017 Brett Harriman. All rights reserved.

No part of this book may be reproduced, stored in a retrieval system, or transmitted by any means — electronic, mechanical, photocopying, recording or otherwise — without written permission from the author.

ISBN: 978-1-5452971-6-2

Printed in the United States of America.

All maps either hand-drawn or designed by © Brett Harriman.

Pictures used throughout the interior of this book were taken by © Brett Harriman, unless otherwise noted.

One particular subject (p. 24-25) sweethearts should embrace. Have your own padlock custom engraved before you hit the road and surprise your significant other by attaching it to the bridge while in Salzburg.

Cover created by © Brett Harriman.

Pictures on the front cover of this guide capturing the floral and architectural beauty of old-town Salzburg were provided by the fab folks at © Salzburg Tourism (www.salzburg.info). Back-cover pictures were shot by © Brett Harriman.

Although Harriman has exhaustively researched the latest information before press time, he accepts no responsibility for stolen street signs, schedule changes, union strikes, late trains, hangovers, overcooked schnitzel, traffic jams, lacking the use of common sense, bad weather, loss of property, inconvenience or injury sustained by any person using this guidebook. It is always prudent to be prepared and confirm all travel information before departure.

GPS data is provided for reference only. Harriman is not responsible for malfunctioning satellites or erroneous coordinates.

All comments, tips, suggestions, or whatever it is you want to get off your chest, please email: Brett@BrettHarriman.com

Please review us on the Web. As a small business, we get pumped about the little things. That's why positive support and word-of-mouth from our readers means the world to us. It let's us know how we're doing, thus we'd greatly appreciate it if you could share your experience about this book by typing a brief review on *Amazon*. If you've enjoyed a particular Salzburg site because of our attention to it, please mention Harriman in your *TripAdvisor* comment. Thanks in advance!

Tour Europe with Brett Harriman(.com). *Pick a tour, pack your bags.*

Salzburg & The Sound of Music

Self-guided

Contents

Salzburg Introduction & Orientation ... **1-10**
  Free Salzburg ... **11**
  Sights ... **11**
    Mozartplatz to Mirabell, Do-It-Yourself Old Town Tour ... **11-28**
    More Sights & Self-guided Tours ... **29-47**
      Best Views & Hikes ... **47**
        Shopping ... **49**
          Entertainment ... **52**
            Good Eats ... **56**
              Good Sleeps ... **62**
                Excursions ... **73**

Oberndorf (*Silent Night, Holy Night*) ... **74**

Werfen (Ice Caves, Medieval Fortress) ... **75**

Salzkammergut (Lake District) ... **79-93**
  Fuschlsee ... **79**
    Wolfgangsee ... **80**
      Mondsee ... **85**
        Hallstatt (on Hallstätter See) ... **86**

The Sound of Music, Do-It-Yourself ... **94**
  Walking Tour: University Platz to Mirabell ... **98**
    Driving Tour: Anif to Moon Lake ... **106**

Tour Europe with Harriman ... **118**

Guidebook: This guidebook is updated every year. It is the very latest resource on Salzburg, the lake district, and DIY Sound of Music to hit the market. (In essence, there is no single regularly printed guidebook regarding these sites and attractions that is more current and comprehensive than this resource.) While many publishers of guidebooks update their material every so often, Brett Harriman is as consistent as the resplendent beds of tulips blossoming every spring in the gardens at Schloss Hellbrunn. Although some details will invariably change after the research has been logged, the vast majority of information is accurate and reliable. Harriman personally visit the sites contained within this guidebook every autumn and therefore it is released with the utmost "freshness" for the coming year. Moreover, it is designed for you to travel like a local, to save time and money, to experience an enjoyable and authentic trip, while leading to new adventures and acquaintances along the way. Thank you for your support, and please tell others about Brett Harriman.

24-hour clock: Please note when using this guidebook, Harriman has written all times using the 24-hour clock. Europeans exclusively use this system to keep time. Here are the conversions.

Temperature: Additionally, Europeans use the Celsius scale to measure temperature: 0°C being the freezing point of water and 100°C the boiling point of water. For those of us who use the Fahrenheit scale, the easiest way to estimate Celsius to Fahrenheit is to double the Celsius number and add 30. For example, let's say the weather report calls for a high of 20°C, thus double it (40) then add 30, equaling 70(°F). It's not perfect, but pretty darn close. Now you try.

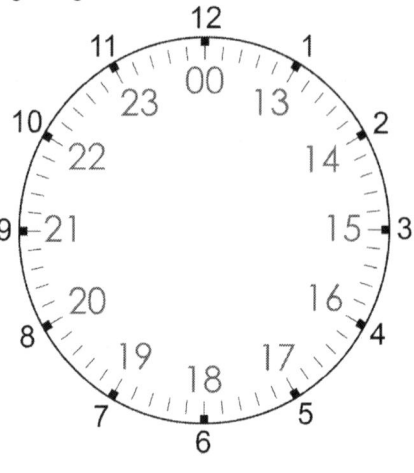

1:00 = 1 a.m.	13:00 = 1 p.m.
2:00 = 2 a.m.	14:00 = 2 p.m.
3:00 = 3 a.m.	15:00 = 3 p.m.
4:00 = 4 a.m.	16:00 = 4 p.m.
5:00 = 5 a.m.	17:00 = 5 p.m.
6:00 = 6 a.m.	18:00 = 6 p.m.
7:00 = 7 a.m.	19:00 = 7 p.m.
8:00 = 8 a.m.	20:00 = 8 p.m.
9:00 = 9 a.m.	21:00 = 9 p.m.
10:00 = 10 a.m.	22:00 = 10 p.m.
11:00 = 11 a.m.	23:00 = 11 p.m.
12:00 = 12 p.m.	00:00 = midnight

Salzburg Old Town as seen from Kapuzinerberg ©Brett Harriman

Salzburg

Population: 154,000 • **Elevation:** 450 m (1,480 ft)
Country-Area code: +43-(0)662 • **License plate:** S

In 45 A.D. Romans granted municipal status to "Iuvavum," a majestic outpost on the banks of a jade-green river that bisected the forested Mönchsberg (Monks' Ridge) and Kapuzinerberg (Capuchins' Ridge). It wasn't long before the region's valuable salt deposits were discovered. The Romans used salt as a food preservative and a commodity to barter goods. They even paid their legionnaires with the "white gold"; hence the term we use today, "salary" (from the Latin "salarium," referring to the salt allotment issued to Roman soldiers for money). Iuvavum blossomed and the population swelled to 4,000. By the year 488, the once vast and mighty Roman Empire had collapsed and Iuvavum fell to nomadic tribes.

In 696 A.D., the Catholic Church dispatched Bishop Rupert from the German city of Worms to form a diocese on the ruins of Iuvavum. He founded St. Peter's monastery, bringing peace, prosperity and Christianity to the region. From these pious roots came the first archbishop, Virgil, and the community's new name: Salzburg (meaning Salt Castle, first mentioned in 755). Appropriately, the jade-green river flowing through Salzburg was also given a name: Salzach, or Salt River—not because of any salt content, but for the prosperous river trade that transported the "white gold" downstream to the Inn River, which flowed into the Danube and eventually the Black Sea and into the coffers of powerful Asian rulers. Bishop Rupert's city of salt flourished, and Salzburg over the next 1,000 years became a wealthy archbishopric, an independent church state ruled by the resident Catholic prince-archbishop, not the Habsburg emperor seated in Vienna. Salzburg is Austria's only city that can claim its own history of autonomy from the imperial family.

In 1803, Napoleon's troops arrived and secularized the millennium-old diocese, forcing the last archbishop (Hieronymus von Colloredo) to flee to Vienna. It wasn't until 1816 that Salzburg actually became part of Austria.

More than a century later, Austria joined forces with Hitler's ill-fated Third Reich, consequently attracting swarms of Allied aircraft to the city of salt. From October 1944 till the end of World War II (May 1945), there were 16 bombing raids over Salzburg, totaling some 750 bombers (mainly B-24s), leaving 46% of the city's buildings either lightly or heavily damaged.

Today, Salzburg, the antique settlement on the Salt River and capital city of the Austrian province of the same name, has never looked better. What's more, since 1996, Salzburg's Altstadt has taken its place alongside the historic old towns of Bruges (Belgium), Dubrovnik (Croatia), and Florence (Italy) as an esteemed member of UNESCO's World Heritage List. For this reason, Salzburg's Old Town has largely been pedestrianized and its buses are mostly smog-free, powered by electricity (via overhead electrical lines).

According to a reliable source, 1 in 4 locals (including those who live in provincial ski resorts) work in the service and tourism industry, and the city's single biggest private employer outside of this broad field is the Stiegl Brewing company with some 700 employees. But tourism remains the city's No. 1 money-spinner, attracting nearly 7 million visitors per year. Next to the federal capital of Vienna, Salzburg is Austria's second most important tourist destination. I, your humble author, have personally escorted some 6,000 guests through Salzburg, and not one was ever disappointed! Now it is *your* turn to marvel at the majesty that is this magnificent municipality.

SALZBURG	Average Rainfall	Sun Hours	Average Temps	Highest / Lowest Temps
January	60 mm (2.36 in)	67	-1°C (30F)	16°C (61F) / -25.5°C (-14F)
February	55 mm (2.16 in)	91.9	1°C (34F)	22°C (72F) / -22°C (-7.5F)
March	79 mm (3.11 in)	130	5°C (41F)	25°C (77F) / -21.5°C (-7F)
April	83 mm (3.26 in)	152.6	8.5°C (47F)	28°C (82F) / -4°C (25F)
May	114.5 mm (4.5 in)	196.4	14°C (57F)	32°C (90F) / -2°C (28F)
June	155 mm (6.1 in)	193.9	17°C (63F)	35.5°C (96F) / 2°C (35.5F)
July	157.5 mm (6.2 in)	221.1	19°C (66F)	38°C (100F) / 4°C (39F)
August	151 mm (5.94 in)	202.8	18°C (64F)	35.5°C (96F) / 4°C (39F)
September	101 mm (3.97 in)	167.7	14°C (57F)	32°C (90F) / -1.5°C (29F)
October	72.5 mm (2.85 in)	129.7	9°C (48F)	28°C (82F) / -8°C (17.5F)
November	83 mm (3.26 in)	81.2	3.5°C (38F)	23.5°C (74F) / -18°C (-1F)
December	73 mm (2.87 in)	62.8	0.5°C (33F)	18.5°C (65F) / -27°C (-17F)

Climate, Salzburg (Salzburg Tourism kindly imparted the following text:) "The city of Salzburg is located next to the Prealps and therefore is very much influenced by the Alpine climate. Winters are usually quite cold and dry; snow can be found pretty often. Summers are hot and friendly, however, rainy periods occur and can last for a couple of days in the 'worst case.' Like with any trip, bringing an umbrella and rain jacket is no mistake—just in case you get acquainted with the famous 'Schnürlregen.'"

In the table above I've entered the results of a 30-year climate study (1971-2000) completed by the Austrian Institute of Meteorology (www.zamg.ac.at). The first three columns average the monthly (air) temperatures, rainfall and amount of sunshine hours in Salzburg over the three-decade period. The fourth column lists the air-temperature highs and lows for that particular month dating from 1971.

Suggested Itinerary — Use Salzburg as your base to tour regional attractions, thus I suggest at least a three-day stay. Mood and weather permitting, divide your time like so:

Day 1: At Mozartplatz set off on my self-guided orientation tour of the city (p. 11). Buy the Salzburg Card (p. 9) and visit sites of interest. Sound of Music fans, combine the aforesaid orientation tour with my SOM Walking Tour (p. 98). Conclude your day on the Stein Terrasse (p. 47) then dinner at St. Peter's Stiftskeller (p. 56), Zum Fideln Affen (p. 57), Bärenwirt (p. 57), or splurge on the Mozart Dinner Concert (p. 53). **Note:** With little time or sore feet, the yellow Hop On Hop Off sightseer bus circuiting the city may be worthwhile to you, otherwise know that all the important sights are listed in this guide for you to do on your own and that public transportation is efficient and 100-percent free with your Salzburg Card. **Rainy day ideas**, see page 10.

Day 2: Continue touring sites of interest with your Salzburg Card or head east for a day in the Salzkammergut (p. 79), conceivably the world's most beautiful lake district, locale of more Sound of Music sights.

Day 3: Consider a trip south to the village of Werfen to experience the lofty ice caves and medieval fortress (p. 75) or travel 25 km southwest to the Bavarian village of *Berchtesgaden (see my *Self-guided Munich, Ludwig's Castles & Hitler's Eagle's Nest* guide out later this year) to tour the Eagle's Nest, Königssee lake, and/or salt mines. (*If traveling by bus purchase the Bayern-Ticket, p. 6.) Back in Salzburg, consider an evening with the puppets at the Marionette Theater or perhaps take in a classical concert in the fortress or Mirabell Palace (p. 54).

Children: On vacation with the little ones and wondering what to do in town to pique their interest? See the boxed entry for Children on the next page.

👍 **Don't miss it!:** (Note: On my do-it-yourself orientation tour of Salzburg I walk you past, or point out, all of the following locations and listings.) Climb the **Glockenspiel** (p. 15) • admire the **Cathedral** (p. 16) • tour the **Fortress** (p. 17 & 33) • stroll through **St. Peter's Cemetery** (p. 18) and into **St. Peter's Church** (p. 19) • indulge in **St. Peter's Stiftskeller** (p. 56) • sample a chocolate **Mozart ball** (p. 49) • window-shop **Getreidegasse** (p. 50) • warm up to a shot at **Sporer wines & spirits** (p. 50) • marvel at the **Mirabell Gardens** (p. 26) • take a spell at one of Austria's most scenic café's, the **Stein Terrasse** (p. 47) • beer drinkers blow the froth off a couple at **Müllner Bräu** (p. 52) or the **Stiegl Keller** (p. 57) • and lastly, the **Salzburg Card** (p. 9) is a must-buy and your key to the city, thus it will open a whole other round of recommended sites and attractions, such as **Mozart's Birthplace** (p. 29), **DomQuartier** (p. 32), **Monchberg Lift** (p. 38), **Mozart's Residence** (p. 40), **Schloss Hellbrunn** (p. 41), **Untersberg cable car** (p. 44).

©Brett Harriman   BrettHarriman.com

☞ **Children:** Popular things kids enjoy to do, see, or eat in Salzburg are the **Fortress** (p. 17 & 33) • **Glockenspiel tour** (p. 15) • **Museum of Natural History** (p. 39) • **Schloss Hellbrunn and zoo** (p. 41-42) • **Hangar-7** (p. 43) • DIY **Catacombs tour** (p. 36) • **Marionette Theater** (p. 54) • DIY **Sound of Music tour** (p. 94—watch movie first at JUFA hostel-hotel, p. 63, combined with cafeteria-style dinner); **Mozart ball** (p. 49) • **Mönchsberg Hiking Trails** (p. 48) • **Untersberg cable car** (p. 44) • **Austria's longest toboggan run** (luge ride) combined with neighboring **salt mines** at Bad Dürrnberg (p. 46-47) • lunch/dinner at "**Café-Restaurant**" (p. 58), **Wilder Mann** (p. 58), **Bärenwirt** (p. 57), or **Bosna Grill** (p. 60).

Tourist Information, (www.salzburg.info • tel. 0662/8898-7330). Salzburg has two TIs, both offering help and advice to umpteen tourists every day. To complement this guidebook, stop by the TI and pick up a free city map. Staff also provide a room-finding service for a fee, or search free online via their Web site.

Old Town: The city's largest TI is on Mozartplatz, centrally located in the Old Town (closed Sunday Oct thru March, otherwise daily 9:00-18:00, July/Aug till 19:00). This main branch has an event ticket agency, and offers a (German-English) guided city tour (departing daily at 12:15, duration 60 min, pay guide 10€ adult or 8€ with Salzburg Card, and Mon-Sat at 14:00, duration 60-90 min, 12€/9.50€); see TI for details.

Railers, most convenient for you is the TI (daily 9:00-18:00, May/June & Sept 9:00-19:00, July/Aug till 19:30) located inside the main train station by the main entrance at Südtiroler Platz (look for green [i] symbol in passage on left heading to tracks 11-12 before exiting station). This branch also sells event tickets, e.g. concerts at Mirabell Palace.

Emergency Tel. Numbers, valid free Austria-wide, dial **122** for the Fire Department (Feuerwehr) • **133** for Police (Polizei) • **144** for Ambulance/Rescue.

Main Train Station, (www.oebb.at). Finally, after years of reconstruction, city officials recently pulled back the curtain revealing Salzburg's new and enlarged Hauptbahnhof (Hbf), originally dating from 1860. Thus, as you step off the train and make your way through the station, be sure to compliment its multimillion-euro shine. Pick up a free city map at the **tourist information office** (look for green [i] symbol in passage on left heading to tracks 11-12 before exiting station at Südtiroler Platz, daily 9:00-18:00, May/June & Sept 9:00-19:00, July/Aug till 19:30). **Toilets** (.50¢) and **lockers** (2€-4.50€/24hr) are located below track 5, in the main hall. The **ÖBB** (Reisezentrum) **train info** and **ticket purchase** office (Mon-Sat 5:30-21:15, Sun 6:30-21:15) are situated in the main hall straight inside the station's front entrance. Note that also represented in the ÖBB info office is a clerk from the **German rail authority**, Deutsche Bahn (DB), daily 7:20-19:10, imparting state rail info as well as selling tickets for Germany, e.g. the discounted Bayern-Ticket (see next page for details). Directly across from the ÖBB info and ticket office in the main hall is a **Spar grocery store** open seven days (Mon-Sat 6:00-23:00, Sun 8:00-23:00). Pick up **free Wi-Fi** inside the station by logging on to "OEBB-station" or you can find an **Internet** shop immediately outside the station (exit right, 3€/hr daily 8:00-23:00). Also outside the station is a McDonald's and Starbucks fronting the "Forum 1" **shopping mall** (exit front of station and angle right). Local **bus connections**, as well as those to Berchtesgaden, are out front of the station. **Taxis** are abundant and also out front. In the aforementioned shopping mall is a **pharmacy** (Apotheke Mon-Fri 8:00-18:00, Sat 8:00-12:00) and a large EuroSpar **supermarket** (all major CCs accepted, Mon-Fri 7:00-19:00, Sat 7:00-18:00). Lastly, outside the station and to the right, you'll discover a fast-food Burger King and just beyond it a **post office** (Mon-Fri 8:00-20:30, Sat 8:00-14:00, Sun 13:00-18:00). Getting to the **airport** from the station ride bus 2 (typically from platform D—check departures board). **Getting to the Old Town** from the station is a painless 20-min *walk, about 8€ by taxi, or ride bus 3, 5 or 6 (typically from platform C) headed direction Zentrum and get off after a handful of stops at Rathaus. *By foot, exit front of station, go left and continue straight along Rainerstrasse for some distance, eventually leading under the train tracks (this half of the walk is unattractive). A few cross streets farther, opposite the church, cut right through the enchanting Mirabell Gardens and traverse the river. **By train from Salzburg to Innsbruck** 2-hour trip (hourly 7:00-22:00); **Vienna** 3-hour trip (2/hr 7:00-22:00); **Berchtesgaden** 75-min trip (hourly with one change), or ride the cheaper and faster bus 840 (see Buses on next page), either way is valid with a Bayern-Ticket (see next entry for details); **Munich** 2-hour trip (2/hr 4:00-21:00), consider purchasing the Bayern-Ticket (explained below). **Note:** Because Salzburg is partnered with the German rail authority, special Deutsche Bahn train tickets (like the Bayern-Ticket) and Eurail passes that include Germany are valid to/fro Salzburg main train station at no additional cost. What's more, if you're traveling within Austria, purchase your ticket at least three days in advance and **save big** on the new **Sparschiene** fares! Go to the Austrian rail site (www.oebb.at), click to book your ticket and follow the prompts. By doing this, I've paid as little as 14€ one way from Salzburg to Innsbruck and 19€ to Vienna. Thus, there's no need to buy an Austrian Eurail pass anymore.

☞ The **Bayern-Ticket** is a terrific buy for individuals (25€) and small groups up to *five persons traveling for the day in 2nd-class seating on non-speed trains within the German state of Bavaria and to/fro Salzburg main train station. *(*The Bayern-Ticket costs an initial 25€ for the first person then add 6€ per person to a maximum of five persons, thus a two-person Bayern-Ticket costs 31€, three-person 37€, four-person 43€, five-person 49€.)* Although the latter ticket is specifically aimed at Bavaria, it's ideal from Salzburg if you're headed across the German border to, for example, Munich or Berchtesgaden, which many of you will be. For instance, you can visit the Bavarian capital for the day, travel on the city's trams and buses and subway as needed, then return to Salzburg main train station for the aforesaid bargain price of 25€ one person or 31€-49€ for small groups up to five persons. For travel to Berchtesgaden, however, the Bayern-Ticket is not recommended for one person since the day ticket sold by the driver of bus 840 is a better deal (see Buses on next page). The Bayern-Ticket is also ideal for parents (and grandparents) who can use it to travel with an unlimited number of their own children (or grandchildren) aged 14 and under. **Note:** The Bayern-Ticket is valid Mon-Fri *after* 9:00 until 3:00 (the following morning) and the whole day Sat/Sun in 2nd-class seating on non-speed trains (heading to/fro Salzburg Hauptbahnhof across the German border) and on all public transportation within Bavaria (but *not* Salzburg) for the pocket-friendly price of 25€ one person or 31€-49€ for small groups up to five persons. But for this price the ticket must be purchased either online (www.bahn.de, print invoice and bring it on train with your credit card) or from the driver of bus 840 (headed to Berchtesgaden) or at a German rail automat in Salzburg main train station (automats accept all major credit cards and are multilingual). To emphasize; if the ticket is bought over the counter you will pay a 2€ surcharge (i.e. 27€ for individuals and 33€-51€ for small groups), and even more if purchased on the train. The Bayern-Ticket is now available in the premier category of first-class seating (add roughly 12.50€ per person to the above-listed prices). Lastly, if you're holding a railpass, e.g. Eurail, you may not find the Bayern-Ticket such a bargain. Weigh your pass-type and destination against the price of the Bayern-Ticket.

Buses, (www.stadtbus.at). Salzburg isn't big enough to warrant a subway system, therefore an efficient and eco-friendly bus network (consisting of some 250 drivers operating 106 electric buses on 12 urban lines) does the trick. Most of the city's attractions can be found in the Old Town, or within walking distance of it, rendering public transportation for many travelers unnecessary. If you do require the service, however, the vast majority of my readers will be holding a valid Salzburg Card and therefore ride for free! Otherwise, bus fares are: **Short Trip Ticket** (Kurzstrecke) 1.30€—valid only for 2 stops on city buses and 1 stop on long-route buses such as Postbus. **1 Hour Ticket** (Stundenkarte)—good value, especially if you're bus busy within a 60-minute period—adult 2€ (or 2.50€ from driver), student 15-18yr 1.50€, youth 6-14yr 1€. **24-Hour Ticket** (24-Stundenkarte)—good for exactly 24 hours from time of validation—adult 4€ (or 5.70€ from driver), student 15-18yr 3€, youth 6-14yr 2€. And the **Week Pass** (Wochenkarte) 15.50€, not available for purchase from driver, is valid for exactly one week from first use and is transferable, meaning another person can use it. **Purchase tickets** at multilingual automats labeled Fahrscheine/Tickets/Salzburg Verkehr or at magazine/tobacco shops. Tickets purchased from the bus driver are prevalidated but cost more money! Small groups consider hailing a cab. **Note:** Stamp ticket in time box on bus to validate; watch locals. Children 5yr and younger ride free; senior discount only applicable with special Austrian railway reduction card. To signal the driver to *stop* the bus, push button on handrail or by exit door that will also trigger the door to open when the bus comes to a complete stop. And note that at Mirabellplatz (one of Salzburg's main transportation hubs) there are three different pick-up points; check posted schedule to make sure you're in the right place.

Bus 840 to Berchtesgaden (5.80€ one way, 50-min trip) departs typically Mon-Fri 8:15, 9:15, 10:15, (*summer also 10:45), 11:15, (*11:45), 13:05, 14:15, 15:15, (*15:45), 16:15, (*16:45), 17:15, 18:15, and Sat/Sun 9:15, 10:15, 11:15, (*12:15), 14:15, 15:15, (*16:15), 17:15 from opposite Salzburg's main train station (across street from "Forum 1" mall, or from **Mirabellplatz, Rathaus, and Mozartsteg a few minutes later. **Note that at Mirabellplatz there are three different pick-up points—you need to wait at the north end, i.e. the bus stop closest to main train station, but check schedule in advance for changes). If you're planning on returning to Salzburg, **purchase the day ticket** (Tageskarte adult 10€, youth 6-14yr 6.30€, family [2+2] 23.50€) from the driver, which will cover all your bus transportation for the day, including to/fro Salzburg and Obersalzberg (bus departure area for Eagle's Nest), as well as to the salt mines and Königssee lake (see my *Self-guided Munich, Ludwig's Castles & Hitler's Eagle's Nest* guide out later this year). But if you are a **small group** of 4 or 5 persons, buy the Bayern-Ticket (explained on previous page) directly from the driver of bus 840 to significantly increase savings. Note that during the week (Mon-Fri) the Bayern-Ticket is officially valid *after* 9:00. The ticket is also valid Sat/Sun but there is neither an 8:15 bus nor an early time restriction on weekends. **Note:** Bus 840 terminates at Berchtesgaden's train station, where buses depart roughly every 30 min to Obersalzberg and elsewhere around town.

Getting to Berchtesgaden: This picturesque Bavarian village is only 25 km southwest of Salzburg (on the German side of the border) and, as you are probably already aware, highly worth a visit, especially mid-May thru October when the Eagle's Nest is open. From Salzburg you have five ways to reach Berchtesgaden: train, bus, taxi, car, pricey tour. **By train:** If you're holding a Eurail consecutive-day or dated Flexi/Select pass, you ride free on the train: 75-min trip (hourly with one change). **By bus:** If you're not holding a discounted rail pass (and even if you are you may want to) forget the train and ride bus 840 to Berchtesgaden. It's quicker and cheaper, (see entry above). **By taxi:** From Salzburg's main train station it will cost around 50€ to Berchtesgaden and 60€ to Obersalzberg. **By car:** Exit A10 autobahn at Salzburg-Süd and head direction Grödig; follow this road straight all the way (roughly 14 km) to Berchtesgaden. But if you're coming from central Salzburg, you need to get to the southeast side of town and connect onto the Alpenstrasse; drive this straight to Berchtesgaden. **Pricey tour:** If interested, tours are available to Berchtesgaden from Salzburg; ask TI or staff at your digs for info.

Drivers/Parking: For street parking pay at nearby automat and leave ticket on car dashboard (applicable Mon-Fri 9:00-19:00, Sat/Sun 9:00-16:00, otherwise free). Price (automat) typically 60¢/30 min, max 3.90€/3hr. There are a few **parking garages** around town, but the best choice for new arrivals is the 24-hour underground **Altstadt Garage** at Hildmannplatz 1 with some 1,300 spaces (starting 1.20€/30 min, 2.40€/60 min, every 10 min thereafter 40¢, max 22€/24hr, CCs ok, but note that many shops in the Old Town can discount your parking ticket to 4€/4hr or 6€/8hr if you make a purchase [thus ask about ticket validation before shopping], or Sporer spirits p. 50 told me they would validate your parking ticket without having to purchase anything, just stop by, browse the liquid refreshment, and show this guide with your ticket). **Getting to the Altstadt Garage** is straightforward—exit A1 autobahn at "Salzburg Flughafen" and follow signs to Salzburg, then Mitte and Hotel route. After about 4 km of wending through city streets you will reach a giant cliff face and a tunnel funneling into Old Town—*don't* drive through tunnel! A short distance before it, on the right, is the entrance to garages A and B (either is fine but take B if possible). After parking, follow signs Festspielhäuser (Festival Halls p. 21) to the Toscaninihof opening to Old Town. (Sound of Music fans, both the Festival Halls and Toscanini Hof were used in the movie and are part of my DIY tour p. 98.) **Note:** Buy a beer and **park free** for the day after 14:40 (14:10 weekends) at Müllner Bräu (p. 52), found at Lindhofstrasse 7 north of the Old Town. Take ticket at gate and have beer cashier validate it with purchase. Drivers who wish to **avoid the city** entirely, leave your car at a **Park+Ride** on the outskirts and ride the bus in. There are two good choices: *Salzburg-Süd*, and *Designer Outlet*. To reach the latter, exit the A1 autobahn at Flughafen and drive direction Salzburg to the Outlet center. To reach the former P+R, exit the A10 autobahn at Salzburg-Süd and continue in the direction of Salzburg—after about 4 km follow TI and Park+Ride signs into parking lot. **At either P+R,** purchase the 15€ Kombiticket that covers your parking and a group bus ticket (up to 5 pers.) for the day.

Note: As a reminder, vehicles traveling on the Austrian autobahn are required to have a "Vignette," or toll sticker (p. 115).

The following examples of **traffic signs** can be commonly seen throughout Austria on its extensive network of roadways (for more examples, see page 116).

Do not enter | Closed to all vehicles | One-way street | No parking | No parking or stopping

Salzburg Airport, locally Flughafen (www.salzburg-airport.com; code: SZG; **free Wi-Fi**—log on to "Freeware"; **free** viewing terrace at terminal 1). Salzburg's W.A. Mozart Airport is idyllically nestled at the foothills of the Alps, which is a spectacular scene when flying to/fro the city of salt. Moving more than 1.7 million passengers annually, Salzburg airport is situated 5 km west of the Old Town with regular *bus connections or a **taxi** will cost roughly 15€ (depending on traffic and where

2017 edition   Salzburg Card   9

you're headed); *daily — bus #2, 25 min to/fro main train station or Mirabellplatz — bus #10, 20 min to/fro Old Town Hanuschplatz or Rathaus/Mozartsteg. **Note:** Consider purchasing the Salzburg Card; see info counter. Aviation aficionados, climb (64 steps) to the viewing terrace (Dachterrasse) at terminal 1 and/or visit Hangar-7 (p. 43) two bus stops (bus 2 direction city) from the main airport terminal.

Horse-Drawn Carriage, locally Fiaker. Romantic rides through the Old Town cost 44€/20-25 min or 88€/50 min, max 5 passengers. Carriages can readily be found on Residenzplatz (large gravel square with horse fountain), or if there's a festival in town they'll move to neighboring Domplatz (Cathedral Square). Note that rides double as a city tour, thus the better English your driver speaks the better your tour.

👍 **Salzburg Card:** I highly recommend you invest in the savings afforded by the Salzburg Card. You will not only gain unlimited use of public transportation within the metro area but also free *one-time* admission into most attractions (for example all sights in the do-it-yourself city orientation tour are free with the Salzburg Card), including discounts on select services and entertainment. The Salzburg Card comes in three validity types: 24, 48, and 72 hours (each available at the TI, airport info counter, and possibly your accommodations). The cost of the card varies on the time of year (for example, the price increases May-Oct): **24-hour card** adult 24€, youth 6-15yr 12€ (May-Oct 27€/13.50€); **48-hour card** adult 32€, youth 6-15yr 16€ (May-Oct 36€/18€); **72-hour card** adult 37€, youth 6-15yr 18.50€ (May-Oct 42€/21€). TIs accept credit cards: VC, MC, DC. **Note:** The Salzburg Card is not valid until you sign and date it, which is particularly important if you plan to use public transportation first, but with respect to visiting attractions the card is not actually activated until its first barcode scan, when the countdown begins.

Bike Rental: Salzburg is a pleasure to cycle around, and "a velo" will help you fulfill this eco-adventure. So get your butt in gear and ride your very own Tour de Salzburg. Cycle to Schloss Hellbrunn, along the river, or pedal sites 10-13 in my DIY Sound of Music tour (p. 106). Rent your wheels (including e-bikes) from Georg or his son Raphael at "a velo" located behind Mozart on Mozartplatz, daily (except in bad weather), April-June and Sept/Oct roughly 10:00-17:00, July/Aug 9:00-19:00. Prices start 12€/4hr, 18€/24hr, 72€/week. Bring ID. **Note:** More rental options at Georg's bike shop open year round at Willibald-Hauthaler-Str. 10, tel. 0662/435-5950.

Internet: You can pick up **free Wi-Fi** at Salzburg's main train station by logging on to "OEBB-station". If you prefer to use a computer terminal or require a printer, use the shop outside the station (3€/hr, daily 8:00-22:00). What's more, you can now pick up **free Wi-Fi**—provided by the city of Salzburg beaming in the Mirabell Gardens (by palace and "Do-Re-Mi" steps), Mozartsteg footbridge, Schloss Hellbrunn, at the Rathaus and on Mozartplatz in the Old Town—under the moniker "Salzburg surf" (click "Einverstanden" to access) but surf time will be limited (www.salzburg-surft.at).

Post Office, Salzburg has three central branches: **(1)** Outside the main train station, next to Burger King, is a P.O. (Mon-Fri 8:00-20:30, Sat 8:00-14:00, Sun 13:00-18:00). **(2)** The most centrally located P.O. (Mon-Fri 8:00-18:00) is hidden behind the cathedral, off Residenzplatz, at the same entrance as the Panorama Museum (p. 14). **(3)** There's also a P.O. (Mon-Fri 8:00-18:30) at Schrannengasse 10, by Mirabell Gardens.

Supermarket: A convenient and centrally located grocery store is the Billa **Corso** (Mon-Fri 7:40-20:00, Sat 7:40-18:00, Sun 11:00-15:00) parked at the bus transportation hub Hanuschplatz, opposite the Makartsteg footbridge traversing the river. But a bigger stockpile of foodstuff can be found at the **EuroSpar** supermarket (all major CCs accepted, Mon-Fri 7:00-19:00, Sat 7:00-18:00, free Wi-Fi) secreted in the "Forum 1" shopping mall outside the main train station. Convenient for Railers and Sunday shoppers, the **Spar** grocery store (Mon-Sat 6:00-23:00, Sun 8:00-23:00) is open seven days a week in the main train station. On the New Town side of the river, a **Spar** grocery store (Mon-Fri 8:00-19:30, Sat 8:00-18:00) can be found at Linzergasse 19.

Laundry: The only laundromat within walking distance of Old Town is **Norge Exquisit Textilreinigung** (Mon-Fri 7:30-18:00, Sat 8:00-12:00, last wash two hours before closing, 15€/load, pay attendant), located at Paris-Lodron-Strasse 16 (on corner of Wolf-Dietrich-Strasse) in New Town. North of Old Town at Ignaz-Harrer-Strasse 32 (corner of Alois-Stockinger-Str.) is the coin laundry **Green & Clean** (daily 6:00-22:00, last wash 20:00, 6€/wash, 2€/dry 10 min, detergent is free and automatically dispensed with wash, combination wash + dry machine 10€); ride bus 1, 2, or 7 to Gaswerkgasse (if riding #2 from the city, exit bus left and walk straight to G & C on the corner ahead).

Holidays in Salzburg, 2017

1. January, Sunday – Neujahr (New Year)
6. January, Friday – Heilige Drei Könige (Epiphany)
14. April – Karfreitag (Good Friday)
17. April – Ostermontag (Easter Monday)
1. May, Monday – May Day (Labor Day)
25. May, Thursday – Christi Himmelfahrt (Ascension Day)
5. June – Pfingstmontag (Whit Monday)
15. June, Thursday – Fronleichnam (Corpus Christi)
15. August, Tuesday – Maria Himmelfahrt (Assumption Day)
26. October, Thursday – National Independence Day
1. November, Wednesday – Allerheiligen (All Saints' Day)
8. December, Friday – Immaculate Conception
25. December, Monday – Weihnachten (Christmas)
26. December, Tuesday – St. Stephen's Day (Christmas Day 2)

What to do on a Sunday or holiday: Shops are closed but most all attractions will be open. At Mozartplatz, set off on my self-guided Salzburg tour (see next page). If you've been there done that, consider my Sound of Music do-it-yourself tour (p. 94). If that's already checked off your list, head to Berchtesgaden, Werfen or the Salzkammergut (see Excursions p. 73). Other ideas include renting a bike and cycling along the river or going for a hike (start with the Mönchsberg p. 48). If none of the above appeals to you, how 'bout quaffing a beer or two under the cooling leaves of a chestnut tree at Müllner Bräu (p. 52). *Prost!*

What to do on a rainy day: When the weather turns sour, consider indoor attractions like the Festival Halls (p. 21), Mozart's Birthplace (p. 29), DomQuartier (p. 32), Museum of Natural History (p. 39), Mozart Residence (p. 40), Brew World (p. 43), Hangar-7 (p. 43), Panorama Museum (p. 37), or Salzburg Museum (p. 14).

Church Service, locally Gottesdienst. Note that hours may have changed; for the latest info and other religious denominations, check with staff at your digs or at the TI. **Roman Catholic** service in German is regularly held at the Dom (cathedral) Mon-Sat 6:30, Sun 8:30, *10:00 and 11:30 (*note the 10:00 service is often celebrated with choral music and the 11:30 service with organ music). **Holy Mass** in English is delivered twice monthly on the second and fourth Sunday at 17:00 at the Sacellum chapel, located opposite the Festspielhaus (corner of Hofstallgasse and Karajan-Platz). The **Evangelical service** in English, formerly held every Sunday at 11:00 in the Christuskirche, has moved to the suburb of Aigen—see TI or staff at your hotel for latest details.

FREE **SALZBURG**

(1) For an economical exploration of Salzburg, set off on my **DIY tour**: Mozartplatz to Mirabell (see below). **(2)** To relive a movie classic, embark on the most popular outing in this guidebook: **The Sound of Music do-it-yourself tour** (p. 94). Watch the movie free every evening at 20:00 at the hostel YoHo (p. 66) or 20:00 at the JUFA hostel-hotel (p. 63). **(3)** Capture a memorable view from the **Stein Terrasse** (p. 47). **(4)** Though technically not without cost, the **Salzburg Card** (p. 9) is mentioned here because it's a really good deal! **(5)** A trip to Salzburg wouldn't be complete without a stroll through the **Mirabell Gardens** (p. 26); and within this magical open-air setting listen out for the free hour-long brass-band concerts held May-August every Wed 20:30 and Sun 10:30. **(6) Aviation aficionados** should visit Hangar-7 (p. 43), an ultramodern showroom housing vintage aircraft, and much more. **(7) Grave seekers** will find Mozart's wife Constanze and his father Leopold in St. Sebastian's Cemetery (p. 41). **(8)** Hike the **Kapuzinerberg** (p. 48).

SIGHTS

Many of Salzburg's attractions are listed within my 3-hour do-it-yourself orientation tour of the city (below). But if you only have enough time to visit one or two sights, the following is a short list of attractions and on which page to find them: Residenz (p. 15) • Cathedral (p. 16) • Fortress (p. 17 & 33) • St. Peter's Cemetery (p. 18) • Festival Halls (p. 21) • Old Market Square (p. 23) • Mozart's Birthplace (p. 29) • river cruise ("boat ride" p. 24) • Mirabell Gardens (p. 26) • Mozart Residence (p. 40) • DomQuartier (p. 32) • Mönchsberg Lift (p. 38) • Museum of Modern Art (p. 39) • Museum of Natural History (p. 39) • Schloss Hellbrunn (including trick fountains p. 41) • Salzburg Zoo (p. 42) • Brew World (p. 43) • Untersberg mountain cable car (p. 44).

DO-IT-YOURSELF SALZBURG TOUR, Mozartplatz to Mirabell—3 hours

You're fortunate, because today you are in Salzburg, one of Europe's most beautiful cities and my personal favorite. I had a guy once on one of my tours to Salzburg who, after each site we visited, said: "Just leave me here." I wasn't quite sure what he meant; maybe he wasn't happy with the tour, so I had to ask him if everything was okay. He replied: "Just leave me here, 'cause I never wanna go home."

You may not fall in love with Salzburg as this tourgoer did, but I do hope to at least educate, as well as entertain and inspire you during our walk together. So come on; let's discover Salzburg—Mozartplatz to Mirabell.

What's more, I've sprinkled this tour with sights made famous in the movie, "The Sound of Music." (Fans can combine this city tour with my SOM Walking Tour, page 98, by following the '**SOM fans**' notes included with each related entry.)

Note: Start early to maximize your time, between 9:00-10:00 is fine. (Tour is best April thru October, when flowers flourish and the Residenz fountain is *not* covered.) Wear comfy shoes; you have a fair bit of walking to do, enough to work off a super-sized strudel. **Allow at least three hours**; this does not include time spent touring the attractions. Note that all the attractions listed in this DIY tour are free with the **Salzburg Card** (p. 9). You can buy the card at the TI where we start our tour on Mozartplatz. I suggest you walk with me through town to orient yourself then head back to sights of interest and begin using your card to maximize its value. Also, I'll point out **toilets** en route starting immediately with those at the Salzburg Museum (off Mozartplatz), and midway through the tour we bounce past a few **food options**: a casual eatery (before cemetery), an established restaurant (after cemetery), and a produce market (by Mozart's birthplace) recommended for a quick bite or a take-away picnic (to throw down in the Mirabell Gardens).

❶ (**Free Wi-Fi** on square, "Salzburg surft," click "Einverstanden" to access): Ready? Let's begin on tourist-trampled **Mozartplatz** in front of the sizeable statue of the square's namesake, Wolfgang Amadeus Mozart. Although the statue is of considerable proportions, I find it unremarkable, liberally splattered in bird ca-ca and more akin to a resident of the Planet of the Apes than that of the legendary composer. And the pen clutched in his right hand looks like a Bic, which I'm certain did not exist in the 18th century. At the base of the statue (rear) is the year of its unveiling, 1842, stamped in Roman numerals. This is the same

year Mozart's wife, Constanze Weber, died. We'll be near her grave, which is adjacent to Leopold Mozart (Wolfgang's father), at the end of our tour.

As you gape at the imposing figure before you, ponder this: **Mozart**, child prodigy born in 1756, began playing various keyboards at age 3, wrote his first symphony at 8 and his first opera at 12. Mozart senior (Leopold) schlepped little Wolfgang around for months at a time during his youth to perform for the royal courts of Europe. During one of these tours, when Wolfgang was about 6, Leopold covered up the piano keys with a cloth to increase playing difficulty. Much to the astonishment of the crowd, Wolfgang tickled the ivories without missing a note. As an adult, Mozart favored the sophistication of Viennese culture over the intolerable holiness of small-town Salzburg. And so, in 1781, Mozart tired of composing "table music" on order of Salzburg's ruling archbishop and moved to Vienna, where he married Constanze Weber. Tragically, four of six children born to them died at birth or shortly thereafter. If things weren't depressing enough for the young couple, Mozart's lavish routine as a spendthrift brought more heartache in the form of poverty. In 1791, the prolific composer became ill and died on December 5, at the young age of 35. Except for the gravedigger and the priest, no one showed up for his funeral, not even his wife. A crestfallen rock star of his time, Wolfgang Amadeus Mozart was unceremoniously tossed into an unmarked commoner's grave (p. 114) for a large amount of people.

And to think the musical maestro, lauded today as one of the greatest composers in history, was born only a few hundred meters from where you now stand. Perhaps he played in this very square as a child, that is, if he had the time.

☞ Face the front of the statue—let's say Mozart is high noon (12:00) on a clock dial. To your left, at 10:00, is the **TI** (closed Sundays Oct. thru March, otherwise daily 9:00-18:00, July/Aug till 19:00). Pick up a free map if you haven't already and, as mentioned above, consider buying the Salzburg Card (p. 9).

Over your left shoulder, in the corner at 7:00, the plaza drops into **Judengasse**, or Jewish Lane. If you were to continue along this quaint shop-lined lane you'd first reach the unusual yet intriguing Easter-egg shop (p. 51) then Mozart's birthplace a few minutes farther (which we'll visit later). But, for now, let's get back to his square and statue.

At 6:00, opposite Mozart and rising above his square, is the two-tone bell tower belonging to St. Michael's Church, dating from circa 800 A.D., thus making it one of the first buildings constructed in Salzburg, but its current Baroque charm is owed to renovations in the mid-1700s. Adjoined is Café Glockenspiel with upstairs Christmas Museum (free with Salzburg Card otherwise enthusiasts pay adult 6€, youth 6-16yr 3€).

❷ At 5:00 (in the direction Mozart is looking) is Residenzplatz (our next stop), and through the archway to Mozart's left is the **Salzburg Museum** set in the 400-year-old New Residence, locally Neue Residenz, commissioned by Prince-Archbishop Wolf Dietrich as supplementary quarters to the Residenz (in the next square) to stroke his indulgent ego. During World War II, the New Residence was appropriated by Nazis as a command center. Postwar, the building was used by the U.S. Army as a regional headquarters until the early 1950s. Today, the city is the rightful owner and the aforementioned museum exhibits Salzburg's storied history, art and culture on multiple floors (allow at least 75 min for a visit, Tue-Sun 9:00-17:00, adult 8.50€, student 4€, youth 6-15yr 3€, family 17€, combo-ticket with Panorama Museum 10€/4.50€, or free with Salzburg Card, audio guide included with admission, www.salzburgmuseum.at; on the upper floor are terrific views of Old Town; scenic café on first floor; kids receive fun passport-like document to stamp at the various Kinder Welt, or Kid's World, exhibits).

Part of the museum's collection, but rarely on display due to its sensitivity to light, is the oldest known sheet music of the Christmas carol "Silent Night" penned by Joseph Mohr (circa 1820) in the town of Oberndorf (p. 74).

To find the museum's free and clean **toilets,** step straight through the archway and again through its entrance in front of you, go right and down the stairs one level.

Connected to the Salzburg Museum is the **Panorama Museum,** a large bi-level hall exhibiting a brilliant series of painted city and landscapes (as seen in the 19th century, from Moscow to New York and the Matterhorn to the Grand Canyon) called cosmoramas that bound the museum's namesake "panorama" (for opening times, details, and a **self-guided panorama tour** see page 37).

> **SOM fans**, in the next paragraph we bid farewell to Mozart but before *you* do, walk behind the statue and angle left downhill to the river. Cross with the traffic light and take a quick trip across the **Mozart Steg** footbridge, see page 104, then return here and…

☞ Bid farewell to Mozart—it's only temporary though, because I'll show you where he was born later on—start walking in the direction of 5:00 to the graveled Residenzplatz and stand by the fountain. En route, a striking but brief view of the fortress will present itself on the left. Also on the left, beneath the clock tower, is the fabric store Salzburger Heimatwerk (for traditional lederhosen, a maiden's dirndl, or dressmaking materials see page 49). Beyond Heimatwerk is the post office (Mon-Fri 8:00-18:00) together with the main entrance into the Panorama Museum.

❸ Marking the heart of **Residenzplatz** is Residenz fountain. Dating from 1658, it is said to be the most beautiful Baroque fountain north of the Alps. Fans of the movie "The Sound of Music" will recognize it as the fountain Maria splashes water in the horse's face while singing "I Have Confidence." (She splashed the horse facing the Hypo building, blue logo. Note that the fountain is covered for winter, typically from early Nov. until the end of March. If this is your time frame, you now have an excuse to return.) Residenzplatz, or Residence Square, is the largest square in town. It is the scene of Salzburg's Christmas market, a number of festivals throughout the year and occasionally the venue for big-time concerts, like the time in June 2000 when I stood here with 10,000 other cheering fans watching Eddie Vedder front Pearl Jam. Other names who have performed here are Neil Young, Simply Red, and Eros Ramazzotti. In recent years, A-list artists such as Elton John, Joe Cocker and Mark Knopfler have performed in Salzburg, but event management now hosts its stars in the contemporary 6,700-seat Salzburg Arena—check Web or TI for latest event listings.

👍 Look back to the New Residence; you now have an up-close view of its high-flying

bell tower, or **Glockenspiel.** Dating from 1703, the Glockenspiel's 35 chiming bells once admired by Mozart now play Mozart tunes thrice daily: 7:00, 11:00, 18:00. **Note:** If you're in town on a Thursday (17:30) or Friday (10:30), April-Oct, join the recommended **Glockenspiel tour** (adult 4€, student/senior 60yr+ 3€, youth 6-15yr 2€; Salzburg Card not valid; reserve your spot in advance with cashier at Salzburg Museum). Know that on this 30-minute tour you'll need to climb more than 100 calorie-burning steps to reach the tower's narrow observation terrace (if you have a fear of heights, like me, go at least as far as the clock mechanism then see if you can manage the few remaining steps to the viewing platform. I did it. I was petrified, but I did it).

❹ Residenzplatz takes its name from the **Residenz,** the prominent building on the square (opposite Glockenspiel) with three rows of windows stacked one on top of the other. Established in 1102 and enlarged during the 17th and 18th centuries, the Residenz is the former state rooms and living quarters of Salzburg's powerful prince archbishops, men who were inspired by Rome and the pope. Alas, much of the original furniture did not survive the cravings of Napoleon's troops in the 1800s or the Habsburgs who chronologically followed. The city, however, has done a superb job of restoring the Residenz to

its former glory, thus I've composed a **self-guided tour** of the whole cultural complex for you, including the Cathedral (see **DomQuartier** p. 32). For example, it was here in the Residenz's lavish Conference Room that Mozart played his first court concert at the age of 6; where Leopold Mozart was portrayed in the movie "Amadeus" asking the archbishop to retrieve his son from Vienna; and in the White Hall where documents were signed in 1816 to officially incorporate Salzburg into Austria.

Right of the Residenz opens into Alter Markt, or Old Market Square, which we'll visit later. At this right corner, on the Residenz's side wall (almost directly opposite the Jahn-Markl store), is a wooden display case notifying passersby of the daily tunes played by the Glockenspiel.

Left of the Residenz, through the arches, leads onto Domplatz, our next stop. Above the arches is a skywalk formerly connecting the archbishops with the Dom, or cathedral, so they could avoid commoners on the way to Mass. Above the skywalk you may see people milling around the Panorama Terrace, part of the recommended DomQuartier (p. 32).

In front of the Residenz, **horse-drawn carriages** (called Fiaker) patiently wait for the pleasure to trot you through Old Town (44€/20-25 min or 88€/50 min, max 5 passengers). Because rides double as a city tour, request a driver who speaks reasonable English before setting off.

☞ Stroll through the arches into Domplatz, the square fronting the cathedral. Along the way you are crossing a former excavation site. A testament to the city's prosperity, some 55 years ago archaeologists discovered a trove of artifacts and ruins dating from the medieval cathedral to Roman times when Salzburg was known as Iuvavum.

Beneath the **left arch** is a stairwell descending below ground where you can explore the excavation site now a **museum**, locally Domgrabungsmuseum (July-Aug daily 9:00-17:00, closed remainder of year, adult 3€, student 1.50€, youth 6-15yr 1€, free with Salzburg Card). Although fascinating for archaeologist-types, the general traveler will find the excavations hard to decipher.

At the **right arch** say "Hi" to my artist friend, Igor Zindovic (pictured), who has been parked here since the mid-1990s painting and selling his artwork. Show Igor this guidebook and he'll give you a deal along with a big dose of friendly conversation.

❺ 👍 From Domplatz (Cathedral Square) we have a divine view of the city's premier house of God, the Salzburger Dom, or **Cathedral** (visiting hours Mon-Sat 8:00-17:00, Sun 13:00-17:00, March-April & Oct daily till 18:00, May-July & Sept daily till 19:00, August daily till 20:00, donations welcome. For Mass times, see Church Service on page 10. If time is on your side, tour the upper level of the Cathedral now part of the **DomQuartier** p. 32).

This Roman Catholic church is the largest Baroque structure north of the Alps, having the capacity to hold more than 10,000 of us. Fittingly, Mozart was baptized here in 1756 (in font left of entry), and the "Hoforgel" organ inside (right) he often played. But before you enter its holy domain, waddle into the middle of the square, stand by the statue of the Virgin Mary and face the cathedral. Above its wrought-iron gates are three landmark dates in the Dom's history: 774, consecration of original structure (long since ruined). 1628, rebuilt in the Baroque-style you see today and reconsecrated (after cathedral was destroyed by fire in the late 16th century). 1959, reconstructed after Allied bombs shattered it during World War II (pictures

2017 edition   Cathedral & Fortress   17

inside cathedral, back left, depict this blasphemous day). Flanking the gates are four figures, (left to right): **St. Rupert** (patron saint of Salzburg), **St. Peter** (holder of the keys to Heaven), **St. Paul** (holding a sword—assumed beheaded by Romans), and **St. Virgil** (first archbishop of Salzburg and creator of the Dom).

Atop the cathedral is a statue of Jesus, flanked by Moses (left) and Elijah (right). Midway up the facade you'll see the four evangelists: John, Paul, George and Ringo. Um, err, I mean Matthew, Mark, Luke and John. Just above them are two angels holding a crown. Now, walk beyond the Virgin Mary in the direction she is facing and stand beneath the middle archway. Once there, line up Mary's head under the angels. When ready, pace forward and the angels crown her. Neat, huh?

While facing the cathedral **look for Vlado** (pictured), another of my artist friends whom I've known since the late 1990s; he is usually standing immediately right of the entrance (April-May, July-Aug & Oct, 11:00-18:00 but not in bad weather). He'll masterfully cut out your portrait like Edward Scissorhands on high-octane turnip juice (5€, but show Vlado this guide and pay 4€. If he doesn't give you the discount, the artist is not Vlado)!

❻ When ready, continue right past the cathedral through the *arches and into the next square, Kapitelplatz, where you'll be graced with a so-close-you-can-almost-reach-upwards-and-touch-it view of the fortress as well as Stephan Balkenhol's larger-than-life man on golden globe (called "Sphaera," erected in 2007). In front of the globe is arguably the Continent's **largest chess set** (board painted onto asphalt), with pieces the size of children. On your right are souvenir stands laden with Mozart mementos, useless knickknacks, scenic postcards, and T-shirts with catchy print like 'No Kangaroos in Austria.'

*If you have the urge, **toilets** (WC) can be found at the arches (bring small change for stall, 50¢. On Kapitelplatz beams **free Wi-Fi**, "Salzburg surft," click "Einverstanden" to access).

❼ 👆 One reason people like myself absolutely adore Salzburg is its history—it's downright mind-boggling! A good example is the massive structure in front of you. Lording over the city for more than 900 years, stark and imposing, the **Fortress of Salzburg** is every bit the castle I envisioned while listening to fairy tales as a child. And here it is, perched upon a forested bluff in western Austria, flexing its muscles; an impregnable curtain of stonework and turrets. Dating from 1077 A.D., Salzburg's fortress was never conquered, and today it registers as one of the largest fully preserved castle complexes in Europe. It is the city's signature landmark, where the ruling archbishops lived before moving down to the Residenz. Needless to say, this must-explore fortress is highly worth your time, thus I've penned a **self-guided fortress tour** for you on page 33 (free with Salzburg Card, including the cable railway lifting visitors to its ramparts—allow at least 2 hours for a visit).

☞ Continue straight through the square; we're headed up the cobbled lane (Festungsgasse) running between the buildings. But before we go that route, I want you to veer right and slip through the corner wrought-iron gate (one of three entrances into St. Peter's Cemetery). Inside on the left is **Salzburg's oldest bakery** (and probably its smallest, Mon-Tue & Thur-Fri 8:00-17:30, Sat 7:00-13:00, closed Wed). It belongs to St. Peter's monastery (which we'll soon visit) and has been baking bread in a wood-fired oven here since the 12th century. Today, the bread is baked mornings 4:00 till 7:00; an on-site video exhibit illustrates how it's done. For something to nibble on during our tour, buy a bread roll. Choose from one similar to rye (.90¢), sourdough (half kg 2€), but definitely hand over 1€ for the sweet raisin-roll. Mmm. (Note that later we'll be walking through an outdoor market selling various meats and cheeses that sandwich well with the bread.)

The adjacent **surging waterway** (called the Almkanal, typically shut down the latter half of September for maintenance) has been flowing in from Germany since medieval times and was an integral part of the city's water supply as well as a canal system used to flush the filth from the streets, power grain mills, and (of course) sustain the bakery.

▶ Retrace your steps back out the wrought-iron gate and go right up the cobbled lane (Festungsgasse) toward the fortress.

Ahead on the right is a **casual eatery** (daily 10:00-17:00, summer till 20:00) affording its guests reasonable prices, a colorful picture menu, and an ivy-blanketed patio-garden with fortress view. The hard-working owner, Helmut, dishes up his locally famed two-course lunch special consisting of soup, schnitzel and potatoes (Kartoffel) for a mere 8.90€. Adjoining the eatery is a souvenir shop managed by Alex, who's worked here for about as long as I've been guiding groups through Salzburg, since 1998.

Beyond the mementos and Mozart chocolates is another wrought-iron gate leading into St. Peter's Cemetery, our next stop. But before we venture through said gate, I first want to point out the **cable railway** (Festungsbahn) in front of you climbing to the fortress (p. 33), the most expedient way up; (note there are free **toilets** inside the railway entrance). And if you were to continue up the cobbled lane you'd soon reach the restaurant **Stieglkeller** (p. 57), beyond it is a crossroads: right climbs steeply to the fortress, straight leads to the Nonnberg abbey from von Trapp fame.

> **SOM fans**, flip to page 101, near the bottom of the page begin reading from "At the top the lane splits direction…." and finish after the Nonnberg abbey entry.

❽ ☞ Mosey through the gate into **St. Peter's Cemetery** (daily 6:30-18:00, April & Sept till 19:00, May-Aug till 21:30), **Austria's oldest active graveyard**, and world famous for hiding the Trapp family in "The Sound of Music." (Actually, Hollywood hid the von Trapps in a studio but this cemetery inspired the director.)

St. Peter's Cemetery is a mix of old and new graves linked via lopsided footpaths and encompassed by a succession of vaulted burial chambers belonging to titled families. Vault **XVI**, for example, belongs to Lorenz Hagenauer, landlord to the Mozart family (Getreidegasse address); and within vault **XXXI** is the architect Santino Solari, famous for building the cathedral, Schloss Hellbrunn, and many of Salzburg's fortifications constructed during the Thirty Years' War. In the center of the graveyard is **St. Margaret's chapel**, the only church in Salzburg that still stands as it did in the 15th century (1491). It's amazing to think that Europeans were already building cathedrals, fighting wars, and brewing beer long before my country was even a twinkle in our forefathers' eyes. (If the entrance to St. Margaret's is shut, the interior may be viewed through two peepholes in the main portal.) Framing the chapel, burial plots dressed in a symphony of multihued flowers are immaculately tended, most burning a red remembrance candle, breaking the black stillness of the night. Meters from the water basin in the center of the cemetery—coins thrown in from well wishers regularly cleaned by entrepreneurial vagabonds—is the plot of U.S. Major General **Harry J. Collins**, commander of the distinguished 42nd Infantry "Rainbow" Division (Seventh Army) from July 1943 thru May '45. After the war, Collins was promoted to military governor of U.S. forces in Austria. It was during this time that he fell in love with Salzburg and one of its offspring, Irene Gehmacher. The general died in the early '60s and is buried here with his wife. His head-

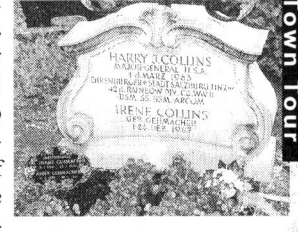

stone reads: "Honorary citizen of the cities of Salzburg and Linz." Behind the general's grave (against the church wall), ironically, is a memorial dedicated to the Axis soldiers who fell in defense of the city during the war.

Going back a few years, before the general and World War II, are Salzburg's so-called **catacombs**, Christian dugouts secreted in the cliff face from the Romans in the 3rd century A.D. At its entrance you'll find the grave of **Mozart's sister**, Maria Anna, affectionately known as "Nannerl."

On page 36 I've written a **self-guided catacombs tour** for you. Either come back later for a visit or whip out your Salzburg Card and tour the dugouts now—it'll take 15-20 minutes.

❾ Exit the cemetery via the arched passageway (beneath church clock tower) and into the next plaza.

You are now standing in the courtyard of **St. Peter's (Benedictine) monastery**, the oldest community of monks in the German-speaking world (in which some 30 pious brothers are still active), and where Bishop Rupert founded Salzburg more than 1,300 years ago, thus it's not surprising that St. Peter's Stiftskeller (to your left) is **Europe's oldest restaurant!**

Although the Stiftskeller (p. 56) was first mentioned in the year 803 by the court scribe Alcuin during a visit by the great Emperor Charlemagne, it is likely the monastic cellar was the monks' regular buffet decades prior to the emperor's visit and is therefore much older. While prices have indeed increased since the founding of Salzburg, I recommend you stop in sometime for a bite to eat, even if it's only for a soup, Salzburger Nockerl (p. 56), or a Mozart dinner concert (p. 53).

👍 The Stiftskeller faces another of Salzburg's pious landmarks, **St. Peter's Church.** Built between 1130-1143, St. Peter's lavish renovations during the Baroque and Rococo periods (17-18th centuries) have transformed the interior of this must-see church into the region's most spectacular. In 1789, Mozart directed his Dominicus Mass in C-minor here while his wife, Constanze, sang soprano. It is within this hallowed structure that Bishop Rupert is interred. Look for the "Grab des Hl. Rupertus" midway along the right aisle.

❶ Mozartplatz
❷ Salzburg Museum
❸ Residenzplatz
❹ Residenz
❺ Cathedral (Dom)
❻ Kapitelplatz
❼ Fortress
❽ St. Peter's Cemetery
❾ St. Peter's Church
❿ Festival Halls
⓫ Old Market Square
⓬ Mozart's Birthplace
⓭ Boat ride & footbridge
⓮ Mirabell Gardens
⓯ Mozart's Residence
⓰ Stein Terrasse
🅐 Mönchsberg Lift
🅑 Museum of Natural History
🅒 Müllner Bräu
🅓 Hotel Sacher
🅔 Marionette Theater

☞ Continuing our platz hop, saunter across the square, paralleling the sheer cliffs that cradle the fortress, and stop beneath the next arched passage. Here you have a memorable view of the church, square, fountain, restaurant and fortress. Snap!

Sashay straight through the passage and into the adjoining courtyard, home to the College of St. Benedict for aspiring monks. Mozart's father, Leopold, studied here for a short while (before he excused himself on account of his love for music). Pass a welcoming Bishop Rupert (patron saint of salt) with a drum of the "white gold" at his feet, and head through the next passage into the Toscanini Hof (**SOM fans** see page 100), a secluded courtyard named after the distinguished Italian conductor, Arturo Toscanini (1867-1957).

To your left, a passageway cuts through the cliff face into the underground **Altstadt Garage**, the ideal parking lot for daytrippers (for more info on the garage, see Parking p. 8). During World War II, the garage was used as an air-raid shelter. It was also here that initial talks took place leading to the surrender of Salzburg after its liberation on May 4, 1945 from the Nazis by "dog-faced soldiers" of the U.S. 3rd Infantry "Marne" Division. (The plaque affixed to the stone wall right of the passageway tells the story.)

In front of you is the House for Mozart, the south end of Salzburg's renowned festival halls. Through its two massive iron doors stage crews regularly wrestle with the loading and unloading of hefty props and technical equipment for the latest productions.

From here the festival halls appear to be rather insignificant. But let's make tracks and get a significant view. To your right is an underpass, roll through this and stop in the middle of the street (Max-Reinhardt-Platz), mindful of the horse dung left by the procession of Fiakers clip-clopping tourists around town.

(Shortly, we'll keep going straight and take the lane running alongside the domed church, but first I want to point out a few sites:) Look right. Do you recognize anything? The far archway is on the edge of Domplatz, where you lined up the angels to crown the Virgin Mary. Now turn around; the enormous building you see extending the entire length of the block accommodates Salzburg's grand festival halls. If you were to walk a few minutes beyond the halls, paralleling the cliffs, you'd reach the **Ⓐ Mönchsberg Lift** (p. 38), elevators which access the Mönchsberg observation terrace, one of Salzburg's most scenic vantage points and where **SOM fans** will be interested to know Maria and the kids sang "Do-Re-Mi." Adjoining the terrace is the **Museum of Modern Art** (p. 39, beige building with castle-like turret), and just down the street from the base of the Lift (towards the river) is the **Ⓑ Museum of Natural History** (p. 39—fun for kids!).

⑩ Festival Halls, locally Festspielhäuser, a massive 17th-century structure formerly the archbishop's stables and riding school. The **large festival hall**, or Grosses Festspielhaus, impressive in its size (at the north end of the complex), has seating for 2,200 of us and is outfitted with one of Europe's largest opera stages, totaling 100 meters in width. The second largest theater, **Haus für Mozart** (at the south end of the building), dates from 1924 and recently underwent a three-year, 29€-million renovation for the 250-year celebration of Mozart's birth. The so-called **Summer Riding School**, or Felsenreitschule, is the most historic venue, dating from 1693 when the archbishop's horses trained and performed here. This striking theater has seating for

1,400 guests beneath a state-of-the-art retractable roof that can open on the flip of a switch (depending on the scene) and features three dramatic tiers of stone arcades hewn into the cliff face (pictured) that moviegoers will recognize in "The Sound of Music" when the Hollywood von Trapps sing "Edelweiss" before escaping to the cemetery.

The only way to visit the Festival Halls, besides paying 50€-500€ to see a performance, is by taking the recommended multi-language tour. (For Sound of Music fans, the tour is a must! Turn to page 99 for more SOM movie trivia regarding the halls.) **Tours of the Festival Halls** (duration 50 min, adult 7€, youth 6-12yr 4€, free with Salzburg Card) run daily at 14:00, July-Aug 9:30, 14:00 & 15:30—but times may change due to events or theater performances—and meet 15 min prior to tour start at the Festival ticket shop (by iron gate and column with mask atop). The **Salzburg Festival** (Salzburger Festspiele) this year is scheduled from July 21 thru August 30, 2017. For tickets and info, either go to the Festival Halls box office, the Mozartplatz TI, or www.salzburgfestival.at.

☞ Take the lane (Wiener-Philharmoniker-Gasse) running alongside the domed church to the **open-air victuals market**, a lively locale to gather lunch (Mon-Fri early till around 18:00, Sat till around 15:00). Choose from a variety of meats, cheeses, fruits, vegetables, pretzels, and grilled sausages, locally Würste. (**SOM fans**, remember the scene when Maria juggled the tomatoes and Gretl dropped hers? It was filmed right here on **University Platz**.)

To your right (before the first food stand), look to the plaque above the Restaurant Zipfer. It reads, "In this house lived W. A. Mozart's sister Nannerl (widowed baroness von Berchtold zu Sonnenburg) from October 28, 1801 until her death October 29, 1829."

Speaking of Wolfgang Amadeus, we began this tour on his square, Mozartplatz, and since then you've learned a few things about the master composer. Now, you're within a pretzel toss of where the master was born. Look to the golden facade in front of you; this is the back of Mozart's birthplace. We'll arrive at its front facade in about 15 minutes; first I want to show you Salzburg's most senior market square.

▶ When ready, go right through the tall, arched passage. Midway through is a petite shop selling the sugary satisfaction of Fürst confectionery (Mozart Balls p. 49), dutifully supervised by the sepia eyes of its founder, Paul Fürst. The next shop along, on the corner, is **Austria's oldest bookstore**, since 1594 (Mon-Fri 9:00-18:30, Sat 9:00-18:00), you'll find its English-language section against the left wall.

Continue straight to the next platz, Alter Markt. (If class is in session, you'll pass an eclectic string of bicycles parked in front of the historic university building, housing the criminal justice department.) Once in the plaza turn left, stop, face the fountain and its flag-bearing statue. This is Florian, patron saint of firefighters.

❶ After leveling the charred houses destroyed by the fire of 1262, the townsfolk decided to build an expansive firebreak to better protect the inner-city residents and their dwellings from a future inferno. So came about Alter Markt, or **Old Market Square,** where locals flocked in medieval times to buy and sell their goods.

In the center of the square is **Florian fountain**, the neighborhood's former water supply, capped by the saint himself depicted in action pouring a bucket of water over a burning castle.

To your left is Café Tomaselli (p. 59), **Austria's oldest coffeehouse**, dating from 1703, where Mozart played cards while contentedly consuming cake and caffeine. Also a regular visitor, Constanze Weber (Mozart's widow) lived above the café from 1820-26 with her second husband. More importantly, pay **toilets** can be found inside Tomaselli's, straight to the back, up the stairs.

Across the square from Café Tomaselli is **Café Fürst** (p. 59), another of Salzburg's authentic coffee institutions and home of the original Mozart chocolate ball. Right of Café Fürst you'll recognize graveled Residenzplatz.

(Move closer to the fountain.) Left of Florian fountain, or third doorway from Café Tomaselli, is formerly **Salzburg's smallest house** (2.2 m wide x 8 m long), dating from 1860, built in a former alleyway. It's not much of a house, more like a gap between two buildings. Add a door, a window, throw on a few tiles for a roof, nail in a gargoyle and call it the smallest house in town. Ha!

Right of Florian is **Salzburg's oldest pharmacy** (Apotheke), dating from 1591, still in operation today (Mon-Fri 8:00-18:00, Sat 8:00-12:00). Two doors farther along is a sweets shop parading chocolate in its front window. Boxes upon boxes, in all shapes and sizes, filled with little chocolate balls wrapped in shiny foil. Compare Fürst's original Mozart ball (p. 49) with the competition's imitation blend.

☞ Skip to the lower end of the square and stop. To your right begins Judengasse. Do you remember this Jewish Lane that leads to decorated Easter eggs and Mozartplatz?

Jog left. This leads to **Getreidegasse** (pictured), meaning Grain Lane, Salzburg's main shopping street, teeming with tourists buzzing beneath a multitude of gilded wrought-iron signs hanging over retail outlets.

Follow the crowds a short distance to the rich-yellow facade at number 9, Mozart's birthplace, looking much like it did in his day, minus the fan frenzy. Right of its entrance portal, notice the building's original doorbells. The middle one jingled Mozart's apartment.

❷ 👍 **Mozart's Birthplace:** The wondrous Wolfgang Amadeus Mozart was born January 27, 1756 in the apartment on the third floor of this six-story dwelling in the heart of Salzburg's Old Town at Getreidegasse 9, now a museum (free with Salzburg Card).

On page 29 I've penned a **self-guided Mozart tour** of his birthplace for you. Either come back later for a visit or whip out your Salzburg Card and tour the museum now—it'll take some 30 minutes.

☞ Continue along Getreidegasse some 50 meters to the archway at No. 24 (right). Stop here. We're headed through this passageway but if you were to continue straight along Getreidegasse to No. 33 (left) you would reach Salzburg's **best curry sausages** (p. 60) and six doors farther at No. 39 you'd strike the lane's narrowest house and a Salzburg tradition, **Sporer wines & spirits** (p. 50). When the time is right, step inside and taste test Sporer's essential orange punch, prepared according to a secret recipe handed down from grandfather Otto.

March through the portal at No. 24, straight down the passageway and out the other end. You're now at bustling **Hanuschplatz**, a major transportation hub where environmentally friendly buses repetitively transfer commuters here and there. For example, you could pick up bus 1 (from across the street) to **Stiegl's Brew World** (p. 43), or to shop with locals at the **Europark mall** (p. 51), or ultimately to the **casino** (p. 45) to possibly win a fortune. More bus connections depart from "Rathaus" a short jog to your right up the street.

Swing left to the crosswalk. Here is the **Corso** (Billa) **grocery store** (Mon-Fri 7:40-20:00, Sat 7:40-18:00, Sun 11:00-15:00) in case you didn't get all you wanted back at the victuals market.

Cross the street via the crosswalk, then once again straight to the river and jump onto the footbridge, known as Makartsteg.

Left of the footbridge you'll see the dock for Salzburg's one-and-only sightseeing boat that cruises tourists up and down the river.

⓭ In 2002, Salzburg built a dock for visitors craving a Schifffahrt, or **boat ride,** on the Salzach River—the first time since 1891. Fatefully, the inaugural craft sunk a few months later in the devastating floods that inundated Europe in August 2002. Today, Salzburg's one-boat fleet (not surprisingly called "Amadeus") offers the popular 8 km city sightseeing cruise (40 min, adult 15€, youth 4-14yr 7.50€, free with Salzburg Card) as well as other leisurely excursions. Powered by two jet engines, each thrusting upwards of 350 hp, the boat opens up to a respectable 45 kph once upriver from the Old Town. (River cruises depart hourly May-Sept, less April & Oct—no departures outside these months: **April & Oct** 15:00-16:00 as well as 13:00 on weekends • **May** 11:00-17:00 • **June** 11:00-18:00 • **July** 11:00-19:00 • **August** 11:00-19:00 (till 20:00 August 1-19) • **Sept** 12:00-17:00. **Note:** During the warm days of summer, book your ticket[s] hours in advance, if possible. Peak season, expect a 3€ surcharge for the seats on the back deck.)

☞ Now that you're on the bridge you just departed the left bank of Salzburg, or Old Town, and are headed to the right bank, or New Town, named because of the city's mass expansion across the river in the 18th century.

On the bridge you noticed the crazy amount of **padlocks** attached to the cable fencing. This ardent craze has spread across European bridges with gusto over the last years. You see, young lovers fasten their engraved padlock to the bridge and toss the key over the side, into the river below to symbolize their eternal union to one another. Now you know the story of the myriad padlocks, perhaps it's a bond you'd like to make with your partner? (If you're reading this in advance of your trip, have a padlock custom engraved—with both your first names and the date your relationship was consummated—and surprise your significant other by attaching it to the bridge while in Salzburg. You can thank me later! If you're reading this while already on the road, ask a local where you can buy a padlock and have it engraved.)

▶ Stop at the midway point of the bridge to take in the stupendous view of Salzburg Old Town. Vying for attention against the backdrop of its landmark fortress crowning the skyline, stylized steeples stand tall like a pageant of beauty queens above immense churches wittingly built by ruling archbishops to showcase their divine authority.

Beneath you is the Salzach, meaning Salt River, not because of any salt content but for the river trade in medieval times that transported the "white gold" downstream from the **salt mines** at nearby Bad Dürrnberg (p. 47) via the Inn and Danube rivers, eventually the Black Sea and into the coffers of powerful Asian rulers. Much closer, 20 km downstream, the Salt River flows through the border town of **Oberndorf** (p. 74), home of the world famous Christmas carol "Silent Night."

Look downstream: the copper-topped church steeple you see rising from the hillside formerly belonged to the Augustinian monastery, home today to Austria's largest tavern and beer garden, **❻ Müllner Bräu** (p. 52).

Turn around and look upstream to the neighboring, motor-trafficked bridge. To its left, facing it (from New Town) is the Hotel Stein, where we'll end our tour on its scenic rooftop café, Stein Terrasse (p. 47).

▶ Mosey down the latter half of the footbridge and onto the right bank. The long, stately structure on the right is the **❹ 5-star Hotel Sacher** (p. 69). In 1964, Julie Andrews and director Robert Wise stayed here while filming "The Sound of Music." Besides deluxe digs, Sacher is best known for its rich chocolate torte. You'll pass its classy sweets shop (Mon-Fri 9:30-18:00, Sat 9:30-17:00) on the right before the crosswalk.

Picnickers, a choice place to enjoy your goodies is along the riverbank—bench or grass—or wait a few minutes until we reach our next stop, the Mirabell Gardens.

Continue straight ahead. At the traffic intersection, cross with the light (left crosswalk) and stop on the forward corner.

We're going to keep walking straight (away from river) but if you were to go left, the next building along is the **❺ Marionette Theater** (p. 54). It was these puppets that inspired the Lonely Goatherd sequence in the "The Sound of Music."

Keep walking straight and stop on the other side of the Landestheater (Provincial Theater). In front of you is the 5-star Hotel Bristol, where the remainder of "The Sound of Music" cast stayed during filming. To your right, across the street, the corner building is the Mozart Residence (the family's second, much larger, apartment). We'll head over there in a short while; our first attraction on this side of the river is the Mirabell Gardens, to your left. After visiting the gardens, we'll shuffle past the Mozart Residence on the way to our final destination: Hotel Stein's rooftop café.

⑭ 👈 Go left, scamper past the quartet of chiseled nudes and into the immensely beautiful **Mirabell Gardens** (free to enter, daily from 6:00 to sundown—**free Wi-Fi** in gardens, "Salzburg surf," click "Einverstanden" to access). Mirabell is the city's most prominent gardens, exhibiting a symphony of color, brilliant reds and yellows and violets, like a painting with tourists. No trip to Salzburg would be complete without a stroll through this fragrant reserve. Fans of the movie "The Sound of Music" particularly love Mirabell because the von Trapp children, plus one governess, donned specially tailored play clothes and frolicked through the gardens singing "Do-Re-Mi" (for more **SOM** highlights in the gardens, see page 105).

Mirabell Palace (in front of you) at the back of the gardens came first in 1606, when Prince-Archbishop Wolf Dietrich von Raitenau built it for his mistress, Salome Alt, who bore him 15 children. At that time the palace was aptly named Altenau and located outside the medieval city. Although the archbishop was truly in love with Salome Alt, their long relationship had to be kept secret on account of his ecclesiastical position as ruler of Salzburg. (In addition to Dietrich's impious behavior, he suffered a number of political and military defeats, which got him deposed in 1612 and subsequently jailed in the fortress as a "prisoner of the pope" until his death in 1617.)

In the 18th century, the immaculate Baroque gardens you see today were landscaped around the palace. After the archbishop surrendered his authority to Napoleon (who in turn surrendered to Austria) in the early 19th century, Emperor Franz Josef officially opened the gardens to the public in 1854 and they've been a cultural magnet to locals and tourists ever since.

Today, **Mirabell Palace** accommodates the offices of local government like that of the mayor (Bürgermeister) and the marriage registry (Standesamt), as well as a popular venue for classical concerts in the sumptuous **Marble Hall**, where Mozart himself once played to the delight of the archbishop. The Marble Hall is also where locals are officially obliged by the state to say their wedding vows (before they can hold the ceremony in the church, or location, of their choosing). But Salzburgers aren't complaining because it is recognized as one of the world's most exquisite wedding halls. Wouldn't it be great to say you were married in a palace (with only the nominal administrative fee of 150 euro to pay required by the state).

▶ If you have a few extra minutes, follow me, let's peek into the palace. Step through the portal next to the Pegasus (winged horse) fountain, jog straight through the building then take the first door on the left, climb 41 steps to the Marble Hall (Marmorsaal) on the right; conveniently opposite is the marriage registry (Standesamt). Have a look around, take pictures, then check out the royal view listed in the next paragraph.

Lastly, before leaving Mirabell, stand in front of the rose garden, where the graveled path arcs into the grass, and behold a view that is befitting of kings and queens, and you! From this spot (GPS: N47 48.294 E13 02.530), the splendor of the gardens, skyline of the Old Town, and the majesty of the Alps await your grace.

☞ Leave the gardens the way you came and carefully cross the road (watching out for cars and buses coming from either direction) straight to the corner building, former Mozart residence.

⓯ **Mozart Residence:** Since Leopold Mozart had made a name for himself as the archbishop's concert meister, in addition to rearing a child prodigy, the Mozarts could afford to move across the river in 1773 to this much bigger, eight-room residence, now a museum journeying visitors through the family's history and former dominions (allow 30-45 min for a visit—free with Salzburg Card—for opening times, details see page 40).

☞ When standing directly in front of and facing the Mozart Residence, go right then swing immediately left (on Theatergasse), weave past the people waiting at the bus stop, and jog straight towards the main bridge connecting New Town with Old Town (2 min).

Stop when you reach the pedestrian plaza opposite the bridge. This is called Platzl, meaning "little square." There's usually a crowd of people waiting at the crosswalk for the traffic light to change and on warm days pants-soaked kids playing in the fountains (streams of water) erupting from the ground.

The Hotel Stein is on the corner in front of you but before we venture inside and up to its roof, we're going to first loop around the hotel.

Step into Platzl, mosey past the fountains and over to Steingasse first on the right—stop here—on the corner is the recommended Darwin's Café-Bar (p. 53).

We're headed down cobbled Steingasse but if you were to continue up Platzl, it narrows into shop-lined **Linzergasse**, climbing to the top of New Town. A short way up, on the ground by the Apotheke (**pharmacy**) at Linzergasse 5 (left), is a trio of brass inlaid tablets remembering the Jewish family who once lived here. The Löwy family, Ernst, Ida and son Herbert, were deported in 1942 by the Nazis and murdered at Auschwitz (concentration camp). Farther up, at Linzergasse 41, is St. Sebastian's Cemetery (p. 41), where you'd find the **graves of Mozart's father, Leopold and Mozart's widow, Constanze Weber**, as well as the aforementioned Prince-Archbishop Wolf Dietrich von Raitenau.

▶ Head down Steingasse. On your left are a trio of petite and atmospheric evening establishments. First up you can get your Kebab fix most anytime at Renya's (classic Döner 3.50€ or Dürüm wrapped like a burrito 4€, vegetarian options available). Next door at No. 3, tempting your spicy Latino side, is the **Pepe Cocktail Bar** (p. 53) with "tasty cocktails and hot music." And next in line is the unassuming **Shrimps Bar and Restaurant** (p. 61), a trendy Mediterranean-style locale specializing in crustacean cuisine.

Ahead, at Steingasse 9, you'll see a *plaque on its facade memorializing the house as the birthplace of **Joseph Mohr** (1792), who penned the world-famous Christmas carol "Silent Night." Adjacent, 256 steps climb to the monastery capping the forested **Kapuzinerberg** (p. 48), where a plethora of hiking trails and eye-popping views entice all who make the trip. (*Note: The plaque was incorrectly placed here decades ago; Mohr's correct birthplace is actually Steingasse 31.)

A few meters farther along the lane, as Steingasse narrows, (we're going to go right at Das Kino but first) check out the extensive crevices that gouge the right corner wall. These originate from the end of World War II when a U.S. soldier eagerly tried to drive his tank ahead to No. 24 to meet his hot date. Frustrated, the soldier had to complete his mission on foot, thus he parked his steel beast and marched the short distance to his lady in waiting, under the red light at the *Maison de Plaisir*.

→ Alas, our next and last stop, the Hotel Stein, as of January 31, 2016, is closed for renovations until summer 2017. Yikes! Cross fingers it's reopened by the time you arrive.

Go right at Das Kino (cinema, occasionally screens English-language films), then right at the street and right again into the freshly renovated Hotel Stein. Shuffle straight through the lobby, past reception, and ride the elevator up to the Stein Terrasse.

⑯ **Congratulations!** You've reached the **Stein Terrasse** (p. 47), the end of our tour. (Sit down, relax, order a beverage. You deserve it.) I hope you enjoyed our walk together and now have a better feel for the City of Mozart, spread before you like the colorful canvas of a Claude Monet painting. If only he ever came here. But you did, thus we celebrate this moment.

I began this tour by saying, "You're fortunate." Look around you; a view of unparalleled beauty extends before your eyes. You're fortunate, and so am I to be able to share this with you. Millions of people around the world can only dream of such a moment, and it's yours to keep, forever.

Before I finish, I want to point out one last site: The red onion steeple you see left of (and beneath) the fortress belongs to the Nonnberg abbey (p. 102). Dating from the 8th century, Nonnberg is the first abbey of nuns north of the Alps to follow the Rule of St. Benedict. Together with St. Peter's monastery, the abbey is the epicenter of the Christian community in Salzburg. More recently, Nonnberg starred in the movie "The Sound of Music." It was an easy choice for Hollywood film scouts. Besides its centuries-old history and architectural splendor, the abbey is where Maria really studied, and where she and the captain really got married. Nonnberg, or Mountain of Nuns, is majestic, solemn and eternal, a place where miracles are said to happen. Perhaps, one has your name on it?

EDITOR'S NOTE: Please review us on the Web. As a small business, we get pumped about the little things. That's why positive support and word-of-mouth from our readers means the world to us. It let's us know how we're doing, thus we'd greatly appreciate it if you could share your experience about this book by typing a brief review on *Amazon*. If you've enjoyed a particular Salzburg site because of our attention to it, please mention Harriman in your *TripAdvisor* comment. ☺

2017 edition   Self-guided Mozart's Birthplace   29

SIGHTS, Old Town

Note: All the attractions listed in this section are either free to enter or are free with the Salzburg Card (p. 9), *except* the Glockenspiel tour (p. 15).

Salzburg Museum (p. 14) • **Glockenspiel** (p. 15) • **Cathedral** (p. 16) • **St. Peter's Cemetery** (p. 18) • **Festival Halls** (p. 20) • river cruise ("**boat ride**" p. 24) • **Mozart's Birthplace** (p. 23 & 29) • **DomQuartier** (p. 32) • **Residenz** (p. 15 & DomQuartier 32) • **Fortress** (p. 17 & 33) • **Panorama Museum** (p. 37) • **Mönchsberg Lift** (p. 38) • **Museum of Natural History** (p. 39) • **Museum of Modern Art** (p. 39).

👍 **Mozart's Birthplace,** locally Geburtshaus, Getreidegasse 9, allow 30 min for a visit, enthusiasts allow at least 2 hours (daily 9:00-17:30, last entry 17:00 • July-Aug 8:30-19:00, last entry 18:30 • adult 11€, student/senior 9€, youth 6-14yr 3.50€ & 15-18yr 4€, family 23€, combo-ticket with Mozart Residence available, or free with Salzburg Card, www.mozarteum.at. Pictured—55-cent postage stamp released in January 2006 by the Deutsche Post to commemorate Mozart's 250th birthday).

The legendary "Amadeus," baptized as Johannes Chrysostomus Wolfgangus *Theophilus Mozart, was born January 27, 1756 in the third-floor apartment at Getreidegasse 9, now a museum, in the heart of Salzburg's Old Town. *Amadeus, as he is so often referred to, comes from Theophilus, which translates to Gottlieb in German, Amadeus in Latin, and "beloved by God" in English. He routinely used Wolfgang Amadeus as his signature and is therefore generally known by these two names.

Wolfgang was the seventh and last child born to Leopold and Anna Maria Mozart. The parents moved into this third-floor apartment in 1747, where they lived for 26 years before relocating across town in 1773 (to the Residence p. 40).

☞ **Self-guided Mozart's Birthplace** (allow at least 30 minutes). The Mozart apartment at Getreidegasse 9 is small, consisting of a storage room, living room, bedroom and study. The entire museum, however, covers much more, three floors totaling 17 exhibition rooms, beginning on the third floor and descending to the first floor. *For the sake of time and interest, this self-guided tour will only cover the third-floor,* totaling 11 rooms. And since our tour begins on the third floor, there are a bundle of stairs to negotiate, some 57 up and the same down. Ready? Follow me, let's check out where the maestro drew his first breath.

→ At Getreidegasse 9, walk through the curvaceous portal and climb 20 steps to the cashier, then another 37 steps to the third floor and communal kitchen.

1: Kitchen: During Mozart's time, kitchens in middle-class residences were built separate from the living area because of poor ventilation and dangers posed by fire. Consequently, we reach the kitchen first with its stone stove shared by building residents outside the Mozart apartment.

2: Hallway: The other end of the hallway you'll see a large family tree on the right wall. The infant mortality rate in the 18th century was sky high, as experienced by Anna Maria Mozart who gave birth 7 times here with only 2 surviving infancy: Wolfgang Amadeus and his sister Maria Anna, affectionately "Nannerl." Wolfgang and his wife, Constanze, bore 6 children but only 2 survived babyhood: Carl Thomas and Franz Xaver Wolfgang. Sadly, neither son married nor had children, therefore when Nannerl's great-granddaughter Bertha Forschter died in 1919, the Mozart line was extinguished. (Note: From this point photography is not allowed in the museum.)

3: Storage room: Step through the (Museum) doorway into the Mozart apartment via the so-called Kabinett, used as a storage room and later Wolfgang's bedroom. Exhibits here introduce visitors to Wolfgang's parents, Leopold Mozart and Anna Maria Pertl. Leopold was born in 1719 (some 250 km northwest of Salzburg) in the Bavarian city of Augsburg and came to Salzburg to study philosophy at the university but never finished, devoting himself entirely to music from age 24. Anna Maria, on the other hand, daughter of the town judge, was somewhat of a local girl, having grown up in nearby St. Gilgen on Wolfgangsee (p. 80).

→ Step over to the display case. The most important document in the room you'll find here, 2nd from right, a letter penned by Leopold announcing the birth of his son on January 27, 1756 at 8 o'clock in the evening. (Note: Leopold Mozart is buried in Salzburg, adjacent to Wolfgang's wife, Constanze, see page 114.)

4: Living room: From the Kabinett step into the living room, the largest and brightest room in the apartment, serving as space for the family to relax, share meals, and practice music. Alas, no furniture from Mozart's day has been preserved, not even the green-tiled heater in the corner, only its location is accurate. Facing you on the wall upon entering are individual portraits of the Mozarts, framed between parents Leopold and Anna Maria are arguably the most famous paintings of the two children. Wolfgang, for example, is pictured here in 1763, age 7, wearing the swanky duds presented to him by Empress Maria Theresa after a highly anticipated appearance at the Viennese court. (Note: If you tour the DomQuartier, page 32, you'll see where Mozart made his first ever court appearance in the Residenz.)

Leopold Mozart was a revered musician and violinist in his own right. He schooled his two children incessantly, right here in this room, thus young Wolfgang literally had music running through his veins. Perhaps unsurprisingly, he learned to play various keyboards at the age of 3 and penned his first symphony at age 8, which some of his first compositions can be seen in the display cases. In the display beneath the aforementioned family portraits are breezy quotes from letters describing characteristic eloquences of the Mozarts, like the humorous mother, the well-behaved sister, the critical father, and the unconventional son. Ha!

5: Birth room: Jump two small steps into the Mozart family bedroom, where it is widely believed that Anna Maria gave birth seven times, the last being at 8 p.m. January 27, 1756 to wondrous Wolfgang, when she was 36 years old and Leopold 37. Since the birth room, locally Geburtszimmer, is indeed the most important room in the apartment, personal objects and treasures are understandably exhibited in this space. It is an absolute treat, for example, to eyeball the very violin Wolfgang played as a youngster, still in excellent playing condition, as well as view Mozart's silk wallet, mother-of-pearl buttons from his jacket, a lock of hair, and more.

6: Study: The last room in the Mozart apartment is the study, likely the locale Leopold used to play music and coach his child prodigy. Today, this space is devoted to Wolfgang's family history with his wife Constanze, whom he married in Vienna in 1782. The two were generally very happy together and she bore him six children, two of whom reached adulthood. The first, Carl Thomas was six years older than his brother Franz Xaver Wolfgang, who was born on July 26, 1791, less than five months before his prolific father passed. Both sons can be seen in the double portrait hung next to their astute mother pictured in 1802 holding a folder containing Mozart's works.

→ Exit the Mozart apartment via the study and head out onto the walkway, passing the toilets and staircase, to the back of the building where the museum continues.

7: Anteroom: In this space a large-scale view of Vienna in the 18th century sets the scene for the next room.

8: Life in Vienna: In 1781, Mozart arrived in Vienna, a bustling city having a population of some 200,000 residents, a big jump from sleepy Salzburg that had a fraction of the inhabitants. Additionally, Vienna was the capital of classical music and seat of the House of Habsburg, rulers of the Holy Roman Empire for centuries. The opportunities were endless in the imperial metropolis, and Mozart worked tirelessly to get ahead, splitting his time between composing, teaching, performing, socializing, and Freemasonry, managing on around five hours of sleep per night. Although Mozart earned a respectable amount of money, he spent more than what was coming in, incurring substantial debt, much to the dismay of Constanze. Sadly, at the young age of 35, Wolfgang Amadeus Mozart, the self-promoting virtuoso light years ahead of his time, died on December 5, 1791 after suffering a long illness and was buried in St. Marx Cemetery, Vienna (p. 114). His musical genius will forever be remembered.

9: Post-death: This room further explores the people closest to Wolfgang Amadeus and documents their lives after his death. Two oil paintings adjacent to one another, for example, feature his two sons. Exhibits in the display case below recount that the oldest son, **Carl Thomas**, despite his musical talents, followed a career of civil service and lived in Italy for some 50 years, returning to Salzburg only three times. The last occasion being in 1856 to celebrate the 100th anniversary of his father's birth. Mozart's younger son, **Franz Xaver Wolfgang**, born mere months prior to his father's death and therefore he did not know him but was said to be likewise a musical prodigy. At age 17, Franz Xaver took his talents to the city of Lemberg, then under Habsburg rule, today known as Lviv, the largest city in western Ukraine, where he lived out his life as a music teacher and composer. The painting of Mozart's sister, **Nannerl**, portrays her at age 50. Living to the advanced age of 78, she was an important witness to the Mozart family history and advocate of her little brother's gifted legacy. In an apartment in the (present-day restaurant) Zipfer Bierhaus, a stone's throw across the square from this room, Nannerl lived out the final 28 years of her life. **Constanze Mozart** lived 18 years as a widow before remarrying. She had met Danish diplomat Georg Nikolaus Nissen years earlier and headed down the aisle with him in 1809. The couple published the first extensive biography on Wolfgang Amadeus. (One of the first copies can be seen in the display case.) She owned the small piano on display while living in Denmark with Georg before retiring in Salzburg.

10: Posterity: This room is dedicated to the Salzburg Mozarteum Foundation, established in 1880 to preserve and commemorate Mozart's legacy. The first monumental fanfare honoring Mozart in Salzburg began on September 6, 1842 with the unveiling of his statue on then Michaelsplatz. Sadly, Constanze died 6 months prior and never saw the majestic tribute. Next came a small exhibition at his birthplace, now the world's oldest museum dedicated to a composer!

11: Mozart Online: In the adjoining room enthusiasts can surf computers for further information about the Salzburg Mozarteum Foundation as well as to populate digitized Mozart compositions and browse original manuscripts.

That's it, folks, the end of our self-guided tour. The museum, however, continues. Head downstairs to the next set of exhibition rooms or keep following the Exit signs that lead outside.

👍 **DomQuartier,** allow at least 2 hours for a visit (Wed-Mon 10:00-17:00, closed Tue, last entry 16:00 • July-Aug daily, Wed till 20:00 • **free Wi-Fi**, log on to "ResidenzSbg" • www.domquartier.at), price includes audio guide and admission into the **Residenz** state rooms and **Residenz Gallery** (www.salzburg-burgen.at), the **Cathedral Museum**, onto its **Panorama Terrace**, and the temporary exhibitions of the **North Oratory**, adult 12€, student 5€, family 27€, child 5yr or younger free, or free with Salzburg Card. **Note:** Tickets are valid all day thus you can break when you wish, just be sure to return before last entry. No photography allowed inside except from the Organ Gallery and, of course, the outdoor Panorama Terrace (steps 5-6 below). From either said location the scenes are sensational, reason alone to visit the DomQuartier.

☞ **Self-guided DomQuartier** (allow at least 2 hours). Billed as Salzburg's Tour de Baroque, the DomQuartier gives visitors an intimate look into the former seat of power held by the ruling prince-archbishops. Set within a handful of adjoining sites in the heart of Salzburg, the newly established cultural center totals some 15,000 square meters, 2,000 exhibits, and spans 1,300 years of history for the price of one admission. From the upper floors, behold terrific views of Old Town lanes, squares and courtyards while touring grand rooms, galleries, and consuming exhibitions.

1: The best place to enter the DomQuartier is via the Residenz. To do that, step through its grand portal off Residenzplatz. From the inner courtyard go straight and climb the broad staircase (61 steps) to the cashier and state rooms, locally Prunkräume. (At the top of the staircase, notice the Fackelstein used to snuff flaming hand-held torches, or Fackeln, in centuries past.)

2: The tour circles back here, thus store your personal items in one of the provided lockers (insert a 1€/2€ coin but you'll get it back upon reopening locker). When ready, show the cashier your Salzburg Card then pick up an audio guide. → **Note:** Throughout the DomQuartier, follow Tour/Rundgang signs leading to the next exhibits. Toilets (WC) can be found on either floor.

3: At your leisure begin touring the **Residenz**, dating from 1102, the former state rooms and living quarters of the prince-archbishops. The second room along is the Conference Room, where Wolfgang Amadeus Mozart played his first court concert at the age of 6 (in front of Prince-Archbishop Schrattenbach). Later in the tour, note the so-called White Hall where documents were signed on May 1, 1816 to officially incorporate Salzburg into Austria.

4: From the state rooms climb 42 steps to the **Residenz Gallery**, hung with paintings from the 16th to 19th centuries by European masters, including Rubens, Rembrandt, and van Dyck. I'm particularly partial to painting No. 64, "Kinder im Fenster" by Waldmüller.

5: When ready, step outside on to the **Panorama Terrace** for a wowing bird's eye view of Salzburg's landmark plazas, saintly steeples, and old-town architecture. An info board positioned either side of the terrace names specific sites and an audio guide key for narration. Fans of the movie "**The Sound of Music**" will recognize Residenzplatz as the setting Maria splashed water in the horse's face while singing "I Have Confidence" as well as for German soldiers marching beneath Nazi flags hanging from the Residenz.

6: Back inside, on the way to the Cathedral Museum, you'll pass the North Oratory on the left (for temporary exhibitions) before encountering more jaw-dropping views at the **Organ Gallery**, home to Austria's largest organ. From here you can peer over the whole of the cathedral's glorious inner sanctum, Salzburg's spiritual center—this breathtaking sight alone is worth your time! → Skip to the other side of the Organ Gallery and face the high altar; the organ to its right (pictured), and partially facing you, Mozart regularly played when he was an organist in the archbishop's court. In total, you count five independent organs; Salzburg Cathedral is the only house of God north of the Alps to maintain this many under one roof. And on special occasions when they're all gloriously played in unison, heavenly spirits seemingly lead saints in song and priests in prayer.

7: Next and last stop on this floor is the **Cathedral Museum**—peruse its pious relics dating from as early as the 8th century A.D. Really! You'll find the large, processional Rupert Cross facing you in the last room. Don't miss it.

8: → When finished perusing the Cathedral Museum, you have two options: **1)** End your tour here and exit the DomQuartier or **2)** continue the tour, which I recommend since we're almost at the end anyway. Moreover, if you have items stored in the locker, take option 2. Those of you who choose option 1 and wish to exit now, take the elevator down to the cashier at the bottom where you can turn in your audio guide. This exit will put you at the cathedral's main entrance on Domplatz.

9: Continuing our tour, descend the spiral staircase (33 steps) to the **Cabinet of Curiosities** collected centuries ago by influential archbishops, like Wolf Dietrich, who sought to gather a world of scientific discoveries and cultural refinement, nature's wonders and creatures to be displayed here, in the original showcases, for us to marvel.

10: From the Cabinet of Curiosities step straight into the well-hung **Long Gallery**, formerly serving as the archbishops' picture gallery from the mid-17th century.

11: From the literal Long Gallery swing right into the **Museum of St. Peter's Abbey**, representing the oldest community of monks in the German-speaking world, showcasing a remarkably rich collection of divine art on display for the first time.

That's it, folks, the end of our tour. The Museum of St. Peter's Abbey is the last station in the cultural complex, leading you back to where we began. Hope you enjoyed our saintly swing through Salzburg's DomQuartier.

✋ **Fortress of Salzburg,** locally Festung Hohensalzburg, allow at least 2 hours for a visit (daily: Jan-April & Oct-Dec 9:30-17:00, May-Sept 9:00-19:00, last entry 30 min before listed closing times • www.salzburg-burgen.at • **free Wi-Fi**, log on to "Festung").

There are **two ticket-types** at the fortress, **Basic** and **Standard**, that cover the three main attractions (listed as A, B, C) within the medieval complex: **[A]** fortress walking tour with audio guide, **[B]** museums, **[C]** royal rooms (locally Fürstenzimmer) and the mediocre Magic Theater.

The **Basic Ticket**—adult 12€, youth 6-14yr 6.80€, family 27€, free with Salzburg Card—includes round trip on the cable railway and attractions [A] and [B], *not* [C] royal rooms. The **Standard Ticket** costs roughly 3.50€ more, is *not* valid with the Salzburg Card, includes the Basic Ticket offerings [A, B] and entry into the royal rooms [C]. **Suggestion:** Pay cashier the extra fee to upgrade to the Standard Ticket and tour the royal rooms. Or better, arrive before 11:00, show your Salzburg Card to the cashier and let him/her know you want to access the royal rooms—it's *free* before 11:00!

Note: Salzburg Card holders, if you're only interested in the Basic ticket (i.e. not the royal rooms) you can skip the line at the cashier by simply scanning the barcode on your Card at the turnstile to enter the funicular. You don't need a physical ticket in the fortress, your Salzburg Card is sufficient. And if you decide later to visit the royal rooms, you can pay the upgrade to the cashier before entering the rooms.

Getting there: Although the vast majority of us will reach the fortress via the easily accessible **cable railway**, or funicular, locally Festungsbahn (departing every 5-10 min), there is actually a second method: **by foot** — steep, 15 min, Basic admission reduced to adult 9.20€, youth 6-14yr 5.20€, or free with Salzburg Card — from outside the funicular station entrance, climb the cobbled lane a few meters and take the steps on the right connecting to the path up to the cashier.

Hikers: Double the exercise and sightseeing, combine the following fortress tour with my self-guided Mönchsberg hike on page 48. Either start below with the funicular to fortress, exit the fort on foot (via path listed at step 6) and trek to the Lift (p. 38), or begin with the Lift up and trek to the fortress following my self-guided hiking tour. Once in the fortress, continue straight and jog uphill to step 4 below and begin the following self-guided fortress tour from there.

☞ **Self-guided Fortress tour** (allow at least 2 hours). And since our tour is set within a big fortress on a big hill, you'll need to negotiate a few hundred steps along the way to reach attractions A, B, and C.

→ Dating from 1077 A.D. and never conquered, Salzburg's fortress (Festung Hohensalzburg) registers today as one of the largest fully preserved castle complexes in Europe. It is the city's signature landmark, where the ruling archbishops resided before moving down to the Residenz (see DomQuartier, p. 32). Our self-guided fortress tour will take in all the highlights, and more. Ready?

1: Let's start by riding the funicular to the fortress, visited by upwards of 1 million tourists each year.

2: Exit the top station left and stroll a short distance to the viewing terrace with guard lookouts. Sensational, isn't it? And I'm pleased to inform you it gets better.

3: Climb 60 (steep) steps to the fortress grounds, go right then swing left and down to the door ahead on the right with the letter A. Stop.

4: Later, I highly recommend you return here and join the 30-minute **fortress walking tour with audio guide [A]**. You'll delve into the history of the fortress, deep into the bowels of its battlements, taking in such highlights as the torture chamber, Salzburg Bull, and **lookout tower** with its jaw-dropping, panoramic views. This attraction alone is worth your fortress visit. (To continue the jaw-dropping awesomeness in Old Town, do my self-guided tour at the Panorama Museum on page 37.)

→ Now that we found the first fortress attraction, let's make a loop around the castle grounds and find the remaining two [B, C].

5: Continue downhill, passing **toilets** on the right, and stop in front of the archway next right. We're going to continue straight but first I want to show you a magnificent view from the **lookout**, thus bounce down the 17 steps. At the bottom, for the sake of orientation, if you were to continue down the next set of steps it would lead you past the Panorama Restaurant and back up to the funicular station where we first arrived. Instead of that route, skip a few meters past the tree to the railing.

→ Below you'll see a lone cottage in the meadow. This formerly belonged to the **town executioner**. (Perhaps nobody wanted to hang out with him.) The last person to wear the noose in Salzburg was in the early 1800s on the knoll behind the cottage. Notice the palatial digs across the street just beyond the cottage—this is the **Altenheim**, or old folks' home. And dominating the background of this dreamy vista is perhaps Austria's most intriguing mountain: **Untersberg**. Fans of the movie "**The Sound of Music**" will remember the opening scene when Maria says it was upon this landmass she was singing. Maria explained passionately to the Reverend Mother Abbess that Untersberg is her mountain, and as a child she used to climb a tree and peer into the convent's garden to watch the sisters at work (obviously with mega-powerful binoculars because the abbey is just to your left around the corner). What's more, when Maria hears the bells chiming while on Untersberg, we now know (from our view point) that not only did Maria have bionic hearing and the vision of a superhero, but she also must have been an Olympic athlete in training to even contemplate reaching the convent in time. No wonder she was late! Pointing to another Sound of Music scene, look behind the Altenheim and to its right and you'll see part of another stately structure. This stunning Rococo palace is Schloss Leopoldskron (pictured on back cover of this book), originally built in 1736 for Prince-Archbishop Leopold Firmian and was used in the movie as the back of the von Trapp villa. (For more on "The Sound of Music" and my self-guided walking and driving tours, see page 94.) Lastly, before we move on, less than half of Untersberg is in Austria and everything to its right and beyond is Bavaria!

6: When ready, bounce back up the steps the way you came and exit right. (Let's continue our fortress tour.) Mosey past the Burgschenke Restaurant-Café and up the slope. (The right lane, however, is the footpath to/fro the fortress, thus if you'd like to **exit the fort on foot**, take this path down.) At the top of the slope walk straight past the cistern wellhead and stop in the middle of the grounds, leaving the wellhead behind you and the tree to your immediate right. From this position I'll point out a few sites:

→ In front of you, in the eastern corner of the fortress grounds, is the **goods railway** responsible for lifting materials, wares and whatnot into the fort. It is arguably the oldest railway of its kind in the world still in use, originally commissioned by then Prince-Archbishop Leonhard von Keutschach circa year 1500.

→ Next to the railway you'll see an arched portal leading to another stupendous **lookout**, having similar vistas over Salzburg Old and New towns as you first encountered off the funicular. Head through the portal later if time is on your side. (From the terrace, look right for "The Sound of Music" abbey with its red onion-domed steeple and directly below the terrace you'll see the steep footpath leading to/fro the fortress.)

→ Over your right shoulder is the former **arsenal** building, dating from 1559, thus the first weapons stored here were swords, sabers, halberds, cannon, and later the flintlock rifle.

→ Turn and face the wellhead. After the months-long siege of 1525 in the so-called Peasants' War, then Prince-Archbishop Matthäus Lang von Wellenburg realized that without water a ruler wields no power. It was a close call, the water nearly dried up during the siege, thus the archbishop commissioned this significant Venetian-style **cistern** capable of filtering and storing some 300,000 liters of rainwater.

7: Jog right (west), beneath the ancient linden tree, through the two archways and climb 58 steps to the first of the fortress museums.

→ **Note:** We're headed to the top of the fortress to attractions [B] and [C], thus if time is short or you're just plain tired and prefer to skip the museums and royal rooms, continue straight past the steps and follow the signs a short distance to the funicular (Festungsbahn) to return back the way you came.

8: After climbing 58 steps you'll reach the first part of the **Fortress Museum [B]**, having multiple rooms exhibiting the fort's history via artifacts from Roman times as well as suits of armor and weaponry from the Middle Ages.

9: Climb another 28 steps to the imperial **Rainer Regiment Museum [B]**, where military enthusiasts will marvel at medals, uniforms, and machine guns from World War I.

→ On this level you'll also find a *cashier sitting before the **royal rooms [C]**, the fort's penthouse equivalent with stunning city views, formerly belonging to influential archbishops whose royal toilet flushed onto the peasants below. Really! (*Basic ticket holders can pay cashier 3.50€ upgrade fee or Salzburg Card holders who arrived before 11:00 get in *free.*) Rooms include the Golden Hall, where classical (e.g. Mozart) concerts are held. While in the hall, pay particular attention to the second marble pillar from the left. Midway up its left side you'll see a cavity where a canon ball struck it during the Peasants' War in the year 1525. No kidding!

That's it, folks, the end of our tour. The exhibition, however, continues. Drop back downstairs and exit through the second part of the Fortress Museum to the castle grounds. Hope you enjoyed our boogie through the battlements and continue to do so. Sashay over to attraction [A] and join the 30-minute walking tour with audio guide. To return to the cable railway descending to Old Town, follow signs to the funicular (Festungsbahn). It's never far.

Catacombs, allow 15 min for a visit, (daily 10:00-17:00, May-Sept till 18:00, adult 2€, student/youth 6-18yr 1.50€, free with Salzburg Card).

In the cliff face overlooking St. Peter's Cemetery (p. 18) are Salzburg's so-called catacombs, dwellings dug out by Christians in the 3rd century A.D. The caverns are still somewhat of a mystery to historians, who will concede that they were used as a hermitage over the past 1500 years. Perhaps Salzburg's founding father, Bishop Rupert, initially resided here in the year 696?

☞ **Self-guided Catacombs tour** (allow 15 minutes).

1: In St. Peter's Cemetery, stroll over to the cliff face to the catacombs, locally Katakomben. These were originally enclosed within the composite rock until a landslide exposed them in 1669. The man-made facade we see today was added later. You won't find any bones in the catacombs as the name suggests. However, at the entrance are the graves of Mozart's sister Maria Anna ("Nannerl") and prominent Salzburg composer Michael Haydn (brother of Joseph Haydn hailed as "Father of the Symphony"). When viewing the two graves, you're standing on top of an ossuary (oodles of bones), which was positioned here as an "intermediate" depository when no graves in the cemetery were available. The painting at the cross depicts the Virgin Mary, Jonah and Mary Magdalene flanking Jesus above weak souls praying for absolution in a raging fire. Either side of the painting is the Dance of the Dead (1660), portraying victims of plague.

2: To your left, climb 48 steps to reach the first level, go right then follow the walkway to St. Gertrude's chapel, dating from the 4th century. The monks from St. Peter's monastery (next door) still periodically use this chapel today, along with the consecrated altar (1862). The column in the center of the room dates from the 17th century and is a remembrance to those who died during the plague. Adjacent are vaulted niches for clergy. In the back of the chapel (through opening) is a section hollowed out for those not yet baptized. The fading fresco above the entrance dates from the 15th century and portrays the martyrdom of St. Thomas Becket (who was the much-adored Archbishop of Canterbury murdered by followers of Henry II, the King of England, in 1170).

3: Waddle outside and climb nine more steps to a petite platform affording dramatic views of the cemetery and Salzburg's soaring collection of church steeples. Inscribed on the bell to your left is the year "1681."

4: Climb the final 36 lopsided steps via the narrow passage to reach the Maximus chapel. At the top you'll discover an unconsecrated altar (inlaid tablet is absent), a tiny doorway that once led to further dugouts, and an empty grave with a Latin inscription dating from 1530. It reads: "In 477, Odoacer, the king of the peoples Ruthenians, Gepids, Goths, Magyars and Herules, fought against the church of God and violently threw Maximus and 50 of his followers to their deaths from this cave where they were hiding on account of their faith. Odoacer's men went on to destroy the entire province of Noricum with fire and swords." (Noricum is roughly the provincial boundaries of today's Salzburgland.)

That's it, folks, the end of our tour. Hope you enjoyed our cruise through Salzburg's catacombs. Exit at your leisure. Please be careful descending the steps. Go slow, hold on to the railing, and I'll see you safe and sound at the next attraction.

Panorama Museum, allow at least 20 min for a visit (daily 9:00-17:00, adult 4€, student 2€, youth 6-15yr 1.50€, family 8€, combo-ticket with connecting Salzburg Museum 10€/4.50€, or free with Salzburg Card, www.salzburgmuseum.at).

Majestic and magnificent, the panorama painted by J.M. Sattler is an enormous 130-square-meter cyclorama, or circular mural, of Salzburg as viewed from the fortress' lookout tower in the year 1829 (if you've done my fortress tour you know the immensity of this tremendous view). Upon the panorama's completion, Sattler and his family toured Europe with it for 10 years (1829-39). At each destination, from Oslo to Prague, the panorama was displayed in a pavilion so locals could marvel at the beauty of Salzburg, often billed as the "Rome of the north" because of its myriad piazzas and church steeples. After the Sattlers returned home, the panorama together with the so-called cosmoramas were exhibited permanently in its own tribute pavilion near the Mirabell Gardens until 1937. Today, Sattler's panorama has been lovingly restored (exceeding 4,400 work hours) and is now on display for you to admire in this purpose-built museum. **To get there**, the Panorama Museum adjoins the Salzburg Museum but its main entrance (recommended) is located off Residenzplatz, behind the cathedral, next to the post office. Come with me, let's peruse the panorama together.

☞ **Self-guided Panorama tour** (allow at least 20 minutes).

1: Enter museum via its main entrance. At the turnstile, insert your entry ticket, you'll see illustrations of the Sattler family and of the original tribute pavilion.

2: Step inside the museum—women's **toilets** are to the right and men's are downstairs—take one of the small description boards located either end of the **cosmoramas** and read along. Originally, some two centuries ago, these toured with Sattler's panorama and were viewed through a small peep hole in a box, intensifying the imagination of travel to exotic and faraway places. Sattler went on long exhibition tours with the cosmoramas, even crossing the gigantic Atlantic to America. (What an amazing journey that must have been in those days.) Browse the cosmoramas at your leisure.

3: When ready, from the lower level, enter the **panorama**, climb 10 steps, and stand in the middle of the platform with your back to the stairs. Let's say high noon (12:00) on a clock dial is in front of you and the stairway behind you is 6:00.

→ Remember, the panorama is a portrayal of Salzburg as viewed from the fortress in the early 19th century, thus the reason you do *not* see the fortress. Today, Old Town is virtually unchanged but the open green fields have largely been converted into housing areas and commercial centers. Note the river was much wilder then. Beer connoisseurs will be happy to know that the church tower at 12:00 (just above the white twin towers) represents the monastic Augustinian complex which joins the Müllner Bräu (p. 52), Austria's largest tavern and beer garden.

At 2:00 (lower part of canvas) is the Dom, or cathedral, where Mozart was baptized in 1756. The twin steeples budding from the distant hill above the Dom (upper part of canvas) belong to the Baroque-style church Maria Plain, a pilgrimage site since the 17th century and today arguably Salzburgland's most breathtaking wedding venue.

At 5:00 (lower part of canvas) is the Nonnberg abbey—dating from the 8th century, it is the oldest known Catholic convent in the German-speaking world. This is the abbey portrayed in the movie "The Sound of Music," where Maria really did study and where she and the captain really did tie the knot.

At 7:00, the snowcapped Tennengebirge mountains in the background is where you need to be to explore the world's largest ice cave (see Werfen p. 75).

At 9:00 is Schloss Leopoldskron (palace built in 1736 for the archbishop but more recently recognized as the back of the von Trapp house in "The Sound of Music." Remember the scene the kids fell in the lake?). And it is upon the imposing mountain (Untersberg p. 44) rising above the lake that Maria confesses she was singing (in the opening scene of the movie).

That's it, folks, the end of our tour. Short, sweet, and a sprinkling of *The Sound of Music*. Use one of the provided telescopes to zoom in on the painting's impressive detail. Enjoy, and I'll see ya at the next attraction.

👍 **Mönchsberg Lift,** locally Mönchsbergaufzug, (daily 8:00-21:00 except Monday only till 19:00, July-Aug till 23:00, round trip 3.60€, one way 2.30€, youth 6-14yr 1.80€/1.20€, family 7.20€/4.50€, free with Salzburg Card, www.salzburg-ag.at). **Note:** Salzburg Card holders, no need to see cashier or wait in line, scan Card's barcode at turnstile.

This elevator, Aufzug in German, lifts visitors to/fro the Mönchsberg (Monks' Ridge) **observation terrace**, one of Salzburg's most scenic vantage points. Historically, a single elevator system was excavated from inside the cliff in 1890, whipping beguiled visitors up the 60-meter shaft in a record 2 minutes. Today, the same trip takes a mere 30 seconds and the 3-elevator system transports approximately 1 million persons per year to a gargantuan view (best in afternoon), the **Museum of Modern Art** (next entry), the scenic and not-so-economical **M32 café-restaurant** (closed Monday).

→ For more on the recommended Lift and my **self-guided Mönchsberg hike**, see page 48.

To get there, the Lift is secreted at Gstättengasse 13. To find it, look above the northwest part of Old Town for a wood-covered shaft running up the cliff face. Walk toward this and follow the cliff farther along to the road Gstättengasse. Above the entrance at No. 13 is the acronym MdM for Museum der Moderne. Step through the portal to the cashier and elevators. Or, buses 1, 4 and 10 stop out front at Mönchsbergaufzug.

Museum of Modern Art, (Tue-Sun 10:00-18:00, Wed till 20:00, adult 8€, student-senior & youth 6-16yr 6€, combo-ticket with Mönchsberg Lift 10€/7€, or free with Salzburg Card, www.museumdermoderne.at). → At a cost of 22€ million in 2004, Salzburg added the voluminous Museum der Moderne (MdM) Mönchsberg to its bevy of A-list attractions. Boasting some 3,000 m² (32,000 ft²) of floor space on three levels largely dedicated to rotating exhibitions, MdM's easily recognizable white facade with castle-like turret planted atop Mönchsberg is readily accessible via the above-listed "Lift." While connoisseurs of contemporary visual arts will embrace the juxtaposition of modernity above Old Town, non-enthusiasts will find the austere all-concrete structure uninspiring and only worthwhile with a Salzburg Card for the exceptional hill-top views and possibly a visit to the adjoining scenic-though-pricey M32 café-restaurant (closed Monday). Note: Store your daypack/personal items in one of the lockers provided (insert a 1€ coin but you'll get it back upon reopening locker). Every Wednesday (18:00-19:30) and Sunday (14:00-17:30) students pay only 2€ (and 1.70€ rt for the "Lift").

Museum of Natural History, locally Haus der Natur, allow at least 2 hours for a visit (daily 9:00-17:00—adult 8€, student and youth 4-15yr 5.50€, family from 20€, free with Salzburg Card—best on a Monday, Thursday or Friday • www.hausdernatur.at). → This fun, educational and exceptional museum, founded in 1924, a favorite with children, is Austria's largest science center, having eight levels of exhibits from outer space matter to sea life and dinosaur displays to reptiles in habitat. Hustle up two flights of steps to the 2nd floor and browse the Galaxy room for your estimated weight (in kilograms) on the various planets in our solar system; start with Erde (Earth). I weigh, for example, 175 kg on Jupiter; that's 385 lbs! Who knew. After exploring the cosmos, swing through the neighboring reptile zoo and check out an alligator, iguanas, and other cold-blooded creatures. See if you can stare down a poisonous snake. Journey into the human body on the 4th (top) floor; learn how we see, hear, and smell. If nature calls you away from the action, **toilets** are seated on every floor. Next door in the adjoining Science Center, having some 80 interactive stations, kids can ride the (Palfinger) basket crane (ground floor) or physically run in a human hamster wheel to generate power to keep the wind turbine and train running (1st floor, solar energy exhibit—I reached around 960 watts before I conked out). Before all that, however, plan your trip here around the following happenings: **Aquarium**: the octopus, archer fish, and reef shark are fed every Monday & Thursday starting at 10:15, piranhas too on Thursday. **Science Center**: big and little kids alike are wowed by the explosive *Magic Chemistry Show typically scheduled at 10:30 every 2nd and 4th Friday of the month in the 2nd-floor Lab (*show in German, duration 45 min, no reservation required). Round off your tour with a visit to the museum's popular café with outdoor terrace on the 1st floor (i.e. one level up). Note: store your daypack/personal items in a locker downstairs (insert a 1€ coin but you'll get it back upon reopening locker). **To get there**, the museum is located in the northwest part of Old Town at Museumsplatz 5, between the river and Mönchsberg Lift (listed on previous page).

SIGHTS, New Town (across river)

Note: All the attractions listed in this section are either free to enter or are free with the Salzburg Card (p. 9): **Mirabell Gardens** (p. 26) • **Mozart Residence** (below) • **St. Sebastian's Cemetery & Church** (next page) • **Kapuzinerberg** (p. 48).

Mozart Residence, locally Wohnhaus, Makartplatz 8, allow 30-45 min for a visit, enthusiasts much longer (daily 9:00-17:30, last entry 17:00 • July-Aug 8:30-19:00, last entry 18:30 • adult 11€, student/senior 9€, youth 6-14yr 3.50€ & 15-18yr 4€, family 23€, combo-ticket with Mozart's Birthplace available, or free with Salzburg Card, audio guide included with admission • www.mozarteum.at).

Note: Photography is not allowed in the museum. Check in advance to see if free Mozart concerts or performances are scheduled. Enthusiasts will be happy to know the museum is home to the Mozart Audio-Visual Collection, the largest of its kind relating to the life and works of Wolfgang Amadeus. The collection can be found on the mezzanine level (as you exit), is free to enter (hours are limited), and contains some 26,000 sound recordings (the oldest dating from 1889) and 3,300 video productions.

Residence: Since Leopold Mozart had made a name for himself as the archbishop's concert meister, in addition to rearing a child prodigy, the Mozarts could afford to move across the river in 1773 to this much bigger, eight-room residence known as the Dancing Master's House after prior resident and professional dance instructor, Johann Pastier. Centuries later, during World War II, the house was partly destroyed by bombs after an Allied air attack blasted the city in October 1944, but of course none of that had any bearing on young Wolfgang Amadeus who lived here until 1780-81 before moving permanently to Vienna, only returning once to Salzburg in 1783. Wolfgang's sister (Nannerl) lived at this residence until 1784, and Leopold died here in 1787.

Room 2: Although there are no original furnishings remaining here from Mozart's day, in the first main room (former ballroom) his personal fortepiano he used in Vienna is fortunately part of the collection, along with a treasured family portrait. Wolfgang's mother, Anna Maria, who sadly passed in 1778 some two years prior to the painting's commission, is prominently featured in the background. If you time it right, a master musician will be there performing a concert of sonatas on Wolfgang's fortepiano for you to savor. (Inquire ahead for planning.)

Room 3: Especially traumatic was young Wolfgang's sojourn in Paris, where his mother suddenly fell ill and died July 3, 1778. Heartbroken, Mozart asked a family friend to convey the sad news to his father and sister. You can view this letter in the 3rd room (after the ballroom) in the display case on the left as you enter.

Room 6: Staggeringly, Wolfgang traveled over one-third of his piano-playing life entertaining the various imperial courts of Europe and other dignitaries. Underscoring this feat, the 6th room in the museum presents visitors with a multimedia show offering 10 topics narrating "Mozart's Travels," such as his numerous concert tours (1762-91) across the continent totaling some 3,700 days, more than 10 years on the road! It certainly wasn't easy in those days, traveling by horse-drawn carriage was not only primitive but grueling, stressful, and terribly bumpy, taking what must have seemed like an eternity to count down the umpteen miles between destinations.

Room 7: In the last room we see a black-and-white photo of Mozart, appearing to be "Wanted" by authorities, illustrating how the gifted musician would have really looked with his large head, prominent nose, penetrating eyes, and petite frame. Stand next to the figure depicting his actual height, about 150 cm (4 ft 10 in).

St. Sebastian's Cemetery & Church, (daily 9:00-16:00, April-Oct till 18:30). Built in late-Gothic style from 1505-1512, St. Sebastian's Church fronts an enchanting, somewhat secluded cemetery landscaped in 1595 under the reign of Prince-Archbishop Wolf Dietrich von Raitenau. It makes sense that Wolf Dietrich chose this memorial park for his mausoleum, forever showcasing his holy eminence within a large stately rotunda marking the center of the grounds. Other eternal inhabitants include **Philippus Paracelsus**, renowned 16th-century alchemist who cured the incurable; (Wolfgang Amadeus) **Mozart's father**, Leopold (d. 1787) and **Mozart's widow**, Constanze Weber (d. 1842). For more on the two Mozarts, flip to page 114. **To get there** from Old Town, GPS: N47 48.259 E13 02.847, cross the river via the Staatsbrücke (main bridge) and climb Linzergasse to No. 60 (right). On your left step through the wrought-iron gate opening into the cemetery. Inside, go straight to Wolf Dietrich and en route you'll pass the Mozarts at the third grave site on the left.

SIGHTS, outside Old and New towns

Note: All the attractions listed in this section are either free to enter or are free with the Salzburg Card (p. 9), *except* for the last two entries: the luge and salt mines.

👍 **Schloss Hellbrunn,** allow 30 min to half a day for a visit (admission and details at bottom of entry). With its elaborate Baroque gardens, reflecting pools, romantic grottos and trick fountains landscaped on a sprawling 148-acre reserve, Hellbrunn palace was built for the playful and privileged Prince-Archbishop Markus Sittikus (1612-1619), who opportunely succeeded his uncle, Wolf Dietrich von Raitenau, whom Sittikus had imprisoned in the fortress. In select circles, these ornate and expansive digs became known as a Lustschloss, or palace of pleasure, where jovial parties and lavish celebrations were customary. The trick fountains, or Wasserspiele—specially modified statues, footpaths and walls—were a favorite of the archbishop, who giddily lured visitors into the gardens to run a gauntlet of spraying water. The big laugh came when Sittikus invited his guests to the luncheon table (pictured), where he seated them onto marble blocks fashioned into stools rigged with concealed water spouts. When Sittikus gave the signal, cold Alpine water shot from the stools—except his, of course—once again saturating his guests, who had to sit unflustered and appreciate that they were the butt of yet another heavenly gag contrived by the archbishop.

A visit to Schloss Hellbrunn is a delightful experience, in particular the trick fountains on a warm summer day. Families will appreciate the open green spaces and playground for kids, not forgetting the Salzburg Zoo and its adorable animals mere meters away (see next entry). Fans of the movie "The Sound of Music" will discover the famed gazebo (see Schloss Hellbrunn p. 108). Adventurers will trek one hour to the Stein Theater (signs point the way), where on August 31, 1617, the first open-air opera north of the Alps was performed: "L'Orfeo" by Monteverdi. Visitors in December will experience the spirit of Christmas in the palace courtyard, with its decorative market and festivities. → Since Schloss Hellbrunn covers many acres and attractions, a visit here could easily take half a day, depending on your agenda. If you're not carrying the

Salzburg Card, I recommend you allow at least 30 minutes to stroll the gardens (free to enter). Consider a picnic? **Toilets** can be found opposite the gazebo as well as near the palace entrance.

During your visit, you'll notice a canary-yellow structure on the hillside. In 1615, Prince-Archbishop Sittikus required an extra guest house for visiting VIPs, thus he ordered one to be built. The archbishop's labor force completed the task within a month, and from this stellar effort the structure originated its name: Monatsschlössl, or Month Villa. Today, it is the state-run (Volkskunde) **Folklore Museum** exhibiting items typifying regional cultures and traditions (April-Oct., daily, 10:00-17:15, 3€/1€, free with Salzburg Card or free with your combo palace-and-fountains ticket).

Stop by the palace April thru Nov 2017, daily (end times denote last tour)—April and Oct (thru Nov 1) 9:00-16:30, May-June and Sept 9:00-17:30, July-Aug 9:00-21:00 (after 18:00 trick fountain tours only), closed Nov-March. The **park and gardens** are free to enter and open daily year round 6:30-17:00, March and Oct. till 18:00, April-Sept. till 21:00. **Price** (combo-ticket palace and fountains), adult 12.50€, student 8€, youth 4-18yr 5.50€, family (2+1/2+2) 26.50€/29€, or free with Salzburg Card, www.hellbrunn.at. **Tours** of the palace interior are at your own pace with an audio guide and take about 30 min (typically no wait time); tours of the trick fountains are led by a palace guide and take roughly 35 min (with wait times upwards of 45 min, depending on weather and crowd size). **Note:** When touring the fountains, if the ground ahead of you is wet, prepare for soakage! On a warm summer's day, however, this is a welcome reprieve (but the line to get in will not be). **To get there**, Schloss Hellbrunn is located 5 km south of Old Town. **By bus** from the city, hop on #25 direction Untersbergbahn and get off at Schloss Hellbrunn, 15-min ride (free with Salzburg Card—bus departs Hauptbahnhof, Mirabellplatz, Rathaus, Mozartsteg every 20 min, and every 30 min after 18:00 Mon-Fri and 17:00 Sat-Sun). **Drivers**, exit the A10 autobahn at Salzburg-Süd and follow signs to Salzburg. At the first traffic light, turn left. On the other side of the village (Anif) you'll see the zoo's natural enclosures (right)—continue past the zoo and turn right at the end of the golden wall. Parking is available in three lots (but I recommend the last one on the right. Take a ticket: first 30 min are free, up to 2hr/2€, 3hr/2.60€, max 3.20€). **Cyclists**, ride pleasant Hellbrunner Allee (via Freisaalweg) to Schloss Hellbrunn—(consider riding riverside path back).

Zoo, Salzburg, allow at least 2 hours for a visit (daily: 9:00-16:30—last entry 1 hour before listed closing times—March open till 17:30, April-May & Sept-Oct till 18:00, June-Aug till 18:30 • adult 11.50€, youth 4-14yr 5€ & 15-19yr 7.50€, senior 65yr+ 10.50€, family [2+1/2+2] 26€/30.50€, or free with Salzburg Card, bag of animal food 3€ • www.salzburg-zoo.at). → In the early 15th century, the archbishop's love for animals motivated his holiness to establish a wildlife habitat 5 km south of Old Town. This evolved into today's 35-acre Hellbrunn Zoo (adjacent to the above-listed Schloss Hellbrunn), attracting upwards of 300,000 visitors annually. The zoo is home to around 1,200 animals (representing 140 species), such as zebras, lions, leopards, kangaroos, tigers, wolves, brown bears, rhinos, lemurs and monkeys, to name a few. Several of the enclosures have been landscaped into the cliff face, providing many animals a natural-as-can-be environment. **Note:** Friday and Saturday nights August thru mid-Sept. 2017 the zoo is open till 22:30 (last entry 21:00), allowing visitors a unique look into the nocturnal world of animals. **To get there**, follow the same directions above for Schloss Hellbrunn except **by bus** get off at the zoo (one stop after Schloss Hellbrunn) and **cyclists** lock the bike up at the palace and stroll through the gardens to the zoo.

Drivers, exit the A10 autobahn at Salzburg-Süd and follow signs to Salzburg. At the first traffic light, turn left. On the other side of the village (Anif) you'll see the zoo's natural enclosures on the right. Free parking out front (take ticket at boom gate and have zoo cashier validate it).

Brew World, locally "Brauwelt," allow at least 2 hours for tour and tasting (daily 10:00-17:00, last entry 16:00, July-Aug till 19:00, last entry 18:00, but plan your trip with the daily 60-min English-language tour departing 15:00 • adult 12.50€, student 11.50€, or free with Salzburg Card • www.brauwelt.at • **free Wi-Fi**, log on to "Stiegl Gast").

The folks at Stiegl have been brewing Salzburg's beer since 1492, precisely when Columbus discovered the Americas. They say he came here too but got lost, thus Stiegl brews a tribute beer entitled "Columbus 1492," a citric pale ale for explorer-types. To complement 500 years of Stiegl tradition, management created Brauwelt, or Brew World, an interactive journey through the history of beer making that you can discover at your own pace on multiple floors, thus umpteen stairs to negotiate. (Follow Exhibition signs thru museum or join 15:00 tour.) **Note:** The first part of Brew World is a 12-minute film, thus notify the cashier you'd like to watch it in English. What's more, included with admission, the cashier will hand you complimentary vouchers for 3 (.2l) Stiegl beers and a remembrance gift (typically a small beer mug). Post-tour, with your vouchers, enjoy a freshly brewed Stiegl on the house anywhere in the house, e.g. in the beer garden, or saloon (Braustüberl) where you can also feed your appetite with the scrumptious Braumeister's schnitzel or meat-lover's Brauwelt-Pfandl from the menu. **Suggestion:** Arrive at 15:00 for the English tour. Salzburg Card holders, even if you're not interested in Brew World, swing by for your free beers and gift. Turn your visit into a cultural smorgasbord and walk from Brew World to Hangar-7 (next entry) or vice-versa, taking only 20 min. Ask staff for directions. **To get there**, Brauwelt is located at Bräuhausstrasse 9, 2 km west of Old Town. **By bus** from the city, hop on #1 direction Europark and get off at Bräuhausstrasse, 10-min ride (free with Salzburg Card—bus departs Hauptbahnhof, Mirabellplatz, Makartplatz, Hanuschplatz every 10 min, and every 20 min after 19:00 Mon-Sat and all day Sun—bus 10 also departs regularly from Hanuschplatz). Exit bus left and make the next left on Bräuhausstrasse. The brewery entrance is a few minutes farther ahead on the right. **Drivers**, from the city it's tough to find—ask directions. From the A1 autobahn, exit at "Flughafen" and follow signs to Salzburg/Brauwelt. After driving through the airport underpass, make your second right onto Karolingerstrasse. Follow this straight to the T-intersection, where you'll turn left. Go straight, the road will curve right, and follow Brauwelt signs closely for the upcoming right turns that circle the brewery and lead into the free visitor parking lot.

Hangar-7, allow at least 30 min for a visit (daily 9:00-22:00 • free entry • www.hangar-7.com). Head over to the airport and into Hangar-7, an ultramodern showroom made of glass and steel to house a collection of vintage aircraft dubbed the Flying Bulls, financed by Red Bull, the energy drink (p. 80). Get acquainted with modern jets and a few of history's legendary aircraft, such as the B-25 Mitchell bomber (pictured), F4U Corsair, Lockhead P-38 Lightning, and a DC-6 (that was formerly Yugoslavia's Air Force One equivalent used to transport Marshal Tito and his centrist guests). Red Bull's expanded collection now incorporates helicopters, F1 motor racing cars, and other vehicle-types. Fans of record-setting Salzburg son **Felix Baumgartner** will find an inspiring exhibition and some of his equipment.

From the display floor, look up. Integrated into the apex of the hangar's ceiling is the translucent **Threesixty Bar** (closed Mon & Thur otherwise open from 18:30), featuring a glass floor giving patrons the feel of walking on air, in a floating bar. Try it, but skirt-wearers beware! → Other reasons to visit Hangar-7 are its first-rate restaurant and bar-lounges, revolving art exhibitions, and one of the nicest restrooms (downstairs) you'll find in Salzburg. At the Michelin-rated **Ikarus** restaurant (daily 19:00-22:00, Thu-Sun also 12:00-14:00, reservations recommended, tel. 0662/21970, e-mail: ikarus@hangar-7.com) not only does the menu change monthly but so does the chef! Each year 12 of the world's best chefs are invited here for the month to prepare their signature dishes alongside those of their native country. Also dissimilar to other restaurants, pilots can literally fly in and park their plane out front. Salzburg's first non-smoking bar, **Mayday** (daily 12:00-midnight, Fri-Sat till 01:00) serves a wide range of hand-shaken drinks and healthy, "smart" cuisine. **Carpe Diem** café-lounge (daily 9:00-17:00, breakfast Mon-Fri 9:00-11:30 and Sat-Sun till 14:00) is a modish place to gel and consume beverages and snacks flown in from around the world while sitting only meters from a World War II fighter-bomber. If it's busy, go to the café first and leave your name before viewing the exhibition. **Suggestion:** Turn your visit into a double-header and walk from Hangar-7 to Brew World (above entry) or vice-versa, taking only 20 min. Ask staff for directions. **To get there,** Hangar-7 is located on the east side of the airport at Wilhelm-Spazier-Strasse 7. **By bus** from the city, hop on #2 direction Airport/Walserfeld and get off at Karolingerstrasse, 20-min ride (free with Salzburg Card—bus departs Wolf-Dietrich-Str., Mirabellplatz, Hauptbahnhof every 10 min, and every 20 min after 19:00 Mon-Sat and all day Sun). From Karolingerstrasse, it's a 5-min walk, exit bus left and march to the forward traffic light. Cross the street, continue straight (on Wilhelm-Spazier-Strasse) and Hangar-7 is a few hundred meters farther ahead on the right. **Drivers,** free parking. When coming from the city, turn left before the airport underpass into Wilhelm-Spazier-Strasse. When coming from the A1 autobahn, exit at "Flughafen" and follow signs to Salzburg. After driving through the airport underpass, make the first right into Wilhelm-Spazier-Strasse.

👍 Untersberg Mountain & Cable Car,

allow 90 min for a visit, not counting travel time to/fro cable car (cable cars run daily every 30 min on the hour and half hour from 9:00-16:00, March-June & Oct 8:30-17:00, July-Sept 8:30-17:30—but note the system will be closed for maintenance April 18-28 & again Oct 23 thru Dec 15, 2017—round trip adult 23.50€, student 16€, youth 6-14yr 11.50€, dog 8€, free with Salzburg Card • www.untersbergbahn.at). → Arguably Austria's most captivating landmass, Untersberg is a mountain of myth and legend spawned by medieval tales immortalizing heroic emperors and fantastic creatures that dwell in its foothills, peaks and valleys. In more recent times, Hollywood discovered Untersberg's charm and portrayed a dirndl-clad girl singing "The Sound of Music" on its meadows that led her to the abbey (p. 102). Midway along Untersberg's extensive plateau, a V-shaped crevice forms the natural border between Germany (Bavaria) and Austria. A short distance away at Obersalzberg, Hitler used to stare past Untersberg's majestic mass and into Salzburg from his giant picture-frame window (at his home, the Berghof). From its valuable marble quarries (still in operation today), Untersberg has been a premier source of building material over the centuries for the construction of numerous structures and statues in the Salzburg region and as far away as Hungary.

But most important, the mountain is home to a sensational **cable car system** (called the Untersbergbahn, built 1959-61) that was used in the filming of the 1968 movie, "Where Eagles Dare" with Clint Eastwood and Richard Burton. If you get a chance, throw your travels into high gear and ride the cable car up to the scenic heights of Untersberg (pictured towering above Salzburg's Old Town). The mountain peaks at 1,865 m (6,117 ft), but the cable car docks at 1,776 m (5,825 ft). This is a perch from which God sits, and from where you can see the world—but more directly the Eagle's Nest, the Watzmann (Germany's second-largest mountain), the inviting lakes of the Salzkammergut, and the glacier ice of the Hohe Tauern. You can enjoy these sights with a hot cuppa or cold beer from the café. The 50-person cabin will climb the mountain and reach the summit within 9 breathtaking minutes. (Simultaneously, a second cabin will descend from the mountain.) You'll notice that only two pylons support the whole system, which can be a petrifying thought to some people. Thus, with the price of your ticket, you may receive an extra pair of underwear! **To get there**, the Untersberg cable car station is located 13 km south of Salzburg's Old Town. **By bus** from the city, hop on #25 direction Untersbergbahn and ride it to the end, 30 min (free with Salzburg Card—bus departs Hauptbahnhof, Mirabellplatz, Rathaus, Mozartsteg every 20 min, and every 30 min after 18:00 Mon-Fri and 17:00 Sat-Sun). **Drivers**, exit A10 autobahn at Salzburg-Süd and head direction Grödig—after 1 km you'll see the cable car station on the right (turn at traffic light).

Casino, Salzburg, Schloss Kleßheim (free entry but must be at least 18 years of age to enter, ID required • open 364 days, 15:00-03:00, slots from 10:00, closed Dec 24 • tel. 0662/854-4550 • CC: VC, MC, DC • www.casinos.at).

Gamblers, try your luck in Salzburg's magnificent casino set in an 18th-century Baroque palace, **Schloss Kleßheim**, former home to Prince-Archbishop Firmian. (The palace was converted into a casino in 1934 but closed during the war and reopened in 1950.) A handful of poker, roulette and black jack tables, along with 200+ slot machines (called Automaten), await your providential touch. Men are required to wear a jacket and an appropriate shirt (or the casino can loan what you need for a nominal fee). No tennis or sports shoes permitted. Ladies, there's no real dress code for you, just look like a winner. Although admission is free, registration is mandatory and a photo ID required. **Note:** Salzburg Card holders, pay 24€ and receive 30€ in chips. **To get there**, Schloss Kleßheim is located 4 km northwest of Old Town. **Drivers**, exit A1 autobahn at Kleßheim, free parking at palace. **By bus** from the city, every second bus 1 stops in front of the casino (direction Red Bull Arena—confirm casino stop with driver), 25-min ride (free with Salzburg Card—bus departs Hauptbahnhof, Mirabellplatz, Hanuschplatz every 20 min until about 22:00). **By shuttle:** The free casino shuttle service (from 17:00) can pick you up in town or drop you off after; have staff at your hotel arrange the transfer or tel. 0662/222-0777 (staffed from 16:30).

Luge Ride, Bad Dürrnberg, (open in good weather **May 5 thru Oct 26, 2017,** daily 11:00-17:00, June 10 thru Sept 10 10:00-18:00, arrive early to beat the crowds • tel. 06245/85105 • www.duerrnberg.at • adult one ride 10€, two/17€, three/23€, Salzburg Card 20% off, students/youths/families receive discount, combo-ticket with Dürrnberg salt mines 26.50€). → Located some 20 km south of Salzburg, above the town of Hallein at Bad Dürrnberg (near salt mines, see next entry), is the mother of all Austrian toboggan runs at 2.2 km (1.4 mi) long! Forget all those other so-called toboggan runs, locally Sommerrodelbahn, this exhilarating and wildly scenic luge ride will make the hair on the back of your neck stand at attention. No kidding! The course is idyllically set upon the peak of a mountain, thus a lengthy yet invigorating chair lift will carry you to the summit, where the flora is lush and the views are sensational! What's more, a short hike from the top station will land you on the German border. When you're ready to ride the luge down, head to the departure area and the operator will supply your sled. Beware, this is not for the faint hearted—it is steep (57% grade), the corners are sharp, and the track is swift! If you want to go full-throttle, allow a few minutes to pass before beginning your run so as not to catch the slowpokes ahead of you. Trust me, if one person before you in the previous 5 minutes throttles at a Sunday pace, your speed record is toast. Argh! Before you ride down, relax at the summit, explore nature, snap memorable photos, straddle the border, enjoy a beverage at the chalet, or throw down a picnic. **Suggestion:** Arrive early to beat crowds. Combine a visit here with the salt mines (see next page). Railers, start here first then mosey downhill 12 min to the mines. **To get there,** the luge is located at Weissenwäschweg 19, Bad Dürrnberg, above the town of Hallein. **Railers**—from Salzburg to the luge is a 45-min trip; Salzburg Card *not* valid; first train then bus, costing 11.40€ round trip (buy ticket in Salzburg)—from Salzburg main station (Hbf) take the train departing :21 min past the hour that connects nicely with bus 41 outside Hallein train station to Zinkenlift (bus departs daily :55 min past the hour *except* Sunday no 9:55 or 13:55, 12-min ride). From the *Zinkenlift stop, exit bus right, cross street and climb steps, then short stroll through a quaint cluster of traditional Austrian-style homes to the luge cashier and toilets. *****Note:** Last bus back to Hallein: Mon-Fri 19:12, Sat 18:12, Sun 17:12! **Drivers**, exit A10 autobahn at Hallein and follow brown signs to Salzwelten (salt mines, denoted by a pick-and-hammer symbol). On the other side of town the road will climb to Bad Dürrnberg; after 3 km the salt mines will appear on the right. (To reach the toboggan:) Continue another kilometer farther to the chair lift and parking area on the left. The cashier and toilets are a short stroll through a quaint cluster of traditional Austrian-style homes. **If you're driving from Berchtesgaden**, ask TI (or a local) for directions because the luge and salt mines are less than 10 km via spectacularly scenic roads.

Salt mines, which one is best? Travelers may be wondering which salt mine is best to visit, Berchtesgaden or Bad Dürrnberg? By far the busier mine is Berchtesgaden because it's cheaper and practically on the way to the Eagle's Nest. However, unlike Berchtesgaden, the Bad Dürrnberg mine offers dynamite views and a reconstructed Celtic village to explore. As for the mines themselves, both are virtually the same: offering deep caverns, wooden slides, and a salty lake. So, to answer the question, which mine is better: they both are (but if I *had* to pick one, it'd be Bad Dürrnberg because of the sweeping vistas across Salzburgland). Bottom line: Visit whichever mine best suits your travel itinerary, this includes the world's oldest mine in Hallstatt (p. 90), which is also excellent!

Salt Mines, Bad Dürrnberg, allow 2 hours for a visit, not counting travel time to/fro mines—note that tours roughly take 70 min (April-Oct tours depart regularly every day from 9:00 until last tour at 17:00, and Nov-March hourly 10:00-15:00, except closed for maintenance Jan 8-26, 2018 • www.salzwelten.at • adult 21€ [with Salzburg Card 16.80€], student/senior 19€, youth 4-15yr 10.50€, family [2+1/2+2/1+1] 44€/53.50€/28€). → Some 2,500 years ago, Celtic peoples migrated to Bad Dürrnberg (mountain above town of Hallein, about 20 km south of Salzburg) to quarry salt. The Celts found tons of the "white gold" here, thus many communities in the region begin or end with the Celtic word *Hall*, meaning salt. From this ancient settlement above Hallein developed a prosperous salt mine, featuring a subterranean labyrinth of deep tunnels (that keep a constant temperature of around 48F/9C), crystal galleries, swooshing slides, and a salty lake. For more than a millennium, "white gold" filled the coffers of Salzburg's archbishops, as well as the Habsburgs who chronologically followed. Today, salt mining on Bad Dürrnberg has gone the way of the dodo bird and the only mining still in operation is the extraction of money from tourists, who throw on white overalls and catch a pit railway deep into the former salt caverns like a themed ride at Disneyland, even cross an international border (between Germany and Austria). Back outside, visitors are treated to a reconstructed Celtic village and distant views of Salzburg. **Note:** The mines are *not* recommended for claustrophobics. If you have a phobia of long lines, book your ticket(s) online in advance during peak season. **Suggestion:** Make a day of it and combine a visit to the salt mines with a sprint down Austria's longest luge (see previous entry). Railers, start first at the luge then roll downhill 12 min to the mines. **To get there,** the mines are located at Ramsaustrasse 3, Bad Dürrnberg, above the town of Hallein. **Railers**—from Salzburg to the mines is a 45-min trip; Salzburg Card *not* valid; first train then bus, costing 11.40€ round trip (buy ticket in Salzburg)—from Salzburg main station (Hbf) take the train departing :21 min past the hour that connects nicely with bus 41 outside Hallein train station to Salzbergwerk (bus departs daily :55 min past the hour *except* Sunday no 9:55 or 13:55, 10-min ride). From the *Salzbergwerk stop, exit bus right then jog left and continue straight to cashier. *Note: Last bus back to Hallein station (Bahnhof): Mon-Fri 19:14, Sat 18:14, Sun 17:14! **Drivers,** see directions for Drivers in the previous entry for Luge Ride.

For more sites and attractions outside of Salzburg, see Excursions on page 73.

BEST VIEWS & HIKES

👍 **Stein Terrasse,** is closed for renovations until summer 2017! *Here are the particulars as they were before its closure:* (daily 7:00-midnight, Fri-Sat till 01:00, breakfast 7:00-11:00, tel. 0662/8743-46700, **free Wi-Fi**). Atop Hotel Stein is the must-visit Stein Terrasse, meaning "stone terrace," a rooftop café featuring astonishing views of Salzburg Old Town crowned by its medieval fortress, making hotshots out of novice photographers. I'd argue this is the most impressive café view in all of Austria! Grab a table, order a beverage, relax, enjoy! (Note, the café can be *very* busy at times, in which case the service may be slow.) **To get there,** Hotel Stein can be found at Giselakai 3, adjacent to the river (right bank) and main bridge (Staatsbrücke) crossing to/fro Old Town. Skip straight through the lobby, past reception, up 11 steps, take the elevator to floor 6 and walk up one level to the Stein Terrasse. **Toilets** located on the 6th floor.

Fortress, locally Festung Hohensalzburg, (p. 17). From the turrets of Salzburg's millennium-old fortress are fabulous views of Old Town and beyond.

Müllnersteg: Exceptional view of Old Town can be captured from the Müllnersteg pedestrian bridge, near Müllner Bräu (best results in afternoon).

Untersberg Mountain & Cable Car, (p. 44). If you have time, especially if you're holding a Salzburg Card, this elevating adventure is not to be missed!

Hiking Trails, Kapuzinerberg (allow at least 30 min). Wander up to the yellowed monastery capping the Kapuzinerberg (Capuchins' Ridge on right bank of river) to reach an abundance of trails and stunning views. The monastery can be accessed via two passageways, at Linzergasse 14 and Steingasse 9. The latter is best. At **Steingasse 9** (GPS: N47 48.098 E13 02.767) you'll see a plaque memorializing the birthplace of Joseph Mohr (1792), who penned the world-famous Christmas carol, "Silent Night." From here, climb 256 steps to the top (steep, 5 min, but after the first 104 steps you'll pass the adorable St. Johannes chapel, dating from 1319). At the top (of the main grouping of steps) <u>stop</u>, you're only meters from two lookout points: one is over your right shoulder, and the other is ahead of you (via the three sets of four steps leading to the monastery). For the better view, climb the 11 steps to your right and go right again. At the bottom of the short path you'll happen upon a battle-worthy turret from medieval times, tremendously scenic views of Old Town, and the beginning of an adventurous hike (left and down). **Note:** If you decide to go for a lengthy hike here, at times you'll feel lost. Just remember, all paths heading west eventually arrive back at the monastery and the other lookout point. However, if you prefer to absorb more wowing views to battling bushes, turn around and skip straight to the other lookout. Adjacent to it is the monastery, and the descending road exits at Linzergasse 14. From there, left drops to the river and bridge connecting Old Town, right climbs to the top of New Town and St. Sebastian's Cemetery (p. 41).

Hiking Trails, Mönchsberg: If you're up for a light nature stroll high above Salzburg Old Town, first turn to "Mönchsberg Lift" on page 38 for prices, times, and directions to the elevator then join me back here and we'll hit the trail together.

☞ **Self-guided Mönchsberg hike** (allow 15 minutes for a quick trip updown to the observation terrace for a postcard-perfect picture, or 45 minutes for hike).

1: At the Mönchsberg Lift, locally Mönchsbergaufzug, step into an elevator. (Salzburg Card holders, no need to see cashier or wait in line, scan Card's barcode at turnstile and go!) Ride it to the top level, exit and climb 13 steps to the **observation terrace**, one of Salzburg's most scenic vantage points (best in afternoon) having the fortress as a stunning backdrop and therefore a choice setting for Maria and the kids to sing "Do-Re-Mi" in the movie classic, "**The Sound of Music.**"

2: Left of the fortress, above the vehicle-trafficked bridge crossing the river, is the yellowed monastery capping the **Kapuzinerberg**, the focus of my Hiking Trails entry above. If you have time later, begin your adventure at Steingasse 9.

3: When ready, climb 15 steps, continue straight (past the telescope) and follow the wooden railing to its end, swing left around then right into the woods via trail. At the fork ahead, go left then jog right at the wooden shack and continue straight. Fortifications will appear on your left and the trail will connect onto a paved route.

4: Follow route down then up and through the arched passage ahead (with little imagination, you've stepped through a time warp to the Middle Ages).

5: At the top, walk over to the plaque (against stone wall right of archway). It reads: "Here the citizens built a defense system consisting of four towers and a wall, as this is the narrowest part of the Mönchsberg. In 1488, citizen watch units were first referred to as the Salzburg Guard, and in 1816 they were dissolved."

6: Over your right shoulder, wander to the benches and check out the terrific view—that's Bavaria in the distance (pointy mountain); below is Salzburg Airport, not surprisingly named after that famed musician, "W.A. Mozart."

7: Walk the trail behind you running alongside the old fortified wall. At the end you'll be rewarded with another spectacular view at the lookout. An info board recalls Salzburg during Roman times with a map illustrating how the settlement, then "Iuvavum," would have looked in the 2nd century A.D., some 1900 years ago!

8: When ready, head back a short distance and step through the narrow portal on the left. On the other side you run bang into the café-restaurant Stadtalm (p. 60). Beyond the café, follow the paved route as it swings left and up to the fork—go straight to the **fortress** (Festung, 15 min) or left and down to **Old Town** (Altstadt). The 330 steps descending to town are called the Clemens Holzmeister Stiege, named after the famous Austrian architect who designed the festival halls (p. 21) located at the bottom. If time is on your side, I recommend the fortress (p. 33). Enjoy!

Mozart Balls

Salzburg is a city of chocolate balls. Boxes upon boxes, in all shapes and sizes, filled with little sweets wrapped in shiny foil. People travel to Salzburg from all over Europe for a taste of an authentic Mozartkugel, or Mozart ball, made of chocolate, nougat, marzipan, pistachio, and more chocolate. Yum. There are actually three different companies that produce Mozart balls. The original balls, however, come from Café Fürst (p. 59) at Old Market Square, established in 1884 by Paul Fürst. Paul created his first ball in 1890 and he soon began winning international awards. It wasn't long before other confectioners copied his idea. Even though Paul's balls were first, you won't regularly see them around town. The Fürst family believes in quality, not quantity, as a statement by Paul Fürst explains: "I am of the basic opinion that the Mozartkugel is a sweet, and not a Mozart souvenir to be sold at unsuitably sunlit street stands." Paul's Mozart balls are still made from the original recipe and are recognizable by their blue-and-silver foil wrapping. Try one, 1.20€.

SHOPPING

In need of some retail therapy? Check out Salzburg's contemporary shopping mall at Europark or window shop medieval lanes in Old Town. And then there's a store that sells only eggs, lots of 'em! But first, I want to point out…

Something Traditional: For an authentic (albeit pricey) gift from Salzburg, like lederhosen or hand-knitted socks, first head over to Salzburger Heimatwerk on Residenzplatz then check out Jahn-Markl across the square. Browse **Salzburger Heimatwerk** (Mon-Fri 9:00-18:00, Sat 9:00-17:00 • all major CCs accepted • www.salzburgerheimatwerk.at • tel. 0662/844-110) to get in touch with authentic Austrian fabrics, handicrafts, dressmaking materials, silks, alpine designs, and traditional Salzburger costume (called Tracht) like lederhosen and dirndls. But don't limit yourself to Heimatwerk, also browse the much smaller but much older **Jahn-Markl** store—Mon-Fri 9:30-18:00, Sat 9:30-15:00, tel. 0662/842-610, www.jahn-markl.at—Salzburg's most venerated dressmaker, since 1408, located in the right corner of Residenzplatz, a couple of doors before Alter Markt, or Old Market Square. Jahn-Markl is pricey, but it's the real deal, having renowned clientele such as the von Trapps, Marlene Dietrich, and Louis Vuitton. Inside its narrow doorway is a room resplendent with lederhosen, dirndls, suspenders, belts, hats, deerskin jackets and slippers, hand-knitted socks and hand-stitched gloves, all handmade locally. They also repair leather garments.

Sporer Wines & Spirits, (Mon-Fri 9:30-19:00, Sat 8:30-17:00 • tel. 0662/845-431 • Getreidegasse 39 • www.sporer.at). This long-established business goes hand-in-glove with the above theme of "traditional" Salzburg. Franz Sporer founded this petite yet atmospheric wine-and-spirits shop and tavern here at Getreidegasse 39 way back in 1903, but the building itself, the narrowest in the lane, was first mentioned 500 years earlier in 1407. Now a fourth-generation family run business, Sporer specializes in an intoxicating selection of Austrian wines and schnapps and brandy, but for Salzburgers Sporer has long been considered a Geheimtip, or "secret" tip, on account of its home-distilled liqueur (e.g. cherry, black currant, peppermint, apricot, cinnamon) and punch (orange, Christmas served warm) that are arguably just as medicinal, or capable of combating ill health, as alcoholic. Many of the "house" blends are stored in 100-year-old wooden casks propped against the stone wall opposite the service counter. Customers readily return with their bottle in hand (any bottle) to refill at a reduced price. The most popular Sporer blend is its orange punch (50% abv, 18€ half liter), first concocted by (grandfather) Otto in 1927 using an agreeable mix of oranges, lemons, liqueurs, rum and a few secret ingredients. When I say the latter orange punch is popular, I'm hardly exaggerating, many Salzburgers keep a bottle of it in their pantry or medicine cabinet. And a friend of mine in town politely told me not to let this Geheimtip out of the bag. But she's just gonna have to forgive my desire to fill you in. So stop by Sporer's small but pleasant non-smoking shop and tavern when you have time and taste test a few local secrets while mingling with a few locals. **Note:** A bottle of punch is a thoughtful gift idea. Staff speak English and will help you choose your tonic. Try a shot of punch (orange, Christmas) or liqueur, but it's cheaper to imbibe by the glass. **Drivers,** if you parked in the Altstadt Garage (p. 8), have a Sporer staff member validate your ticket so you only pay 4€/4hr or 6€/8hr to park.

Getreidegasse, meaning "grain lane," is Salzburg's historic shopping street, an adoring pedestrian thoroughfare chock-full of tourists and locals alike scampering beneath an eclectic array of gilded wrought-iron signs hanging over retail stores. Because many people were illiterate in medieval times, signs like these were commonplace, symbolizing the trade performed at each place of business; for example, a loaf of bread meant a bakery, or a shoe suggested a cobbler (footwear specialist), or a big golden M indicated hot fries and burgers. Getreidegasse gets really congested around the rich-yellow facade at No. 9, Mozart's birthplace (Geburtshaus). At its western end, Getreidegasse runs into Old Market Square (p. 23) then Judengasse that flows into Mozartplatz where you'll find the TI and a statue of Mozart punctuating the square.

Easter-Egg Shop (open 365 days, Mon-Sat 9:00-19:00, Sun 9:00-18:00, from 3.90€/egg, CC: VC, MC). Yes, those are decorated eggs you saw in the window. Back up, walk by again, but you'll see the same thing: Easter eggs (and most all are hand painted by artists who reside in Austria, thus each is unique). Trays stacked upon trays of the colorful hard-shelled objects fill the shop. And not just chicken eggs, there are quail eggs and turkey eggs and ostrich eggs, too. The owner told me she has upwards of half a million eggs, but not just for Easter, also Christmas and Halloween! You've gotta see this place for yourself. **To get there**, the shop is located at Judengasse 9. If you're standing in front of and facing Mozart's birthplace at Getreidegasse 9, go left and continue straight. After Old Market Square (Alter Markt) the lane becomes Judengasse and the egg shop is ahead on the left. Or, when facing the Mozartplatz TI, jog left then right around the corner and down into Judengasse to the shop ahead on the right.

Judengasse: You'll discover antique and specialty shops on this Jewish Lane as well as the quaint lanes running off it. While here, pop into the above-listed Easter-egg shop—use its directions to find this part of Old Town.

Europark, (www.europark.at • Mon-Thur 9:00-19:30, Fri 9:00-21:00, Sat 9:00-18:00). This Olympic-sized shopping mall is the pride of retail Austria and a cash cow for Salzburg. If you're ever wondering where all the locals are, come here. Europark is home to more than 130 eateries and shops, including Ikea, Lacoste, Zara, Esprit, Levi's, H&M fashion, Saturn computer ware and electronic gizmos, and an enormous Inter Spar supermarket with restaurant. **To get there**, Europark is located at Europastrasse 1, 3 km northwest of Old Town. **By bus**, ride #1 to Europark (which departs from the city at Hauptbahnhof, Mirabellplatz, Hanuschplatz every 10 min, direction Europark/Red Bull Arena, 25-min ride); buses 9 and 28 also depart regularly from Hanuschplatz. **Drivers**, from the A1 autobahn, exit at "Kleßheim." Parking is free and won't be a problem since there are literally thousands of spaces available, many of which are in one of Europe's largest combined underground garages.

Designer Outlet, (www.designer-outlet-salzburg.at • Mon-Thur 9:30-19:00, Fri 9:30-21:00, Sat 9:00-18:00). Although this newish, indoor Designer Outlet center (opened Sept. 2009) is a novel concept for Salzburg, I found that even with discounts of 30-70% the merchandise still to be costly (with much of the apparel seemingly priced in the hundreds of euros). One thing for sure, I'm no clever fashion shopper; perhaps you will find a bargain. There are some 100 retail outlets here featuring name brands such as Calvin Klein (Jeans), Escada, Karl Lagerfeld, Hugo Boss, Columbia, Nike. **To get there**, the outlet center is situated at Kasernenstrasse 1, Wals-Himmelreich, off the A1 autobahn by Salzburg airport 5 km west of Old Town. **Drivers,** exit the A1 autobahn at "Flughafen"; park free the first two hours then 2€/hr thereafter (but waived if you spend 150€+ shopping—show receipt to Center Info desk). **By bus** from the city, hop on #2 direction Airport/Walserfeld and get off at Designer Outlet (DOC), 20-min ride (bus departs Wolf-Dietrich-Str., Mirabellplatz, Hauptbahnhof every 10 min, and every 20 min after 19:00 Mon-Sat and all day Sun); buses 10 and 27 also depart regularly from Hanuschplatz.

ENTERTAINMENT

Another Salzburg plus is its welcomed absence of in-your-face neon signs promoting the latest bar, pachinko parlor, or kitschy café. Maintaining age-old tradition, this form of advertising is strictly *verboten*. With a little patience you'll discover a wealth of nightlife behind inconspicuous, 19th-century facades—especially along the riverside. **Note:** Famished night owls consider a kebab (p. 61) before hitting the hay.

Those of you who enjoy drinking beer with history on your side, note the following four establishments: Müllner Bräu, Stieglkeller, Die Weisse, and the Stiegl brewery (Brew World page 43).

👍 **Müllner Bräu,** dating from 1621, is Austria's largest tavern and beer garden (daily 15:00-23:00, weekends from 14:30, Augustiner beer 6.20€ liter, 3.10€ half liter, <u>cash only</u>! • www.augustinerbier.at). → A venerable complex of beer halls adjoined by a leafy 1,400-seat beer garden, Müllner Bräu is not surprisingly situated in the district of "Mülln," named after the umpteen mills that once populated the landscape. In 1605, Augustinian Hermits settled the area, becoming a frothy monastic district of prayer and beer making (not to be confused with Munich's Augustinian brand). Since the 19th century, dry-mouthed citizens have been pouring into Mülln for the spiritual specialty: (Märzen) beer. At the on-site brewery (tours possible with advance booking), the monks store their beer in wooden kegs, giving it an all-natural taste intoxicatingly popular with locals and beer buffs. **Inside** Müllner Bräu, a row of food counters dish up Austrian fare and old-world beer halls feature coffee-colored wood paneling, stained-glass windows, and Gothic typeface drafted upon *smoke-stained walls. (*Saal [hall] "1" is now non-smoking, Saal "2" is smoking.) **Outside,** heady patrons bask under a forest of chestnut trees (Kastanienbäume) quaffing liter-sized brews in Austria's largest traditional beer garden. **Note:** Pay for your beer at the cashier, pick out a clay mug from the cabinet, give it a rinse in the purpose-built fountain, head to the Schenke (place where beer is served), and hand your receipt to the Kegmeister along with your empty mug. To complement your brew, choose some grub from the aforesaid food counters inside or you are allowed to bring in your own picnic items (but drinks must be purchased here). When leaving Müllner Bräu, stop by the nearby pedestrian bridge (Müllnersteg) for a phenomenal view of Old Town. **To get there** (Müllner Bräu), **by bus** from Hanuschplatz (catch bus on river side heading north), ride either 7, 8, 9, 21, 27 (also departs from main train station direction Airport), or 28 a couple of stops to LKH/St.-Johanns-Spital. **By foot** from Old Town, follow the river (north), pass the boat dock and parallel the Mönchsberg cliffs. Continue straight and the cliff face will taper to a soaring copper-domed church steeple; next door is your oasis. **Drivers**, park in their lot (*free* Mon-Fri after 14:40, Sat-Sun after 14:10) at Lindhofstrasse 7—take ticket at gate and have beer cashier validate it with purchase. <u>Note</u>: If you're day parking and wish to reach Old Town, either follow the river (south) on foot (20 min) or buses regularly pick up from here (ask driver if he's going to Zentrum/Hanusch Platz). Upon return, crown your day with a mug of Salzburg's best beer (have beer cashier validate your park ticket).

The **Stieglkeller** (p. 57) boasts Salzburg's most scenic Biergarten, nestled above the Old Town rooftops and below the fortress. Taste it!

Weissebier fans will cherish **Die Weisse** (Mon-Sat 10:00-midnight, Sudwerk 17:00-02:00), Salzburg's century-old wheat beer microbrewery (since 1901) having an atmospheric tavern, beer garden, and nightspot called **Sudwerk**. Die Weisse's two house specialties are its on-tap "hell" and bottled "dunkel," or light and dark wheat beers, both 5.2% abv. Complementing their award-winning brew, Die Weisse also serves traditional Austrian grub (dinner reservations recommended, tel. 0662/872-246). Courting Die Weisse's serious patrons, the brew master kicks it up a notch with its potent seasonal batches and the all-year Jubilator, an extra-strong (8% abv) *doppelbock!* **To get there**, Die Weisse is located at Rupertgasse 10, corner of Bayerhamerstrasse, at the top of New Town via Linzergasse, within a 15-min walk of Old Town.

For an alcoholic slice of the Emerald Isle, pub and clubgoers begin your evening in Old Town at No. 12 Rudolfskai (one-way road running along left riverbank) at either Guinness-inspired tavern: **Shamrock** (Mon-Wed 12:00 noon till 03:00, Thur-Sat till 04:00, Sun till 02:00, non-smoking back area, www.shamrocksalzburg.com) is a fundamental component of Salzburg nightlife with **live music** most evenings and clouds of cigarette smoke. Or for less commotion and free Wi-Fi, try **O'Malley's** next door (daily, 20:00 till late, non-smoking front area). Both pubs neighbor each other behind old stone facades and serve a pint of Guinness for around 5€. To me Irish mates, *sláinte!* **Note:** Depending on where you're coming from, the easiest way to reach either pub is via Shamrock's back door at Judengasse 1, just off Old Market Square.

Continue the fun across the river in New Town at the evolutionary **Darwin's Café-Bar** (Steingasse 1, on corner behind Hotel Stein, daily 8:00-23:00), whose award-winning bartenders blend scientific theory with top shelf distilled beverages to create dreamy daiquiris and intoxicating elixirs that can be enjoyed inside or outside but always with an upside. A couple doors down from Darwin's on cobbled Steingasse the microevolution continues at **Pepe Cocktail Bar** (Tue-Sat 19:00-03:00), a small joint that hooks its guests on a sultry menu of Latin American and Caribbean concoctions consisting of margaritas and daiquiris (pineapple, peach, banana, strawberry, mango), gins, whiskeys, vodkas, rums, tequilas, exotic cocktails and piña coladas, Corona beer, red and white wine, nachos with cheddar cheese and jalapeños. Wednesdays at Pepe's means Havana party night, sip mojitos (5.50€ ea.), dance salsa, and smoke Cubans (buy at tobacco vendor en route). Or join the week-long happy hour Tue-Sat 19:00-21:00 when all cocktails are 5.50€ (usually 6.60€-7.50€).

👍 St. Peter's Stiftskeller (p. 56, adjacent to St. Peter's church and cemetery) hosts the perennially delightful and recommended **Mozart-Dinner-Concert** (duration 2.5 hours, concert and 3-course dinner, drinks not included, adult 59€, student 44€, youth 6-14yr 36€, *exclusive package 98€/person [*preferred seating, extended gourmet menu, welcome drink, program booklet], doors open at 18:30, dress smart-casual, CC: VC, MC). → Show starts at 19:30 in the Stiftskeller's historic Baroque hall (upstairs); the best of Mozart is performed by the "Amadeus Consort Salzburg" in period dress. During intermissions, wait staff stride between candlelit tables delivering a multicourse dinner (e.g. cream soup, chicken breast with vegetables, and dessert) prepared according to recipes from the 18th century. **Tickets** can be purchased at the TI, by phone (0662/828-695), online (www.salzburg-concerts.com), or last minute at the door but at this late hour you risk the show being sold out (particularly May-June Sept & Dec). **Note:** Salzburg Card holders receive 5% discount. Lastly, drinks are pricey and *not* included in the dinner-show price, thus whatever your bill, a tip (e.g. 10%) would be appreciated by your waiter but it is not expected.

"The Sound of Salzburg Dinner Show" (mid-May thru October almost daily, few performances rest of year • www.soundofsalzburgshow.com) performed live entirely in English by the "Salzburg Sound of Music Singers" is a pleasurable, albeit kitschy, proposition at the Sternbräu restaurant (at Griesgasse 23) in Old Town, doors open 18:30, dinner 19:00, show begin 20:30, show end 22:00, 3-course dinner plus show 57€, student 46€, youth 7-14yr 36€, or show only [without dinner] plus one drink 36€/25€/18€, free admission for children 6yr and under, Salzburg Card holders receive healthy discount. Note: CC payment incurs 1€ charge per ticket. Free shuttle bus to show available, optional 5€/person return, ask TI or staff at your digs to reserve.

I enjoyed watching the "Salzburg Sound of Music Singers" (two guys and two gals clad in traditional costume) perform the show, a series of entertaining song-and-dance routines set to the best of the movie soundtrack as well as classical and folk hits played by a live pianist. That said, if you're pained by SOM overkill, give this show a miss. However, if you're keen for more SOM hits, join in the toe-tappin' fun. Heck, you may even get plucked from the audience to sing a chorus with the cast.

Classical concerts sound year round in Salzburg and are a dream in the sumptuous Marble Hall of the Mirabell Palace (www.schlosskonzerte-salzburg.at) as well as in the fortress' lofty Golden Hall (www.mozartfestival.at). For either venue, check online or with TI for schedule and availability. **Note:** Salzburg Card holders receive a 10% discount off the following ticket prices at Mirabell Palace, listed in two seating categories: I & II. *Cat. I* (reserved seating rows 1-7) 38€ per adult—*Cat. II* 32€ (non-reserved seating behind Cat. I)—student 24€/18€, youth 14yr and younger 14€/14€, box office tel. 0662/828-695.

Folks who are inspired by **organ concerts** (see TI for the various recitals planned around town or) check out the latest schedule at the Franciscan church (Franziskanerkirche with pointy tower and sheer roof soaring between the cathedral and festival halls), where there's usually an uplifting symphony of flue pipes summoning all angels.

Spend a fascinating afternoon/evening in the grand Baroque **Marionette Theater** (located at Schwarzstrasse 24, adjacent to the Mirabell Gardens and one block from the 5-star Hotel Sacher • www.marionetten.at • tel. 0662/872-406). → Watch clever puppeteers nimbly manipulate small wooden people to dance and lip-sync and act like super humans not bound by gravity, bouncing and sometimes even levitating on stage. The string puppets and the art of their skillful masters are, to say the least, captivating to behold. Their repertoire includes big-time theatrical productions that run the gamut from Mozart's "The Magic Flute" to the Brothers Grimm "Snow White and the Seven Dwarfs." (**Note:** Productions run about two hours and are performed to recordings by distinguished orchestras, singers and vocalists in their original language with English subtitles. Performances are typically scheduled a few times per week in May and most every day June-August & October; the remainder of the year the theater troop is either rehearsing or on tour entertaining audiences across the globe.)

Historically, the Salzburg Marionette Theater was founded by Anton Aicher in

1913 in a gymnasium near the Mirabell Gardens, where it remained for 49 years. At the start of World War II, the marionettes were sent to the front (first Norway then Russia) to entertain troops. The war tragically dragged on and the theater company was forced to close late 1944. Immediately after the war, 1945, the puppets were back in business entertaining American soldiers. In 1962, the theater company moved across the river to an auditorium near the cathedral on Kapitalplatz. In 1963, Hollywood contacted the puppeteers and the Lonely Goatherd sequence for the movie "The Sound of Music" was born. Finally, in 1971, the Salzburg marionettes found their present and permanent home (back across the river) at Schwarzstrasse 24, adjacent to the Mirabell Gardens.

In 2013, the Salzburg Marionette Theater proudly celebrated its 100-year birthday! Over the decades the theater has achieved mountains of success but in 2007 it perhaps landed its biggest industry coup with the purchase of the rights to perform the Broadway musical, "**The Sound of Music**." With this pricey acquisition a new stage backdrop had to be created along with a small army of intricately carved puppets. Because the marionettes cannot change their costumes, most members of the Trapp family had to be fashioned thrice. The 21 puppets, for example, representing the captain's seven children posed a stringy challenge for the 10 puppeteers working the musical. After months of rehearsal, the European premiere of the "The Sound of Music" at the Salzburg Marionette Theater opened with great fanfare on May 9, 2008. So you can better plan your opportunity to see the von Trapp puppets in action this year, I've listed their **2017 Salzburg schedule** (show duration 105 min; show times ¹17:00, *19:30): **April** *11, *13 • **May** *5, *12, *19, *26 • **June** *2, *6, *9, *13, *16, *20, *23, *27, *30 • **July** *4, *7, *11, *14, *18, ¹20, *21, *25, ¹27, *28 • **August** *1, ¹3, *4, *8, ¹10, *11, *18, *22, *25 • **September** *26, *28 • **October** *3, *12, *19, *25.

Prices at the Marionette Theater are the same for all (full-length) performances and you have a choice between four seating categories: **I** (37€, rows 1-9)—**II** (32€, rows 10-14)—**III** (27€, rows 15-20)—**IV** (20€, row 21 and two sets of side seats opposite row 9)—youth 12yr and under 15€. All major CCs accepted. Buy tickets online, at the theater box office (Mon-Sat 9:00-13:00 and two hours before every performance), or over the phone (0662/872-406 same hours as box office). If you purchase your ticket(s) online, avoid the "shipping" fee by picking up your ticket(s) at the box office.

Suggestion: Because the puppets are petite creatures, sit as close to the stage as your budget allows, thus anything in category I is fine. Rows 10-13 in category II are also respectable but row 14 is the first one beginning the second section to the back (which is ideal for tall folks seeking legroom) but it is also where the stage and puppets start becoming distant and I had to occasionally squint. If only row 14 is available from category II, consider saving the 5€ per seat and opt for row 15 or 16 in category III (then if the theater's not full, move forward). But the best value are the two (category IV) side seats (called Nische) opposite row 9 (but be quick because there are only four of these seats total, two either side of theater). Avoid rows 17-20 unless you're okay with the likelihood of confusing Hänsel with Gretel.

EDITOR'S NOTE: Please review us on the Web. As a small business, we get pumped about the little things. That's why positive support and word-of-mouth from our readers means the world to us. It let's us know how we're doing, thus we'd greatly appreciate it if you could share your experience about this book by typing a brief review on *Amazon*. If you've enjoyed a particular Salzburg site because of our attention to it, please mention Harriman in your *TripAdvisor* comment. ☺

RESTAURANTS, CAFÉS, KEBABS & CURRY SAUSAGES

I begin this section by making a general statement that will always apply in my opinion regarding customary cuisine in Austria: "It's difficult to find a bad meal." People often ask, "Where's a good place to eat?" My answer sounds as if I'm shrugging them off: "Anywhere traditional." Additionally, servings are substantial, thus no need to order an appetizer in Austria. Speaking of appetizers, below are a few appetizing places to kick-start your gastronomic tour of Salzburg. (Vegetarians, consider Spicy Spices on page 61.)

But first, here's a short description of **Salzburger Nockerl** (pictured). Salzburger what? You'll see this dish on menus in the finer, traditional-style restaurants around town (for example at St. Peter's Stiftskeller). It refers to a classic local dessert; a sweet soufflé consisting of whipped egg whites and yolks, sugar, flour, lemon peel, vanilla, milk and butter beat into stiff mountain-like peaks served hot out-of-the-oven. Nockerl is airy yet filling, enough for three people, thus order one to share with your companion(s). And since it is prepared upon your request, never order one if you're in a hurry! It's not uncommon to wait 30 minutes for your specially made meringue to arrive at your table.

Lastly, if you're traveling in Salzburgland (or most anywhere in Germany) mid-April thru May, you'll be happy to know it's **Spargelzeit**, or "asparagus season." And like most resident kitchens, the majority of restaurants celebrate this spring time of year by complementing their dishes with the in-season specialty: white asparagus, harvested in a field near you as Spargel. I say "white" because these medium-length stalks of asparagus are pulled out of the ground (by hand) before reaching sunlight and turning green, the color we most associate with asparagus. Spargel is typically boiled and served with any manner of sauces or seasonings to time-honored palate-pleasing perfection. So, if it's Spargelzeit, ask your waiter for a sampling of the succulent spear-shaped vegetable.

Old Town

St. Peter's Stiftskeller (17€-30€ main dish, veal schnitzel 24€ • daily 11:30-15:30 & 17:30-23:00 [kitchen 12:00-14:30 & 18:00-21:15], open later July-Aug & during Advent [kitchen till around 23:30] • all major CCs accepted • English menu available • tel. 0662/841-2680 • www.stpeter-stiftskeller.at). → Located on the grounds of St. Peter's monastery and administered by the church, this sizeable 1,200-year-old restaurant with its various vaulted rooms undoubtedly needs to be mentioned first since it has been in business for ages, literally. The court scribe Alcuin first recorded the Stiftskeller, or monastic cellar, into the history books during a visit by Emperor Charlemagne in the year 803 A.D., thus it is regarded as **Europe's oldest restaurant!** The prices are reasonable, the cuisine delectable, the setting historically unique, and the ambiance divine. Stop by for a bite to eat, even if it's only a soup or dessert (like the Salzburger Nockerl, a Stiftskeller specialty). Consider spending an evening here listening to poetic strains of Mozart over dinner (p. 53).

🥢 **Stieglkeller** (12€-19€ main dish, schnitzel: veal 18.50€/pork 12.50€ • daily 11:00-22:00, summer till 23:00—Jan-March closed Mon-Tue, all of Feb and for private events on April 5, June 10 & 17, July 22, Oct 12, 2017—kitchen 11:30-21:00 • CC: VC, MC • tel. 0662/842-681 • www.stieglkeller.at). → All over town you've seen the word "Stiegl," the name of Salzburg's beer and brewery, established in 1492. In 1820, the brewery expanded its revenue base by investing in the voluminous Stieglkeller restaurant, having multiple themed halls and a beer garden nestled above the rooftops of Salzburg (built into fortress hill at Festungsgasse 10, up from the cable railway). If the weather is nice, climb the cobbled lane then 52 steps up the broad stone staircase to indulge in a delicious Austrian meal complemented by a thirst-quenching Stiegl beer and precious views from Salzburg's most scenic Biergarten. Arrive before sunset and watch Old Town transcend from the sun's golden rays reflecting off church steeples to the mesmeric twinkling of nocturnal lights. **Drivers,** park in the Altstadt Garage (p. 8) and have the waiter validate your ticket.

🥢 **Bärenwirt** (11€-20€ main dish, schnitzel: veal 19€/pork 11€ • daily 11:00-23:00, kitchen 11:30-14:00 & 17:30-21:30 • CC: VC, MC • tel. 0662/422-404). → In the year 1562 it is said a black bear amazingly swam up from the river and rested here on the bank, thus today's storied Bärenwirt (Bear Inn) on Bärengässchen (Bear Lane) in the district of Mülln. Although the bear is long gone, its legacy lives on in this historic Wirtshaus (Inn) and its authentic Austrian fare, favored by locals. Dishes are prepared in large portions by generous chefs: start with the frothy beer soup (4.30€), or goulash soup (4.90€), then consider the wild boar sausage served with potatoes and cabbage in a skillet (13.90€), tafelspitz (boiled beef) with vegetables and roasted potatoes in a pot (17.50€), the roast pork (Bierschopfbratl) with sauerkraut and a bread dumpling practically the size of a bear's head (11.80€), or the house specialty: fried chicken, said to be Austria's best! Wash it down with freshly tapped Augustiner beer served in a stoneware mug and brewed in the neighboring Müllner Bräu. The trick here is to leave room for dessert, like the Black Forest Cherry Dream ice cream (6.90€). With all the scrumptiousness here, it can get busy, thus reserve a table if possible. **To get there,** Bärenwirt is located at Müllner Hauptstrasse 8, about a 20-min walk north along the river from Old Town. **By bus** from Hanuschplatz (catch bus on river side heading north), ride either 7, 8, 9, 21, 28 one stop to "Bärenwirt," or from the main train station pick up bus 27 direction Airport to "Bärenwirt". Exit bus left and go straight to the restaurant just ahead. **Drivers**, park three hours free at Müllner Bräu (Lindhofstrasse 7) around the corner from Bärenwirt—take ticket at gate and have your waiter validate it. **Note:** Combine a visit here with Müllner Bräu (p. 52). To get there from Bärenwirt, exit the restaurant right and make the first left (across street) up cobbled Augustinergasse. At the top of the lane enter below the sign "Augustiner Bräustübl," then step through the last door on the left and skip down the stairway to heaven.

SALZBURG Good Sleeps & Eats

MAP NOT TO SCALE — To walk from the train station to Mozart's Birthplace is 20 min.

Map labels:
- Train Station
- coin laundry
- Müllner Bräu
- Bärenwirt
- Mirabell Gardens
- Die Weisse
- laundry
- Spicy Spices
- Zum Fideln Affen
- Kapuzinerberg
- Platzl
- foot bridge
- Hanuschplatz
- kebabs
- Hotel Stein
- Sporer wines / Curry sausages / Zum Wilder Mann
- Getreidegasse
- Old Market Square
- Shamrock & O'Malley's
- Hospital
- Mozart
- Uni-platz
- Res. Platz
- Mozartplatz
- Altstadt Garage
- Residenz
- Neutorstr.
- Domplatz
- Cathedral
- Salzach River
- Festival Halls
- Café's Fürst & Tomaselli
- St. Peter's Stiftskeller
- Stiegl Keller
- "Café-Restaurant"
- Fortress

Legend:
- scenic viewpoint
- post office
- grocery store

❶ Art Hotel Blaue Gans
❷ Bergland Hotel
❸ Gabi's Apartments
❹ Gästehaus Bonauerhof
❺ Hotel Goldgasse
❻ Hotel Sacher Salzburg
❼ Hotel Schloss Mönchstein
❽ Hotel Untersberg
❾ JUFA
❿ Motel One Mirabell
⓫ Star Inn Gablerbräu
⓬ Star Inn Zentrum
⓭ Trapp Villa
⓮ YOHO

GOOD EATS

Gasthaus zum Wilder Mann (main dish from 11€, schnitzel: veal 18€/pork 12.50€ • Mon-Sat 11:00-22:30 but kitchen till 21:00 • cash only—no CCs accepted • tel. 0662/841-787). Secreted in a pedestrian passage off Getreidegasse, this rustic inn grows from lively locals hungry for something suggestive of their mother's kitchen and Stiegl beer on tap. Patrons share wooden tables while lederhosen-clad Robert and his dirndl-donning partner Eva-Maria hustle delicious Austrian meals in ample portions from 11€. Popular choices are the beef stew with dumpling (Gulasch mit Knödel 12€), and the farmers' favorite Bauernschmaus (14€) containing roast pork, ham, sausage, dumplings, potatoes and sauerkraut! For dessert, try the rolled pancakes with nuts, chocolate sauce and whipped cream (Schokonuss Palatschinken 6.50€) or the apple strudel with vanilla sauce (5.50€). **To get there**, when facing Mozart's birthplace on Getreidegasse, go right to No. 22 (right). Proceed through the archway and down to Wilder Mann (left). Or, from Griesgasse (bus transportation hub at Hanuschplatz), enter passage via the archway at No. 17.

"Café-Restaurant" (daily 10:00-17:00, summer till 20:00 • pork schnitzel 8.90€ • English menu available). Located at Festungsgasse 2, meters from the Stieglkeller (p. 57), this casual eatery run by hard-working Helmut affords its guests pocket-friendly prices, a picture menu, an ivy-swathed patio-garden with fortress view (best on warm days), and the cheapest (pork) schnitzel in Old Town. As you stroll up cobbled Festungsgasse toward the fortress, look for Helmet's sign advertising his daily special: soup, schnitzel, and potatoes (Kartoffel) 8.90€.

Café Fürst: The historic home of the original Mozart ball, locally Mozartkugel, Café Fürst outshines the bunch. Stop in for homemade chocolates, pastries, cakes and classic Austrian coffeehouse tradition. Café Fürst's flagship operation is located in Old Town on Old Market Square (Alter Markt, neighboring Residenzplatz • Mon-Sat 8:00-20:00, Sun 9:00-20:00 • all major CCs accepted • tel. 0662/843-7590 • www.original-mozartkugel.com). Fürst has another, much smaller, location at Getreidegasse 47 (west end of pedestrian lane, Mon-Sat 10:00-18:30, Sun 12:00-17:00) as well as a third location across the river at Mirabellplatz 5 (Mon-Fri 9:00-19:00, Sat-Sun 9:00-18:00), opposite Mirabell Gardens. For more on the original Mozart ball, see page 49.

Café Tomaselli (cash only • Mon-Sat 7:00-19:00, Sun 8:00-19:00 • mid-July thru Aug till 21:00 • tel. 0662/844-4880 • look for Tomaselli's signature green-and-white table umbrellas fronting the storied café on Old Market Square across from the above-listed Café Fürst). → **Austria's oldest coffeehouse,** dating from 1703, Café Tomaselli set up shop not long after retreating Turkish soldiers hastily left sacks of coffee beans on the battlefield outside Vienna. Over the centuries Tomaselli's has seen many distinguished persons walk through its doors, including celebrities, politicians, artists, and one very famous composer: Wolfgang Amadeus, whose preferred drink here was said to be 'almond milk.' (Even Mozart's widow, Constanze, lived above the café from 1820-26.) Inside, pastry waitresses wearing kitchen-maid uniforms and tuxedo-clad waiters serve customers who sit contentedly on wooden chairs positioned around marble-topped tables, sipping coffee, eating cake, chatting, reading, people watching—the setting here is comparable to a 19th-century oil painting by Édouard Manet. Step into Tomaselli's storied ambiance and be a part of the scene. Keeping to tradition, Wi-Fi is trumped here by the old-and-reliable newspaper rack in the corner respectfully squeaking with every twirl commanded by customers seeking the latest domestic and international publications. The adjacent staircase climbs to the best seats in the house on the terrace; you're in luck if a table is available (you can also reach the terrace via the outdoor staircase right of the café spiraling up from the square). Plop down and relish life. Order your coffee, traditionally served with a glass of water and sugar, then select a delectable dessert from the Kuchenmädchen (pastry waitress) making the rounds with irresistible sweets freshly made in the house bakery finely presented on a sterling-silver tray. **Note:** While here, check out "Kiosk" Tomaselli (Mon-Fri 11:00-18:00, Sat 10:00-18:00), built in 1860, meters from the café for more choice sweets and a scoop of Tomaselli's very own home-made ice cream. Yum!

Curry Sausages at the Bosna Grill (Mon-Fri 11:00-19:00, Sat 11:00-17:00, and July-Dec also Sun 16:00-19:00, but don't wait until the last minute because they often sell out and close early!). Arguably Salzburg's favorite sausage has Bulgarian origins and can be found at the Bosna Grill, a literal whole in the wall since 1950. You typically won't find many tourists here, mostly locals waiting in line to take away a spicy and fatty taste of bliss prepared with special seasonings secreted in a time-honored recipe. The person working behind the window (with little more than elbow room to move) faithfully serves up the so-called "Bosna": two sausages jammed in a hot-dog-like bun loaded with condiments. You have five choices, each 3.60€: **1)** with onions and curry spice • **2)** with onions, curry spice and mustard • **3)** with mustard and curry spice • **4)** with onions, ketchup and curry spice • **5)** with ketchup and curry spice. **To get there**, when facing Mozart's birthplace on Getreidegasse, go right to No. 33 (left). Proceed through the archway into the cobbled passage to the whole in the wall some 10 meters ahead on the right.

Café-Restaurant Stadtalm (daily April thru Oct 10:00-18:00 [kitchen 11:30-17:00], May till 19:00-22:00, June-Aug till 23:00, but closed during bad weather • tel. 0662/841-729 • www.stadtalm.at). Here you can eat and drink high above Old Town in a medieval watchtower or outside on one of the umbrellaed picnic tables parked along the cliff's edge where sweeping vistas of Salzburg come with the (oft poor) service. Nestled upon Mönchsberg (Monks' Ridge), Stadtalm is part of the city's historic defense wall built by the citizen guard in 1487. Hike the forested Mönchsberg and make the reasonably priced Stadtalm part of your adventure, if only for a glass of one of my favorite beers: Wieninger. Budget-minded travelers with few bags may be interested in Stadtalm's bunk-bed lodgings (from 21.50€/B&B), affording first-class views for a pauper's price and hallway toilets-showers. **To get there**, <u>GPS</u>: N47 47.977 E13 02.357, look above the northwest part of the Old Town for a wood-covered duct leading up the cliff face—the battlement at the top is the Stadtalm. Ride the Lift (p. 38) up Mönchsberg then read Mönchsberg Hiking Trails (p. 48).

Restaurants, Cafés, Kebabs & Curry Sausages (cont. from page 56):

New Town

Zum Fideln Affen (12€-19€ main dish, schnitzel: veal 19€/pork 12€ • Mon-Sat 17:00-24:00, kitchen till 23:00 • CC: VC, MC, AE • tel. 0662/877-361). At this popular, non-smoking historic gasthaus (dating from circa 1650) kitchen chefs prepare each meal with art-like presentation (from ingredients supplied by local farmers) while guests share wooden tables wrapped around a service bar and indulge in authentic Austrian cuisine that is plate-lickin' good! Zum Fideln Affen, local jargon meaning "To the Merry Monkey," is a cosy, convivial place with limited seating and hours, thus to arrive *without* a reservation would be akin to being a monkey's uncle. Savory suggestions include the Wiener schnitzel and potatoes served in a skillet, tafelspitz (boiled beef) with vegetables, the multi-layered monkey (Affen) steak, and the delightful pumpkin-cream soup (Kürbiscremesuppe) served in a preservatives jar (seasonal thus in autumn). But, beware, the bread rolls and pretzels kept irresistibly in front of you cost a pretty penny (up to 1.50€ each). **To get there**, zum Fideln Affen is located at Priesterhausgasse 8 in New Town, across from the Star Inn hotel. Head up Linzergasse to No. 14 then jog left to the Affen ahead on the right.

Stein Terrasse: This penthouse café is a must-visit, if only for a quick picture and a cuppa (p. 47).

Shrimps Bar & Restaurant—16€-*32€ main dish, *surf and turf • daily 17:00-midnight, later Fri-Sat but kitchen till 22:30 • located at Steingasse 5, behind Hotel Stein • tel. 0662/874-484 • www.shrimps.at—newly renovated in 2013, has been serving a cross between Asian-fusion and Mediterranean-influenced salads, pastas and seafood specialties for over 30 years to the penchant of its fashionable customer base. Shrimps, true to its name, is a small, stylish establishment seating about 39, thus a reservation is suggested (and wholly recommended on weekends). With welcoming weather, choose a table outside and enjoy the best of Shrimps amidst the medieval charm of cobbled Steingasse that fronts the restaurant. Inside, soft lighting coupled with candlelit tables (most with a view to the chef preparing the dishes) and ambient background music strike the right mood to go with your meal. After dinner, consider the evolution of coffee and cocktails in neighboring Darwin's café-bar (p. 53).

Kebabs: There are two kebab joints to mention, both in New Town, meters from each other. First up is **Renya's** (open late at Steingasse 3, behind Hotel Stein), classic Döner 3.50€ or Dürüm wrapped like a burrito 4€, vegetarian options available. Along the river at Giselkai 15, some 7-8 doors southeast of Hotel Stein, kebabs can only be had nights and early mornings at the whole-in-the-wall **Troja grill** (Tue-Sat 20:00 thru 05:00, kebabs are 4.30€ but pay the extra .90¢ for the Dürüm).

Café Classic (Makartplatz 8 • Mon-Sat 8:00-19:30, Sun also mid-July thru Aug • CC: VC, MC • tel. 0662/882-700 • www.cafeclassic.at). Directly next door to the Mozart Residence (p. 40), consider a break at this "classic" coffeehouse not only for its specialty beverages and pastries and refined atmosphere but also for its daily food specials that make this café a sensible stop for lunch or any-time snack.

Spicy Spices "Bio Bistro" (vegetarian and organic foods, daily special 8€ • open daily 11:30-21:00 • Wolf-Dietrich-Str. 1, top of Linzergasse • tel. 0662/870-712). The piquant aroma of herbs and spices tastefully fill the air in this petite Indian bistro (effectively a restaurant within a shop), an excellent choice for vegetarians or anyone looking for a healthy, steam-cooked meal with lentils. The owner and friendly staff (typically Nirmal dutifully on duty) take pride in the government-issued certificate hanging on the wall guaranteeing that only the best-quality organic ("Bio") foods are used. Heck, you'll even find organic beer and juices on the menu to wash down all the Bio scrumptiousness, like naan chapati bread, panir cheese and lentil dal, tofu specialties, soya with peas, and most popular the **daily special**: typically a large Basmati or natural rice dish with vegetables in mild-curry sauce (add a fresh salad or soup for 1.50€).

Ikarus: Here 5-star cuisine is served in the company of billionaire *Dietrich Mateschitz's vintage aircraft collection at Salzburg airport (for more on Ikarus, see Hangar-7 p. 43). *Founder of the Red Bull energy drink (p. 80).

GOOD SLEEPS

In this pedestrianized city of salt there are more accommodations than you can poke a stick at. Not that I endorse stick poking, or any other poking of sorts. Below is an abridged list of restful lodgings to simplify, from cheap to steep, both for **Railers** and **Drivers** (the latter found in the latter half of this Good Sleeps section). Unless otherwise noted, all accommodations come with breakfast and have a shower and toilet in the room. → Lastly, add 1.50€ per person per night to your room rate for **city bed tax**.

> ☞ To help you better navigate this section, I've rated each accommodations entry with a dollar symbol based on the price of **double occupancy** per night. For example, one **$** symbol means the price of a double (twin) at the respective property is 70€ or less; two **$$** symbols mean the price of a double (twin) is generally between 70€ and 120€; three **$$$** symbols mean the price is generally between 120€ and 190€; four **$$$$** symbols mean the price exceeds 190€.
>
> **$** — pocket-friendly, 70€ or less
> **$$** — moderately priced, generally between 70€ and 120€
> **$$$** — upper end, generally between 120€ and 190€
> **$$$$** — superior, from 190€

Note: Room prices throughout town typically increase a great deal during the 45-day Salzburg Festival, mid-July thru August. As you already know from reading this guide, I urge you to buy the Salzburg Card (p. 9)—which may be for sale at your accommodations. Note that when "dbl" is written below it refers to a private room for two persons, not necessarily a private room having a double bed. Typically in Austria a double bed is two singles, or twins, pushed together to form a double. If it is a twin you're after, request when booking that the beds be separated.

The weather in Salzburg rarely sizzles in summer but in case you arrive during a heat wave, you risk a sleepless night due to the open windows in your room amplifying the possible street racket like bullhorns at a union rally, unless of course your accommodations are **air-conditioned**. The following digs from this section have AC: Art Hotel Blaue Gans (p. 65) • Star Inn (Gablerbräu and Zentrum p. 68 & 71) • Motel One (p. 68) • hotels Schloss Mönchstein and Sacher (p. 66 & 69).

Budget-minded travelers seeking a private room should also consider the hostels YoHo (p. 66) and JUFA (see next page).

Railers, from the main train station, YoHo hostel is a 10-min walk and all the remaining digs are within 30-min or, easier, reachable via bus. **Drivers**, digs more suitable to you are listed in the latter half of this Good Sleeps section, beginning p. 70.

Families, consider the following digs which offer rooms conducive to parties of 3 or more persons: JUFA (see next page) • book connecting rooms or rooftop suite at Hotel Goldgasse (p. 64) • Art Hotel Blaue Gans (p. 65) • YoHo (p. 66) • Star Inn Gablerbräu (p. 68) • Gästehaus Bonauerhof (kids love the farm animals and open space here, Drivers, p. 70) • Star Inn Zentrum (Drivers, p. 71) • Bergland Hotel (Drivers, p. 72).

Suggestion: Like a hearty breakfast, start the day with *ORF III*. You see, in Austria, I wake to soothing music and scenes televised (till 9:00) on channel *ORF III*, owned by the Austrian national broadcaster Österreichischer Rundfunk (ORF), which telecasts the local weather with wowing panoramas from its lofty cameras positioned across the country. You can also try channels *3sat* and *BR Fernsehen* (Bavaria).

Good Sleeps, OLD TOWN

$-$$ (hostel-hotel) **JUFA,** short for Jugend & Familiegästehaus (Josef-Preis-Allee 18 • tel. 05/708-3613 • www.jufa.eu • **free Wi-Fi**). This large 4-story youth-and-family hostel-hotel, located within easy reach of Old Town (under 10 min by foot), has recently undergone major renovations that deserve your attention. The lobby is spacious and sunlit, inviting and airy, a place to make new friends, exchange ideas and stories, pick up the latest brochure, plan the day's itinerary, relax with a beverage from the café-bar or watch the movie "**The Sound of Music**" (daily screening 20:00, ask reception to start movie). Adjoining the lobby, the **cafeteria** offers a heaping dinner menu with vegan alternatives (18:00-20:00, around 10€ all-you-can-eat buffet). Stop by; dig in. All told, this wheelchair-accessible hostel-hotel has 350 beds, an elevator, laundry facility, and large views to the fortress! **Note:** Price includes sheets and an excellent breakfast buffet with scrambled eggs—dorm beds, private and family rooms available. All major CCs accepted. Rates change regularly depending on availability. Check-in from 13:00. No common kitchen. All private rooms have a shower and toilet. Individual travelers looking for a dorm bed only have the 6 & 8-bed options (which are small rooms located one level below ground with meager ventilation). Lockers are provided in the hallway and work with a 2€ deposit (coin is returned upon reopening locker). **Suggestion:** Devote an evening to the film classic "**The Sound of Music.**" Have dinner here around 19:00 then watch the movie at 20:00. If you're not done with your meal by the time Maria takes to the hills, finish it in the TV lounge. If the movie is not playing, ask reception staff to start it. To complement your von-Trapp experience: beer, soda, hot drinks, sandwiches, fruits, and whatnot are available for purchase at the snack bar. **To get there: Drivers**, park in JUFA lot out front of property, 8€/day. **Railers,** from the main train station, a taxi will cost around 9€, or ride either bus 5 (direction Birkensiedlung) or 25 (direction Untersbergbahn) to Justizgebäude (10 min) —exit bus left and walk some 50 meters to the crosswalk (at traffic light) and cross over. On the other side of the road continue straight along Josef-Preis-Allee to your digs at the end. **Railers,** from Salzburg airport, a taxi will cost around 15€, or ride bus 2 from outside the airport to the Hauptbahnhof (main train station) then change to bus 5 or 25 (follow directions above for Railers).

$$ Gabi's Apartments, (Herrengasse 10 • www.salzburgplacetostay.com • email: apartments@sp2s.com • tel. +43-676-316-5080 or +43-660-525-9092 • **free Wi-Fi**). Experience the romantic flavor and medieval charm of Salzburg in one of Gabi's historic apartments, wonderfully located in the heart of Old Town, between the cathedral and fortress. Elegantly furnished, these non-smoking digs are so enchanting you'll want to call them your own! All apartments are self-contained and include the 21st-century comforts of home, having a queen-sized bed, own kitchen, Nespresso coffee maker, flat-screen TV, DVD player (Gabi has a limited selection of movies on loan, such as *The Sound of Music*), but shared access to the washer & dryer. You only need to bring your own shampoo and shower soap. Recipes, too, in case you decide to stay in for an evening and cook. In Salzburg Old Town, everything is synonymous with romantic, starting right here at Gabi's apartments! **Note:** Minimum stay 2 nights • cash only • Sgl/Dbl 110€-120€ per apartment per night, (Trpl possible add 30€/person), plus one-time 40€ cleaning/laundry fee per stay • 50% deposit in euro is required via PayPal and the remaining balance due upon arrival (but first email Gabi the dates you wish to stay and she'll reply to your query in perfect English) • Deal: Stay 7 nights and pay 6! **Apartments:** Gabi has 4 apartments—none with air-conditioning but instead have a fan—all located at Herrengasse 10. **Apt. 1** (110€) is cozy and nestled on the ground/1st floor, thus easy to access. **Apt. 2** (120€) is a quaint wood-beamed studio, located on the 2nd floor, thus up a few steps. **Apt. 3** (120€), on the 3rd floor, has a separate living and bed room with dynamite Old Town views to boot. **Apt. 4** (120€), on the 4th floor, thus a number of steps to climb but an even loftier view, including to the fortress! **To get there: Drivers**, park in Altstadt Garage "B" then 10-min walk. (Enter garage at Hildmannplatz 1, 22€/24hr. On foot, exit garage Festspielhäuser to Toscaninihof opening to Old Town.) **Railers,** from the main train station, it's about a 30-min walk to Herrengasse, around 13€ with a taxi, or catch bus 3, 5, 6 or 25 direction Zentrum and get off at Rathaus (5th stop)—exit bus and take lane running beneath archway. Continue straight through the square (Alter Markt), veer left and connect onto Residenzplatz, swing right (keeping the Residenz to your right) and ahead jog beneath the arches into Domplatz, continue straight (passing the cathedral on your left), through the next set of arches into Kapitelplatz. Here, skip past the painted chessboard and giant golden globe to the back left corner of the square. Behind the historic fountain, march uphill between the buildings and veer left onto Herrengasse to your digs second on the right. Ring doorbell on left side of wooden door where it reads: G. Frost. Welcome home! **Railers,** from Salzburg airport, a taxi will cost around 18€ (depending on traffic), or ride bus 10 toward town (departing every 15 min, every 30 min after 19:00 Mon-Sat and all day Sun) and get off at Rathaus (20-min ride), then follow the above directions for Railers: "—exit bus and take lane…." Another option, take the more frequent bus 2 from outside the airport to the Hauptbahnhof (main train station) then follow directions above for Railers.

$$$$ **Hotel Goldgasse,** (Goldgasse 10 • www.hotelgoldgasse.at • tel. 0662/ 845-622 • **free Wi-Fi**). Tucked onto a crooked pedestrian lane in the heart of Old Town that takes its name from the goldsmiths who formerly applied their trade here, at Hotel Goldgasse you'll get an authentic feel of Baroque life in Mozart's day. Dating from the 14th century, this boutique hotel is one of Salzburg's oldest inns, complete with a rich Austrian tradition and a venerated restaurant serving regional cuisine (daily 7:00-23:00, kitchen till 22:00). That said, Hotel Goldgasse (formerly the Goldene Ente) changed ownership and underwent a complete renovation. Since its reopening spring 2015, each of the hotel's 16 sophisticated rooms and suites are individually outfitted with contemporary design elements, oak-wood flooring, a marble bathroom, safe, flat-screen TV (playing *The Sound of Music* at your request), Italian SMEG fridge with complimentary mini-bar, DeLonghi espresso machine and Nespresso capsules, organic tea selections, and a Dyson fan on request (because there is no AC). Upon arriving, climb stairs (or ride elevator) one level to reception where a staff member is ready

to welcome *you* to the new 4-star Hotel Goldgasse and sensational Salzburg! **Note:** Check-in from 14:00, check-out by 11:00. CC: VC, MC, AE. **To get there: Drivers,** park in Altstadt Garage "B" then 10-min walk. (Enter garage at Hildmannplatz 1, 22€/24hr. On foot, exit garage Festspielhäuser to Toscaninihof opening to Old Town.) **Railers,** from the main train station, it's about a 25-min walk, around 10€ with taxi, or catch bus 3, 5, 6 or 25 direction Zentrum and get off at Rathaus (5th stop)—exit bus and take the lane running beneath the archway. Turn left ahead then go straight, keeping the square (Alter Markt) to your right, make the first right then go left on Goldgasse to your digs ahead on the right. **Railers,** from Salzburg airport, a taxi will cost around 20€ (depending on traffic), or ride bus 10 toward town (departing every 15 min, every 30 min after 19:00 Mon-Sat and all day Sun) and get off at Rathaus (20-min ride), then follow the above directions for Railers: "—exit bus and take…." Another option, take the more frequent bus 2 from outside the airport to the Hauptbahnhof (main train station) then follow directions above for Railers.

$$$$ **Art Hotel Blaue Gans,** (Getreidegasse 43 • www.blauegans.at • tel. 0662/8424-9150 • **free Wi-Fi** in room and use of Internet computer in lobby). This trendy art hotel could hardly be better situated in the hub of Old Town, on Salzburg's historic shopping street, Getreidegasse, meters from Mozart's birthplace. The Blaue Gans, or Blue Goose, dates from the 16th century and, although the historical shell remains, these digs have been fully refurbished to an air-conditioned house of contemporary design studios for tasteful travelers like you and me to lay our heads. Rooms are minimalist yet bright and fashionable, a product of modern art, each individually created but similarly outfitted with flat-screen TVs and Wi-Fi. Adjoining the hotel is the recommended traditional-style Blaue Gans restaurant and next door is the intoxicating Sporer wines & spirits (p. 50). **Note:** The lobby area is small; if the front desk is unattended upon your arrival, wait a minute and the receptionist will be right with you. The single, small double and regular double rooms are petite in size, thus opt for a medium double or larger room if your budget allows. All major CCs accepted. Reception sells Salzburg Card. **To get there: Railers,** from the main train station, a taxi will cost around 10€, or hop on bus 1 direction Zentrum (departs every 10 min, and every 20 min after 19:00 Mon-Sat and all day Sun) and get off at Herbert von Karajan Platz (3rd stop after crossing river but push button on handrail after 2nd stop, Mönchsbergaufzug, to signal driver to stop). Exit bus left, cross the street (left) with the traffic light, to your digs on the left (enter through back door and head straight to front desk). **Railers,** from Salzburg airport, a taxi will cost around 12€, or ride bus 10 toward town (departing every 15 min, every 30 min after 19:00 Mon-Sat and all day Sun) and get off at Herbert von Karajan Platz (15-min ride). Exit bus straight to your digs in front of you (enter through back door and head straight to front desk). Other than bus 10, another option would be to catch bus 2 outside the airport then connect onto bus 1, like so: ride bus 2 toward town (departing every 10-20 min until about 22:55) and get off a few stops later at Hans-Schmid-Platz (mention this to bus driver upon boarding). From here cross over to bus 1 direction Messe/Arena and get off after a handful of stops at Herbert von Karajan Platz (first stop after tunnel; push button on handrail to signal driver to stop). Exit bus straight to your digs in front of you (enter through back door and head straight to front desk). **Drivers,** you have two options: **1:** drop bags off first then park or **2:** with few bags I recommend you park first then walk. **1:** (Enter Herbert-von-Karajan-Platz into your GPS navigation system.) Once you arrive at Herbert-von-

Karajan-Platz, pull into the first available space on the left to unload your bags. The outdoor café-restaurant belongs to the Blaue Gans; enter through back door and head straight to the front desk; have receptionist point you to the parking garage and explain the discounted 18€/24hr tariff. **2:** Park in Altstadt Garage "A" then short walk. (Enter Hildmannplatz 1 into your GPS navigation system; on foot exit garage Altstadt/Getreidegasse then cross road to hotel.)

$$$$ **Hotel Schloss Mönchstein,** (Mönchsberg Park 26 • tel. 0662/848-5550 • www.monchstein.at • **free Wi-Fi** and use of Internet computer). "Enchanting" is the first word that comes to mind when considering Schloss Mönchstein, a luxurious 5-star castle hotel perched upon the bluff rising above Salzburg Old Town. Needless to say, the views from here are stupendous! The property, secluded by 4 acres of private forested reserve, was first mentioned in the year 1350 as Tetelheimer Tower. In the coming centuries, aristocrats and prominent persons caught wind of the beloved castle estate and became regular visitors. Today, valued guests are treated to welcome drinks and rooms furnished with antiques and contemporary comforts, creating a truly exquisite and personal atmosphere. All told, the hotel has 24 exclusively designed rooms and suites, an award-winning restaurant, a romantic wedding chapel, and a restorative health spa (in which many treatments are available, including an aroma-relax massage and body peel). Recent renovations make Hotel Schloss Mönchstein one of Salzburg's finest choices for accommodations. **Note:** Hotel rates include exclusive a-la-carte breakfast with buffet and free use of spa. All major CCs accepted. Once settled into the hotel, your means of connecting Old Town will be on foot (pleasant 25-min walk down) or quicker via the nearby Mönchsberg Lift (p. 38). **To get there: Drivers,** (enter Müllner Hauptstrasse 10 into your GPS navigation system), free parking on property—the only way up the bluff is via the district of Mülln, home of the Augustinian brewery and former monastery (marked by the copper-topped church steeple)—see hotel Web site for print-friendly directions (pdf file). **Railers,** a taxi from the main train station will cost around 9€ or a taxi from Salzburg airport will cost about 15€ (depending on traffic).

Good Sleeps, NEW TOWN

$ (hostel) **YoHo,** (Paracelsusstrasse 9, 15-min walk from Old Town • www.yoho.at • tel. 0662/879-649 • **free Wi-Fi** in lobby or use of Internet computer for a small fee). If you're looking for a hostel with a lively atmosphere, look no further. YoHo (with its 3 floors) is the No. 1 choice in town for backpackers, affording its guests friendly staff, discounted tours, bike rental, laundry facilities, daily screening of the movie "**The Sound of Music**" (at 20:00), inexpensive meals (breakfast buffet 7:30-10:30, dinner 19:00-20:30), movies and Nintendo Wii console on loan from reception, and an in-house bar with a very "happy hour" (2€ beer/wine 18:00-19:00 & again 22:00-23:00). **Note:** Room/bed rates fluctuate according to availability; sheets and key included but require a 5€ deposit. Family room possible. CC: VC, MC. Check-in from 12:00, check-out by 10:00. **To get there: Drivers**, street parking where space is available (free weekends or pay Mon-Fri 9:00-19:00 max 3hr); discounted garage parking possible (see reception). **Railers,** from the main train station, YoHo is roughly 7€ by taxi or a 10-min walk. By foot, exit front of station and go left some 200 meters to the traffic light, then walk left through the tunnel. Continue straight and make the second right into Paracelsusstrasse. Your digs are on the second block, right side. **Railers,** from Salzburg airport, a taxi will cost around 16€ (depending on traffic), or hop on bus 2 toward town and get off at Stelzhamerstrasse, 30-min ride (5th stop after main train station, push button on handrail to signal driver to stop; bus departs every 10 min, and every 20 min after 19:00 Mon-Sat and all day Sun)—exit bus left then make the first left (Lasserstrasse), at the forward intersection go left again and cross the street to your digs.

SALZBURG Good Sleeps & Eats

MAP NOT TO SCALE
To walk from the train station to Mozart's Birthplace is 20 min.

❶ Art Hotel Blaue Gans
❷ Bergland Hotel
❸ Gabi's Apartments
❹ Gästehaus Bonauerhof
❺ Hotel Goldgasse
❻ Hotel Sacher Salzburg
❼ Hotel Schloss Mönchstein
❽ Hotel Untersberg
❾ JUFA
❿ Motel One Mirabell
⓫ Star Inn Gablerbräu
⓬ Star Inn Zentrum
⓭ Trapp Villa
⓮ YOHO

$$ **Motel One (Mirabell),** (Elisabethkai 60 • www.motel-one.com • tel. 0662/885-200 • **free Wi-Fi**). Don't be misled by the name. This non-smoking budget-design hotel is such good value that I look forward to recommending the chain whenever possible across Europe, already having excellent locations in Berlin, Munich, Vienna, Brussels, Edinburgh, London, and Prague. Motel One is a new pocket-friendly hotel group that is true to its marketing slogan: Viel Design für Wenig Geld (meaning "a whole lotta design for little money"). No matter which Motel One you visit, the design and concept are the same. Although the rooms are small, you can count on 24-hour reception; air-conditioning; free Wi-Fi; modish décor accented by the company's aqua-colored theme, starting with the stylish lobby to its trendy room furnishings, including a flat-screen TV, ceramic vessel sink in the bathroom and a soothing shower with "rain" showerhead. Opened December 2012, this Salzburg "Mirabell" property scenically sits alongside the Salzach River, between the main train station and Mirabell Gardens, a pleasant 15-min walk along the river to Old Town. **Important:** All odd-numbered rooms have river views and even-numbered rooms face the ugly apartment block across the back lane, thus be sure to request a river view. **Note:** If available, book a Dbl room with balcony for a few more euro (hotel has only 9 of these room-types—note that in this room wall buttons lower/raise window shade). All major CCs accepted. Check-in from 15:00, check-out by 12:00. Buffet breakfast 9.50€/person. One child up to 12yr is free in parents' room, and child up to 6yr receives free breakfast to boot. During special events and the 45-day Salzburg Festival July-August, add 20€-70€ to the room rate. **To get there: Drivers**, in-house parking, 13€/day. Unload out front and notify reception. **Railers**, from the main train station, Motel One Mirabell is roughly 7€ by taxi, a 10-min walk, or catch *bus 1 (direction Messe) or *bus 2 (direction Airport/Walserfeld—*departing every 10 min, and every 20 min after 19:00 Mon-Sat and all day Sun) and get off at St. Julien Strasse (2nd stop) to your digs across the busy road. **Railers,** from Salzburg airport, a taxi will cost around 15€ (depending on traffic), or hop on bus 2 toward town and get off at St. Julien Strasse to your digs across the busy road (20-min ride, push button on handrail to signal driver to stop; bus departs every 10 min, and every 20 min after 19:00 Mon-Sat and all day Sun).

$$ **Star Inn Gablerbräu,** (Richard-Mayr-Gasse 2, a short walk across the river from Mozart's birthplace • www.starinnhotels.com • tel. 0662/879-662 • **free Wi-Fi**). Located in the heart of New Town, a schnitzel toss from Old Town, this freshly renovated (May 2012) 3-star property in the econo-class Star Inn, 'by Quality' family adds 71 air-conditioned rooms in varying categories (from standard to business suites and small apartments) with modern design, queen-sized beds, and flat-screen TVs to Salzburg's heaping accommodations pool. Unlike its "Zentrum" sister property (p. 71), these centrally located digs afford its guests the option of small apartments and one sweet rooftop suite! First documented in the year 1408 (then a brew house under a different name), the storied Gablerbräu property boasts a rich tradition of serving its Salzburg clientele. **Note:** Check-in from 15:00, check-out by 12:00. All major CCs accepted. Breakfast buffet 15€/person. Ask for room away from (possible noisy) elevator area. Two children up to the age of 11 accompanied by their parents stay for free, including breakfast (if parents booked their own). During the 45-day Salzburg Festival mid-July thru August and Advent, expect a significant increase to room rates. Reception sells Salzburg Card, tours, and concert/event tickets. **To get there: Railers**, from the main train station, it's around a 20-min walk, around 10€ with taxi, or (typically

from platform C) catch bus 1, 3, 5, 6 or 25 direction Zentrum and get off at Makartplatz (4th stop)—exit bus right and at the top of the street go right across the cross walks straight into Dreifaltigkeitsgasse, then make the first left into Richard-Mayr-Gasse to your digs ahead on the right. **Railers,** from Salzburg airport, a taxi will cost around 17€ (depending on traffic), or ride bus 2 from outside the airport to the Hauptbahnhof (main train station) then change buses (follow directions above for Railers). **Drivers,** tough to reach due to one-way streets and pedestrian zones, get directions and barrier code from reception in advance. Unload out front and get discount voucher from reception to the Mirabell garage on Mirabellplatz (5-min walk).

☞ To help you better navigate this section, I've rated each accommodations entry with a dollar symbol based on the price of **double occupancy** per night. For example, one **$** symbol means the price of a double (twin) at the respective property is 70€ or less; two **$$** symbols mean the price of a double (twin) is generally between 70€ and 120€; three **$$$** symbols mean the price is generally between 120€ and 190€; four **$$$$** symbols mean the price exceeds 190€.

   $ — pocket-friendly, 70€ or less
   $$ — moderately priced, generally between 70€ and 120€
   $$$ — upper end, generally between 120€ and 190€
   $$$$ — superior, from 190€

$$$$ Hotel Sacher Salzburg, (Schwarzstrasse 7 • www.sacher.com • tel. 0662/889-770 • **free Wi-Fi**). Nestled on the right bank of the Salzach River and facing Old Town, Hotel Sacher has a reputation of impeccable service, accommodations and tradition that far exceeds the boundaries of Austria. Since its grand opening in 1866 (then the Österreichischer Hof), Hotel Sacher's sumptuous 5-star digs have been a popular rendezvous for celebrities, royalty, jet-setting tycoons, political heavyweights, Hollywood movie stars, honeymooners, and free spirits like you and me who care to splurge once in awhile for that deserving occasion. Among Sacher's famous residents, Julie Andrews and director Robert Wise stayed here in 1964 during the filming of "The Sound of Music." Tom Hanks, the Dalai Lama, John Denver, Sylvester Stallone, Placido Domingo, and First Lady Hillary Clinton have also been guests at Hotel Sacher, an esteemed property belonging to The Leading Hotels of the World (www.lhw.com). Individuality and personal service are top priorities at Hotel Sacher Salzburg, privately owned and run by the Gürtler family since 1988. Guests are welcome to indulge in his or her taste of luxury. Painstakingly planned by management and industry professionals, each of Sacher's 111 rooms and suites have been individually decorated and are a showcase of antique art pieces and Oriental rugs, silk wallpaper and original oil paintings. Delicate and soothing color schemes complement sophisticated design elements. Rooms are clean, sharp, spirited, homey, fashionable, air-conditioned, each outfitted with a satellite flat-screen TV with international channels, safe, minibar, DVD player, the latest sound system. Savor the finest cuisine in Sacher's three restaurants; experience traditional

Austrian coffeehouse culture at Café Sacher; or meet in the Sacher Bar (daily 9:00 till late) and chill with a cocktail to the air of a live pianist (typically Mon-Sat from 18:00). At Hotel Sacher, everything is possible, even a room facing the river and Old Town (which I recommend you request, the alternative is to face the busy road on which you arrived). **Note:** Breakfast buffet 34€/person (or may come with room depending on rate-type). All major CCs accepted. Hotel Sacher Salzburg is the sister property of Hotel Sacher Vienna. Did you know, since 1832, as per a closely guarded secret recipe, Franz Sacher and family have been whipping up the world's most **famous torte:** a rich chocolate cake with a hint of apricot. The 4-portion *Piccolo* size cake presented in a classic-style wooden box with Sacher imprint is a sweet gift idea (24.90€, maximum freshness within 14 days of purchase). To order your Original Sacher Torte, show up in person (café or gift shop) or go to the hotel's Web site. **To get there: Drivers**, a doorman awaits your arrival, parking roughly 35€/day. **Railers**, a taxi from the main train station will cost around 9€ or a taxi from Salzburg airport will cost about 15€ (depending on traffic; tell the driver you want to be driven through the city [the alternative route is longer via the autobahn]).

Good Sleeps, better suited for Drivers

$$ (hostel-hotel) **JUFA** listed on page 63 also works well for Drivers since it has a small parking lot (8€/day) out front and is within easy walking distance of Old Town.

$$ **Gästehaus Bonauerhof,** (Kapellenweg 5, Viehhausen • tel. 0662/853-361 • www.bonauerhof.at • **free Wi-Fi**). I adore these digs, and I think you will too. If you're looking for a quiet bed on a working farm in the 'burbs bursting with fresh country air and vast pastoral vistas, this is for you. Gästehaus Bonauerhof is a family run farmhouse by the Götzinger clan, who offer seven studio apartments with kitchen, each with its own balcony, and big hospitality typically associated with country folk. Located in the village of Viehhausen, 7 km west of Salzburg Old Town, the Götzingers have plenty of room for you and their stable of horses, dairy cows, and handful of rabbits, all whom the children love. Aside from the petting zoo, go for a dip in the natural, spring-fed pool or you're welcome to borrow the family bikes to cycle through the pretty pastures. Your first stop can be the charming chapel across the street to view the historic scene (left of its front door) depicting the raging infernos that swept through the village in 1874. Right of the chapel door is a memorial to the locals who fell during both world wars. **Note:** Minimum stay 3 nights. Room rate per night does *not* include breakfast, cash only, Dbl 72€, Trpl 93€, family (up to 4 persons) 125€. Book early! There are only 7 rooms. Consider buying the Salzburg Card (p. 9) to save on the sights as well as bus fare to/fro Old Town. Bus 27 regularly shuttles between Viehhausen and Salzburg Old Town (Hanuschplatz) every day until last bus at 22:40. **To get there,** GPS: N47 46.985 E12 59.252. **Railers**, from the main train station, hop on bus 1 direction Zentrum (departs every 10 min, and every 20 min after 19:00 Mon-Sat and all day Sun) and get off at Hanuschplatz, then pick up bus 27 direction Airport and get off at Viehhausen Ortsmitte (20-min ride; either notify driver of your intended stop or push button on handrail to signal driver to stop; bus departs daily from Hanuschplatz every 15-20 min until last bus at

22:40). From Viehhausen Ortsmitte it's a short walk; exit bus left then ahead go right at the chapel into (lane) Kapellenweg to your digs on the left. **Railers,** from Salzburg airport, a taxi will cost roughly 7€, or ride bus 27 direction Salzburg Zentrum and get off at Viehhausen Ortsmitte (5-min ride; either notify driver of your intended stop or push button on handrail to signal driver to stop; bus departs every 15 min, and every 20-30 min after 19:00 Mon-Fri until last bus at 23:05, and every 30-40 min Sat-Sun until last bus at 22:44). From Viehhausen Ortsmitte it's a short walk; exit bus right then go right around the corner and ahead go right at the chapel into (lane) Kapellenweg to your digs on the left. **Drivers,** Gästehaus Bonauerhof is just off the A1 autobahn at exit "Salzburg West." **If you've** just connected onto the A1 from the A10 or Germany, after exiting at Salzburg West turn right toward Salzburg and immediately right again at the Viehhausen sign. Take this road a few hundred meters then turn left at the chapel; this is Kapellenweg and your digs are on the left. **If you're** coming from the east on the A1 (e.g. from Linz or Vienna), after exiting at Salzburg West go all the way around the turning circle direction Salzburg, then ahead (just after the Himmelreich sign) turn right at the Viehhausen sign. Take this road a few hundred meters then turn left at the chapel; this is Kapellenweg and your digs are on the left.

$$ **Motel One (Mirabell)** listed on page 68 also works well for Drivers since it has in-house parking (13€/day) and is within a pleasant walk of the Old Town.

$$ **Star Inn Zentrum,** (Hildmannplatz 5 • www.starinnhotels.com • tel. 0662/846-846 • **free Wi-Fi**). These 3-star non-smoking digs with few frills but modern design and flat-screen TVs add some 86 air-conditioned rooms to Salzburg's accommodations pool for Drivers. Conveniently positioned just outside the west end of Old Town, in front of the Siegmundstor (gate) cutting through the Mönchsberg (Monks' Ridge) to the festival halls and main shopping street, Star Inn's proximity to Mozart's birthplace and other major attractions is just the proverbial cow chip chuck away. **Note:** Check-in from 15:00, check-out by 12:00. All major CCs accepted. Breakfast buffet 13€/person. Two children up to the age of 11 accompanied by their parents stay for free, including breakfast (if parents booked their own). During the 45-day Salzburg Festival mid-July thru August and Advent, expect a significant increase to room rates. **To get there: Drivers,** exit the A1 autobahn at "Flughafen" and follow signs to Salzburg, then Mitte and Hotel route. After about 4 km you will reach a giant cliff face and a tunnel funneling into Old Town—don't drive through the tunnel! Before it, on the right, are your digs. Park by hotel and unload. Have reception explain parking situation, including hotel discount, 16€/24hr. **Railers,** from the main train station, a taxi will cost around 11€, or hop on bus 1 direction Zentrum (departs every 10 min, and every 20 min after 19:00 Mon-Sat and all day Sun) and get off at Reichenhaller Strasse (15-min ride; when the bus goes through the tunnel, Reichenhaller Strasse is the next stop. Push button on handrail to signal driver to stop). Exit bus right, stroll back to the crosswalk and your digs are across the street. **Railers,** from Salzburg airport, a taxi will cost around 13€, or ride bus 10 toward town (departing every 15 min, every 30 min after 19:00 Mon-Sat and all day Sun) and get off at Reichenhaller Strasse and your digs (10-min ride). Other than bus 10, another option would be to catch bus 2 outside the airport then connect onto bus 1, like so: ride bus 2 toward town (departing every 10-20 min until about 23:10) and get off after a few stops at Hans-Schmid-Platz (mention this to bus driver upon boarding). From here cross over to bus 1 direction Messe/Arena and get off after a handful of stops at Reichenhaller Strasse and your digs.

$$$ **Bergland Hotel,** (Rupertgasse 15 • www.berglandhotel.at • tel. 0662/872-318 • **free Wi-Fi**). These well-appointed digs secreted behind an unremarkable facade at the top of the New Town, 15 minutes by foot from Old Town, are a great choice for Drivers who can park out front for free. The owners, Peter and Inga (pictured), a convivial husband-and-wife team, whose family has been the innkeepers for more than 100 years (since 1912), affectionately run the non-smoking Bergland Hotel and make overnighting in Salzburg a homey experience in a friendly, urban neighborhood. An elevator lifts guests to the upper floors, filled with individually decorated rooms, from traditional to minimalist. Upstairs is a restful terrace, an ideal place to conclude a dreamy day of sightseeing in Salzburg, with a glass of wine in hand. Musically inclined guests can chill in the cozy confines of the music room and play piano or strum guitar. In the evening, local cuisine and entertainment begin just a few doors along at Die Weisse (p. 53) or down Linzergasse to a smorgasbord of choices. **Note:** The hotel's delicious thus recommended breakfast costs 8.50€/person or only 4.50€ if you book your room directly with the hotel. CC: VC, MC, AE. Parking is free but limited to a handful of spaces, thus upon booking notify reception if you require one. Check-in from 13:00, check-out by 11:00. Reception is open roughly 7:00-21:30, thus notify staff if checking in late. **To get there: Drivers**, free parking out front, enter Rupertgasse 15 into your GPS navigation system. **Railers**, from the main train station, a taxi will cost around 9€, or hop on bus 2 direction Zentrum/Obergnigl and get off at Bayerhamerstrasse (6th stop but push button on handrail to signal driver to stop; bus departs every 10-15 min, and every 20 min after 19:00 Mon-Sat and all day Sun). Exit bus left then go right into lane just past gas station—at end of lane are your digs (left). **Railers,** from Salzburg airport, a taxi will cost around 15€ (tell driver to take you through the city [the alternative route is longer via the autobahn]), or hop on bus 2 toward town and get off at Bayerhamerstrasse, 30-min ride (6th stop after train station but push button on handrail to signal driver to stop; bus departs every 10-15 min, and every 20 min after 19:00 Mon-Sat and all day Sun). Exit bus left then go right into lane just past gas station—at end of lane are your digs (left).

$$$ **Hotel Untersberg,** (Dr. Friedrich Ödlweg 1, St. Leonhard • tel. 06246/72575 • www.hoteluntersberg.at • **free Wi-Fi** and use of Internet computer). More bucolic bliss can be found here at Hotel Untersberg, a 4-star rustic retreat with a bona fide Austrian feel idyllically nestled at the foot of Untersberg mountain, on the road connecting Salzburg with Berchtesgaden, 13 km (or 8 mi) to either destination. Country-style furnishings accent spacious rooms that fill with fresh alpine air puffing in from scenic summer balconies dripping with vibrant geraniums while every half hour a cable car ascends to the summit of Untersberg mountain (p. 44, see reception for your cable-car discount as well as free use of a bicycle for pedaling around the edelweiss). **Note:** Room rate includes breakfast buffet and use of sauna (open 16:30-21:00—ask reception for bathrobe). Hotel Untersberg groups its rooms into two comfort categories: 'Salzburg Land' and 'Kaiser Karl'. Although both are fine, choose the superior Kaiser Karl category which is situated in the main building. All major CCs accepted. Family apartment available. For your dining pleasure, Hotel Untersberg has a traditional Austrian restaurant seeking to indulge your palate. Consider buying the Salzburg Card

(p. 9) from reception to save on the sights as well as bus fare to/fro Old Town. **To get there: Railers**, I don't recommend this hotel for you because of its distance from Old Town, but just in case you need the directions: from the main train station hop on bus 25 direction Untersbergbahn (departing every 20 min, and every 30 min after 18:00 Mon-Fri and 17:00 Sat-Sun) and ride it to the end, 30 min. **Drivers**, free parking on property; exit A10 autobahn at Salzburg-Süd and head toward Grödig—after 1 km you'll see the hotel's (flowering) facade on the right (turn at traffic light). After you've checked in and are ready to head into Salzburg, either catch bus 25 (departing every 20-30 min from behind hotel) or drive into town and park (see Drivers/Parking p. 8).

$$$ **Hotel-Garni Schernthaler & Gasthof zur Post:** Although a fair distance from Salzburg, 27 km to be specific, I've listed these two digs here because if you're heading out to the lake district (Salzkammergut p. 79) and are open to spending the night in a lake-side village, consider either accommodations (p. 84) located on the tremendously scenic Wolfgangsee.

$$$ **Trapp Villa,** (Traunstrasse 34, Aigen). At these digs you have the opportunity to overnight in the former residence of Salzburg's most famous family, p. 112.

EXCURSIONS

Salzkammergut, (p. 79): 15 km east of Salzburg begins this breathtakingly beautiful lake district.

Berchtesgaden, (see my *Self-guided Munich, Ludwig's Castles & Hitler's Eagle's Nest* guide out later this year). Some 25 km southwest of Salzburg (on the German side of the border) is Berchtesgaden, a quiet Bavarian village nestled amongst the edelweiss-encrusted Alps. Here you'll find the Eagle's Nest, salt mines, and Königssee lake. To get there from Salzburg is easy, see page 7. Or, if interested, pricey tours are available to Berchtesgaden from Salzburg; ask TI or staff at your digs for info.

Mauthausen: Consider visiting Austria's former notorious concentration camp —now an affecting memorial—on the way to Vienna. **Railers**, have the railway clerk from your point of departure print out an itinerary (Fahrplanauskunft) to the town of Mauthausen (OÖ) and then back again from Mauthausen to St. Valentin to connect with the Salzburg-Vienna rail line. **Drivers**, Mauthausen is about 150 km northeast of Salzburg via the A1 autobahn direction Vienna; get off at exit 151, St. Valentin, then follow signs to Mauthausen and KZ Memorial.

☞ Similar to the Bayern-Ticket in Bavaria, the **Einfach-Raus-Ticket** is a terrific buy in Austria for small groups (up to five persons) traveling on non-speed trains for the day in 2nd-class seating on the Austrian rail network: ÖBB. The price starts at 33€ for two persons (irrespective of age), then add 4€/person thereafter up to five persons, thus 37€/three, 41€/four, 45€/five persons valid Mon-Fri 9:00 until 3:00 (the following morning) and the whole day Sat/Sun on ÖBB's suburban and regional service trains as well as on the Raaberbahn (R, REX and S-Bahn). **This group ticket would be ideal**, for example, for a day trip from Salzburg to Werfen (p. 75) or Hallstatt (p. 86), or five persons to Oberndorf (below). **Note:** Unlike the Bayern-Ticket, the Einfach-Raus-Ticket is not valid on buses or the subway, only suburban and regional ÖBB trains. Einfach-Raus-Tickets are available for purchase online (www.oebb.at), at ÖBB automats, or over the counter at the train station.

Oberndorf bei Salzburg

Population: 5,995 • **Elevation:** 394 m (1,292 ft) • **Country-Area code:** +43-(0)6272
License plate: SL (short for Salzburgland, the rural district around Salzburg)

Some 22 km north of Salzburg is Oberndorf, a cute border town huddled on the Austrian side of the Salzach River (on the opposite bank is its medieval twin: Laufen, Germany). Oberndorf flourished through the ages as a key partner along a trade route flushed with merchant vessels hauling salt, regarded then as "white gold." Although Oberndorf has a rich history dating from the 12th century, it is a single incident that transpired over the course of just a few minutes that forever labeled the riverside community as an international tourist destination. On Christmas Eve, 1818, Joseph Mohr (the village priest) required a carol to accompany midnight Mass at St. Nicholas' church. Mohr handed Franz Xaver Gruber (school teacher and part-time organist) a poem that he had written and asked him to compose a simple melody befitting the text. Gruber finished the melody in time for midnight Mass and the two men, along with the choir, sang the newly composed carol to a delighted crowd. The carol was called *Stille Nacht*, or more famously, "Silent Night."

Throughout history, communities were preferably settled on the banks of rivers as a means to a robust trading economy. A geographic location such as this, however, could also spell disaster! You see, in the year 1890, Mother Nature dialed up a devastating flood, in which the Salzach River overflowed its banks and St. Nicholas' church standing in the path was irreversibly damaged. Today, the former church grounds on Stille Nacht Platz consist only of the small "Heimat" museum (explaining history of town, salt merchants, and Silent Night story, Thu-Sun 10:00-18:00, closed Mon-Wed, except daily July-Aug and Advent till Jan 6 [Epiphany], adult 4.50€, student/senior 4€, family 12€) and an even smaller memorial chapel (pictured, consecrated 1937), big enough for about 15 of us (daily 8:00-18:00). Inside, notice the stained-glass windows of Mohr and Gruber. Allow at least 15 minutes for a visit to the grounds. From home or your mobile device, check out the chapel via the Web cam at this site: www.stillenacht.info.

Every year on December 24, tour buses usher in hundreds of tourists to join locals in a Silent Night memorial service, when hot-spiced wine (Glühwein) is sipped from collector's mugs, traditional Christmas shooters chase away evil spirits, and joyous revelers sing the world-renowned carol. The memorial service begins at 17:00 and lasts about 45 minutes (but plan to arrive by 16:15 to allow for people and car traffic). During the weeks leading up to Christmas, the Silent Night Post Office will be open for business (daily from about December 8 thru Christmas Eve, located in the "Heimat" museum, where souvenirs are also sold and information given). Bring in your letters and postcards to be mailed and the clerk will strike them with a specially designed "Silent Night" postmark. **To get there,** GPS: N47 56.736 E12 56.200. **Railers**, from Salzburg's central station, trains depart for Oberndorf (bei Salzburg) typically every 30 min at the top and bottom of the hour (25-min trip, www.oebb.at). From Oberndorf train station, it's a 10-min walk to the memorial chapel. (Note the train departure times so you can neatly plan your return to Salzburg.) Exit station left and at the main road go right. Immediately cross the street and jog left on Alte Landstrasse. Follow this road straight all the way into Stille Nacht Platz and the memorial chapel. **Drivers**, the scenic drive from Salzburg to Oberndorf is roughly 30 min. Take route 20 on the German side of the border. To find it, head to Freilassing in northwest Salzburg. After crossing the border you'll meet route 20; follow signs to Laufen, 13 km. Once in Laufen follow signs to Oberndorf, which will lead through the town's medieval gate (circa 1400) and narrow streets. Soon you'll cross the Salt River (Salzach)—halfway across the turn-of-the-century iron bridge is Austria—the other side is Oberndorf. (In June 2003, both Germany and Austria commemorated this striking Art Nouveau-style bridge on a postage stamp to mark its 100th birthday. Pictured is the German stamp.) If it's a clear day, notice the sweeping vista of the Alps to your right as you cross. Continue straight towards the church in front of you; at the T-intersection, turn left. After 1 km look for a parking space (preferably on the right curve). The chapel (Stille Nacht Kapelle) is accessible via a footpath on the left (just prior to right curve). If there are no parking spaces available, turn left into the lane at Gasthof Bauernbräu for more options. When heading back to Salzburg, take route 156 on the Austrian side. This is the main road running through Oberndorf, which southbound will land you in Salzburg (16 km).

Werfen

Population: 3,000 • **Elevation:** 547 m (1,794 ft) • **Country-Area code:** +43-(0)6468
License plate: JO (short for Sankt Johann, district of Pongau, which Werfen belongs)

When heading south from Salzburg you'll encounter massive, sheer mountains flanking your journey—an overwhelming spectacle, indeed. Among this chain of Alps is the town of Werfen, 40 km south of Salzburg. Most of the time it's hard to distinguish one village from another in this region since they all feature an idyllic church steeple soaring above a cluster of well-kept houses accentuated by colorful flowers spilling over their balconies. However, there is one thing that differentiates Werfen from neighboring communities, and that is one hunka-chunka castle: Burg Hohenwerfen, kid brother to the Salzburg fortress. It is truly an awesome sight to behold this medieval citadel perched above Werfen, defining its skyline. Moreover, Werfen possesses the world's largest ice cave. In addition, classic moviegoers will be interested to know that Werfen appeared in "The Sound of Music," and in a much bigger role it was the town portrayed in the 1968 movie "Where Eagles Dare" starring Clint Eastwood and Richard Burton. (In German, the film was called *Agenten sterben einsam*, meaning "agents die alone.") And so, when you marvel at this tremendous scenery in person and envision its natural beauty to be right out of a Hollywood movie, you can be certain that it is.

Suggestion: If you're planning on doing both the ice cave and castle, do the ice cave first then the castle to avoid crowds on, and in, the mountain (especially July-Aug). To save time, in the shuttle bus back down from the ice cave, have the driver drop you off at the trailhead to the castle (Burg Hohenwerfen). **To get there: Railers**, from Salzburg's central station, trains depart hourly for Werfen (45-min trip, www.oebb.at). From Werfen train station, you can pick up the shuttle to the ice cave (for times see Ice Cave below), or mosey 10 min into town to the TI (cross bridge over river and continue straight), or march 30 min to the castle (cross bridge over river and go right along riverside path following signs to fortress). **Drivers**, Werfen is a 30-min drive from Salzburg via the A10 autobahn south, direction Graz-Villach. You are allowed to park on the main drag cutting through the center of town for one hour free with your parking dial (p. 115) during the hours Mon-Fri 8:00-18:00, Sat 8:00-12:00; all other times the dial is not required.

Tourist information (Mon-Fri 9:00-12:00 & 14:00-17:00, November only Tue-Wed • www.werfen.at • tel. 06468/5388) is located at Markt 24, on the main drag in the center of town, a 10-min walk from the train station. Friendly staff can assist you with any local questions or finding accommodations.

The **post office** (Mon-Fri 7:00-12:00 & 14:30-18:00, Sat 7:00-12:00) is located within the magazine shop Nadegger at Markt 41.

A **pharmacy** (Mon-Fri 8:00-12:00 & 14:30-18:00, Sat 7:30-12:00), locally Apotheke, is situated at Markt 23, across the street from the above-listed tourist information office. Remember, in Austria, even if it's just plain aspirin you require, it can only be purchased at an Apotheke (this goes the same for Germany).

An "Mpreis" **grocery store** (Mon-Fri 7:30-19:00, Sat 7:30-18:00) is located at Markt 26, mere meters from the above-listed tourist information office.

Hand-made Austrian hats: Among the many worthwhile sites and attractions in this quaint corner of Austria, **Hutmacher Zapf** (Markt 13 • Mon-Thu 9:00-12:00 & 14:00-17:00, Fri 9:00-12:00 & 15:00-17:00 • www.zapf.at • tel. 06468/5227) has been crafting traditional hats for men, women, and hunters since 1893 in the heart of Werfen (15-min walk from the train station, a few min past the TI). Hat enthusiasts can peek behind the curtain on one of Zapf's 30-minute guided tours through their 15-step manufacturing process (free, call or email at least 2 days in advance to arrange tour time • hats from 115€).

Burg Hohenwerfen, allow at least 2 hours for a visit, **open April thru Nov 12, 2017**: April, Oct & Nov Tue-Sun 9:30-16:00 (closed Mon) • May-Sept daily 9:00-17:00 • July 17 thru Aug 20, 9:00-18:00 • www.salzburg-burgen.at. **Price** (includes birds-of-prey show, national falconry museum, and the castle tour departing most every hour on the hour, 20% off with Salzburg Card), adult 12€ (with cable railway 15.50€), student 10.50€ (with cable railway 13.50€), youth 6-15yr 6.50€ (with cable railway 8.50€), family 28.50€ (with cable railway 36.50€). **Note:** Purchase ticket in advance on castle Web site for discounted options. Time your arrival to coincide with the birds-of-prey show (flight demonstrations daily 11:15 and 15:15, except July 17 thru Aug 18 at 11:15, 14:15 and

16:30), duration 30 min. To avoid the 15-min hike up to the fortress, take the **cable railway** directly from the castle parking lot (see Drivers below).

Dating from 1077 A.D., this imposing castle rests upon a forested bluff towering over the village of Werfen. Its powerful bulwarks firmly entrenched into the rock-solid earth persuasively served throughout the Middle Ages to imprison high-value convicts as well as further protect the trade route connecting Italy. Today, the citadel stands as a footprint of history alongside a sleek autobahn delivering adventurers and moneyed tourists who keenly pay admission to marvel at the castle's medieval matrix and mesmerizing birds-of-prey show. **Special programs** for big and little kids alike are fun, fascinating and held frequently at the fortress, thus I've listed the following dates and happenings to help you plan your Werfen visit. I recommend the "Mittelalterliches Treiben auf der Burg," or medieval festival with jugglers and fencing in period dress and knights' tournament for children, scheduled in 2017 from 10:00-17:00: June 4-5 & 24-25 • August 26-27 • September 9-10 & 30 • October 1. **To get there**, the fortress can only be reached on foot or by cable railway; there is no shuttle service. If you're without wheels and aren't up to the walk, call a **Taxi**—*Taxi Hippolt* (tel. 06462/20333) or *Taxi Pongau* (tel. 06462/4343)—to take you to the castle parking lot to connect with the cable railway (note there are no taxis waiting at the train station therefore call one in advance to schedule your pick-up). **Railers**, at your point of departure, small groups consider purchasing the "Einfach-Raus-Ticket" (p. 73, from Salzburg catch the 9-o'clock train). Once at Werfen train station, you can reach the fortress either via taxi to the cable railway (see Taxi above) or on foot (roughly a 30-min trek, cross bridge over river and go right following path and signs to the fortress; first flat, then steep). **Drivers**, Werfen is a 30-min drive from Salzburg via the A10 autobahn south, direction Graz-Villach, (Vignette required, p. 115). The castle parking lot (GPS: N47 28.983 E13 11.121, free parking and toilets) is located below the fortress on route 159. From the A10 autobahn south, get off at the exit "Pass-Lueg" and drive route 159 south a handful of kilometers to the castle parking lot, found a short distance after the village of Tenneck. From the lot, you can either hike up to the fortress (15 min) or if foot-weary ride the cable railway lifting straight into the castle grounds.

SOM fans, you'll see the abovementioned fortress (Burg Hohenwerfen) in the movie "The Sound of Music." Forward to the scene where Maria and the kids are playing in a grassy meadow while wearing their play clothes and learning to sing "Do-Re-Mi." The significant structure in the background is Werfen's castle, and the meadow they are in is called Gschwandtanger. I recommend a visit here if you have time—plan your stop around midday to complement the dreamy locale and views with a picnic. In 2015, for the movie's 50th anniversary of its Hollywood release, Werfen opened **The Sound of Music Trail** leading from the center of town up to the Gschwandtanger, taking around an hour. **To get there**, SOM meadow, GPS: N47 28.413 E13 10.847. **Railers**, the Trail begins next to the tourist info office. If the TI is open, staff will give you a map and point you the way, otherwise the Trail is well signposted. If you have little time or weary feet, arrange for a taxi pick-up (see entry above, Taxi). **Drivers**, follow the directions I've written for you in the above Burg Hohenwerfen entry to Werfen and castle parking lot, but continue past the parking lot then turn right off route 159 toward Gasthof Dielalm. Climb the frightfully narrow, two-way zigzagging road a little more than 1 kilometer. Once on the other side of the forest, the view will become familiar—on the left is the SOM meadow. Continue driving and soon you'll see two benches ahead beneath a cluster of maple trees—just beyond them, before the curve, is a good place to pull over. **Picnickers,** in Werfen, pick up your goodies at the "Mpreis" grocery store (see previous page) and/or the deli at Markt 36 (when facing the TI, go left several doors to the flowering facade of the Fleischhauerei). **Note:** When absorbing the views on Gschwandtanger, look above the castle about three-fourths of the way up the mountain. Now move your eyes left and you'll see a white structure; this belongs to the ice cave (next entry). If you have a fear of heights, scratch this attraction off your list of things to do. Really, scratch it!

Ice Cave, locally Eisriesenwelt, allow at least 3 hours for a visit, **open May thru October 26, 2017:** cashier daily May-June & Sept-Oct 8:00-15:00 but last cable car at 15:20, July-Aug cashier till 16:00 but last cable car at 16:20 • www.eisriesenwelt.at • **price** includes cable car and guided cave tour: 24€, student 22€, youth 15-18yr 18€, child 5-14yr 14€, family 1+1/2+2 34€/66€, without cable car 7€-12€ but it's about a 90-min hike • **last cavern tour:** May-June & Sept-Oct 15:45, July-Aug 16:45 • **tour duration:** 70 min • overall, expect a visit to take between 3 and 4 hours • if interested, commercial tours are available to the ice cave from Salzburg, ask TI or staff at your digs.

For a chilling experience, visit the world's largest ice cave concealed within the Tennen Alp range—more than 40 km of caverns have been explored! The giant ice cave, discovered by a wandering naturalist in 1879, is located at a dizzying height upon the mountain opposite Burg Hohenwerfen (other side of autobahn). Today, it is a nationally protected landmark and may only be entered with a guide. To reach the mouth of the cave is serious business, not for the faint hearted. First, either by car or shuttle bus, travelers must climb the mega-steep (21% grade) 5 km mountain road to arrive at the parking lot and visitor's center. From here, it's a 20-min walk uphill to the cable car—Austria's steepest cable-car ascent, 500 m (1,640 ft) in 3 minutes—which will lift a dozen passengers (many of whom will see God in the vertical mountain face on the way up) to the elevation of 1,575 m (5,166 ft). The vista, needless to say, is phenomenal! From here, one teeters high above the valley floor while trekking another 20 minutes to reach the mouth of the cave. At this point, many adventurers will be sweating from head to toe, but it is essential to throw on a jacket or sweater, or both. Once the entrance to the cave is exposed, bystanders will be belted by an arctic blast as if being hurled into a giant freezer. *Burrr.* Inside is pitch black, except for the light emanating from the lamps provided by the guide—a surreal environment of ice, rock, and darkness. **Note:** Travelers who are out of shape, have a fear of heights, or suffer from vertigo—save your money and delete this attraction from your itinerary. Travelers who are in good health and have a sense of adventure should find the time and money to experience the world's largest ice cave. Wear good hiking shoes and pack warm clothes (because the temps inside the cave are literally freezing, 0°C/32°F, year round)! Adjacent to the upper cable-car station, a scenic chalet-style restaurant is keen to serve you. Views are paralyzing! Photography inside the cave is *verboten!* (That said, your guide might not enforce it.) **To get there:** The **shuttle bus** (7€/adult, 5€/<15yr) to the ice cave visitor's center and ticket cashier departs Werfen regularly, about every 25 min, from the big parking area along the riverbank, a 5-min walk from the train station. **Railers,** from outside Werfen train station, the shuttle bus (7€/adult, 5€/<15yr) to the ice cave visitor's center and ticket cashier departs 8:18, 10:18, 12:18 and 14:18 (if you missed the shuttle then cross the bridge, go right and follow the path 5 min to the big parking area where the shuttle departs every 25 min), or it's possible to **hike up to the cable car** departure area (5 km, steep) taking around two hours. **Drivers,** follow signs Eisriesenwelt. Slip car into first gear and admire the views *after* parking.

Salzkammergut

This strange-sounding name translates to "salt storage estates," referring to the region's rich salt deposits that have been mined since the Iron Age, i.e. in Hallstatt. Today, however, the Salzkammergut (www.salzkammergut.at) is better known as the **lake district**—a collection of glacial lakes strung out like shimmering pearls across three Austrian states: Salzburgland, Styria (Steiermark), and Upper Austria (Oberösterreich). Besides its stunning beauty, another exclusive feature of the Salzkammergut is that many of the alpine lakes boast crystal-clear drinking-quality water. It's pure!

Within reach of Salzburg, the main lakes of interest are **Fuschlsee**, **Wolfgangsee**, **Mondsee** and **Hallstätter See**, hence this Salzkammergut section focuses on these destinations. While reviewing the aforesaid names, you'll notice they all have one thing in common: the suffix "see," which in German (pronounced 'zay') means "lake."

Sound of Music fans will be interested to know that a few scenes from the movie were filmed in this region, principally the wedding scene at Mondsee (p. 85 & 111).

Suggestion: If it's a warm day, bring your bathing suit and pack a picnic. Those of you who are planning on spending the night, choose between Wolfgangsee and Hallstätter See—either destination is stunning. **Note:** From Salzburg, consider riding the multilingual (Green Line) **Hop On Hop Off bus** departing April 9 thru last week of October, daily, every 90 minutes, (round trip 2.20 hours if you were to stay on the bus), to/fro Fuschlsee, Wolfgangsee, Mondsee and Salzburg (adult 25€, child 6-14yr 12€, family 2+2 55€, see TI or staff at your digs for more info). To obtain a discount on most every attraction mentioned in this chapter, including public transportation, consider purchasing the **Salzkammergut Erlebnis Card** (adult 3.90€/4.90€, valid May thru October for the duration of your stay, available at most any TI/info stand and hotel in the Salzkammergut).

Fuschlsee

Situated 15 km east of Salzburg, Fuschlsee is the first lake you'll reach after leaving the city limits. Its glistening turquoise-colored waters, warming up to a pleasant 24-degrees Celsius (75°F) in summer, allure even the most hardcore urbanites. Drivers and their passengers will parallel the four-kilometer-long Lake Fuschl before reaching the main village upon its shores, aptly named **Fuschl am See**. Although petite, Fuschl am See commands a devout loyalty from vacationers who return annually with their campers and tents to claim a sliver of shoreline for yet another sizzling season on one of the warmest lakes in the Salzkammergut.

In contrast to the pocket-friendly joys of camping are the ultra-exclusive digs of **Schloss Fuschl** (Schloss Strasse 19, Hof bei Salzburg, www.schlossfuschlsalzburg.com, tel. 06229/22530), a 15th-century estate recently converted into one of Austria's leading resort hotels (that is largely out of view from passing motorists). Originally built in the year 1450 for the archbishop as a summer hideaway and hunting lodge, Schloss Fuschl is idyllically snuggled on the water's edge, surrounded by a 35-acre nature reserve. (To get there, turn at the [Sheraton] Hotel Jagdhof, located on the west [Salzburg] side of Lake Fuschl, just after the town of Hof.) World War II buffs will be interested to know that Joachim von Ribbontrop, Hitler's foreign minister, acquired

Schloss Fuschl in 1938 for his holiday home. After the defeat of Nazism, the property became an R&R resort for Allied soldiers until 1950.

As you approach (the town) Fuschl am See, on the right you'll see a number of buildings (there is a bus stop here if you'd like to pull over for a quick picture), among them a pair of saucer-shaped structures standing like dormant volcanoes rising from a man-made lagoon (pictured) that pinpoints the world headquarters of the caffeine-rich energy drink and billion-dollar brand, **Red Bull**. The company's founder, local-resident Dietrich Mateschitz, is a marketing mastermind, who proposed to sell an unknown and overpriced product for which there was no existing market, then successfully sold copious amounts of the product to land him on the list of the world's richest people. Remarkable! In 1984, 40-year-old Mateschitz founded Red Bull in Austria, where it is still exclusively produced. The brand burst onto the German market a decade later, then the world in 1997 (California being the first US market that year). Today, Red Bull (www.redbull.com) is a multibillion-dollar company, having more than 11,000 employees in 171 countries, including Austria where it is the nation's most profitable single brand. To view Mateschitz's collection of vintage aircraft, swing by Hangar-7 (p. 43) in Salzburg.

Wolfgangsee

This area is so stunningly beautiful that anyone who is planning to travel throughout Austria should adhere to the old adage: "Save the best for last." Those who come here first will dream of the delightful shores of Lake Wolfgang for the remainder of their journey—even Austria's Romantic Road meanders past Wolfgangsee to include its splendor. The two main resort towns adorning the lake's shoreline are St. Gilgen and St. Wolfgang. The latter is a storybook village dating from the year 976, when Bishop Wolfgang founded a chapel here. Nestled on the far shore, St. Wolfgang is punctuated by a 213-foot-tall steeple belonging to the town's 15th-century pilgrimage church with museum-like interior. Another town attraction is the celebrated but pricey Weissen Rössl (White Horse Inn, since 1878), romantically rooted on the waterfront.

Of the two resort towns, **St. Gilgen** (pop. 3,700 • elevation 542m/1,778ft) is by far the most visited by English-speaking travelers since it's closest to Salzburg and it sits at the junction between Fuschlsee, Mondsee, and Hallstätter See. What's more, St. Gilgen is the birthplace of Wolfgang Amadeus Mozart's mother, Anna Maria Walburga Pertl, who is remembered at the Mozart Museum (p. 82). And many of you have already seen St. Gilgen (pictured) in the opening of the movie, "The Sound of Music." St. Gilgen was first mentioned in 1376 and takes its name from Saint Giles (locally *der Heilige Ägydius*), whom the parish church is dedicated (you'll see its bulbous tower rising above town).

Wolfgangsee is situated 27 km east of Salzburg, 7 km beyond Fuschlsee and 15 km from Mondsee. The lake is 11 km long, a recreational paradise encircled by a curtain of majestic peaks, and like Fuschlsee it also warms up to an inviting 24-degrees Celsius (75°F) in summer. One of the aforesaid peaks, positioned across from St. Gilgen, is Sheep Mountain (p. 83), where a 110-year-old cogwheel train (seen in the movie SOM) lifts tourists to jaw-dropping views. Rising above St. Gilgen, multicolored cable cars quietly ascend to the summit of Zwölferhorn mountain (see next page), where hikers absorb sweeping vistas and adrenaline-pumped junkies paraglide off the edge and soar like hushed eagles. Farther along the mountainous skyline is the super slick toboggan run (p. 83) challenging speedsters down the hillside on an aluminum track (1.3 km long) with only a flimsy joystick as a brake. Other area activities include boat rides, swimming, cow tipping, and picnics on alpine meadows.

Tourist information (Mondsee Bundesstrasse 1a, St. Gilgen • Mon-Fri 9:00-17:00, longer hours May-Sept including weekends, e.g. July-Aug Mon-Fri 9:00-19:00, Sat 9:00-18:00, Sun 10:00-17:00 • **free Wi-Fi** • tel. 06227/2348 • www.wolfgangsee.at) has English-speaking staff, umpteen brochures, and an ATM (but this money machine may incur a significant withdrawal fee). TI is located on the main road (route 158) running along St. Gilgen, adjacent to the Spar grocery store—within a 15-min walk of the ferry dock. **Railers**, the bus stops within a 5-min walk from TI. **Drivers**, when descending into town from Fuschlsee, go right on the traffic circle (direction Bad Ischl) and the TI will be on the right.

Railers, from Salzburg to St. Gilgen either catch the Hop On Hop Off bus for 25€ (p. 79) or ride bus 150 (direction Bad Ischl) from the Hauptbahnhof or Mirabellplatz (hourly, 50-min trip, adult one way 6.70€, day ticket 13.40€, youth 15-18yr 4.70€/9.40€ and 6-14yr 3.40€/6.80€, www.salzburg-verkehr.at) • **from Mondsee** to St. Gilgen take bus 156 (20-min trip, adult one way 3.50€, day ticket 7€, youth 15-18yr 2.50€/4.80€ and 6-14yr 1.80€/3.60€, but plan ahead because bus 156 departs only 3 times per day in summer and much less in winter).

Drivers, from north Salzburg, follow signs to St. Gilgen (after crossing railway bridge on Linzer Bundesstrasse turn right—this road goes to Fuschlsee then Wolfgangsee). If you're coming from **Salzburg** on the A1 autobahn (heading east direction Vienna), take exit No. 274 (Thalgau) and drive towards Hof then Fuschlsee to St. Gilgen. If you're coming from **Vienna** on the A1 autobahn (heading west direction Salzburg), take the Mondsee exit (No. 264) and drive along the lake to St. Gilgen. (To reach **St. Wolfgang** is roughly 20 km beyond St. Gilgen; follow signs direction Bad Ischl and at the end of the lake turn left.) **Note:** The best way to drive into St. Gilgen, from the traffic circle continue direction Bad Ischl and 1 minute ahead turn left at the cable car station. At the bottom of the street turn left (Aberseestrasse) then make the next right at Haus Tirol (Sonnenburggasse) and in the lot ahead you'll find **free parking** (for three hours, daily 8:00-18:00, otherwise unrestricted) as well as **free toilets** (WC). If the lot is full, drive down to the lake and try your luck with the metered spaces running along the road (daily 8:00-18:00, 50¢/30 min for a max of 90 min, or pay 4€ for all-day parking in one of the two central lots).

Grocery Store: Next to the TI is a Spar grocery store (Mon-Fri 7:00-19:00, Sat 7:00-18:00, Sun 7:30-11:00); another option is Billa (Mon-Fri 7:15-19:30, Sat 7:15-18:00) located above town, on the right when descending into St. Gilgen from Fuschlsee.

Mozart Museum, located at Ischler Strasse 15 (a brief walk from the ferry dock), allow 25 min for a visit (open June-Sept, Sat-Sun only 10:00-12.00 [last entry], closed remainder of year • adult 4€, youth 6-18yr 2.50€ • www.mozarthaus.info). This small memorial museum, known as the "Mozarthaus," features a well-composed *exhibition that remembers Wolfgang Amadeus Mozart's mother, Anna Maria Walburga Pertl, who was born at this address on Christmas day 1720, but mostly the museum focuses on the life of Mozart's sister, nicknamed "Nannerl," who lived here from 1784-1801. (*Note that few period furnishings exist from Mozart's time and Anna Maria's birth room is upstairs and typically off-limits.) Anna Maria's father (Mozart's grandfather) originally built the house, which doubled as the district courthouse. The contemporary yet unremarkable fountain outside remembers Anna Maria as a young girl.

Mozart's Square, GPS: N47 46.021 E13 21.851. In the heart of St. Gilgen is Mozartplatz, a picturesque square featuring a statue of W. A. Mozart playing violin. Behind him is the three-story Rathaus, or town hall, arguably the most eye-catching building in town, having an adorable bay window and decorative facade. Opposite is the recommended Gasthof zur Post (see Good Sleeps below), where Mozart's sister was married in 1784. When standing in front of and facing Mozart, his right elbow is pointing to Hotel Schafbergspitze at the summit of Sheep Mountain (see next page).

Zwölferhorn, (www.12erhorn.at). Locally known as Erlebnisberg (Adventure Mountain), the Zwölferhorn rising above St. Gilgen can be scaled in just 16 minutes by riding a colorful cable car to its summit (1,522m/4,993ft). Tourist information has an excellent brochure listing the hiking trails here as well as the details of surrounding mountains. The cable car (round trip adult 24.50€, youth 5-14yr 15€, one way 17.50€/12€) is open year round, daily 9:15-16:00, March-May & Sept till 17:00-17:30, June-Aug till 18:00, except closed Nov. When ready to descend off the summit to the lake, paraglide down. If you're a novice like me, go tandem (130€, tel. 07612/73033, mobile 0664/111-6099, www.paragleiten.net).

Boat Rides, (www.wolfgangseeschifffahrt.at, tel. 06138/22320). A cruise on Wolfgangsee is a summer joy. Hop on a **ferry boat** in St. Gilgen (dock GPS: N47 45.942 E13 22.082) and ride it to St. Wolfgang, 45 min. Boats depart St. Gilgen: May-Oct every 60-90 min from morning (9:00-10:00) until early evening (18:00), and April Sat-Sun 11:55, 14:10, 16:20 (but note last boat back from St. Wolfgang is 17:30). Round trip from St. Gilgen to St. Wolfgang 15.20€, to Strobl 20€ (other end of lake), or purchase an all-day ticket (Tageskarte) adult 20€, youth 4-14yr 10€, family 45.50€. Another way to cruise the lake is to rent an **electric boat** at the ferry dock (in good weather May-Sept 10:00-18:00, max 5 pax): 14€/30 min, 20€/60 min, 54€/3 hr. Other watercraft available, mobile 0664/585-0891, www.wassersport-engel.at.

Sheep Mountain, locally Schafberg. The Sheep Mountain railway, or Schafbergbahn, as it's called, can be found leisurely climbing the 1,732 m (5,682 ft) high Sheep Mountain, adjacent to St. Wolfgang, across the lake from St. Gilgen. The railway operates on old-timer cogwheels that interlock with the grooved track to prevent slippage. Thus the journey to the summit takes 35 minutes to scale the six-kilometer stretch, which was constructed from 1892-93 by some 350 Italian workers. (**SOM fans**, there are a pair of cogwheel trains here; one of them is the historic steam train that was briefly shown in the movie during the "Do-Re-Mi" curtain-wearing sequence, and it's possible for you to ride!) Be sure to visit on a good-weather day; from the summit you'll behold spectacular views of pristine lakes, lush meadows and majestic mountains. Catering to the appetite of famished tourists, Sheep Mountain accommodates two restaurants (one is set within Hotel Schafbergspitze, overnight Dbl with breakfast 108€, or package incl. railway 163€, considerable discount when staying a second night, cash only, tel. 06138/3542, www.schafberg.net). → The **Sheep Mountain railway** (www.schafbergbahn.at, tel. 06138/22320) departs April 29 thru Oct 15, 2017 daily, every hour from about 9:20 till 15:30 depending on weather; last train down 17:00 (but times vary, thus check at summit then reserve your seat down). Price, adult rt 35€, youth 4-14yr 18€, ow 25€/12€, family rt 80€, combo boat and railway adult 48€, youth 4-14yr 24€—add 10€ to ride the historic **steam train**, locally Dampfzug, departing every Sunday July 9 thru Aug 27, 2017 at 9:30 in good weather (reservation suggested). The Schafbergbahn railway is reachable via boat from the ferry dock at St. Gilgen (35-min trip), or Drivers follow signs to St. Wolfgang then Schafbergbahn.

The **Toboggan run** by the town of Strobl (GPS: N47 42.977 E13 26.495), locally Riesenrutschbahnen, meaning "giant sliding chutes," is an exhilarating ride with stupendous views to boot, located directly on route 158 (just past the towns of Abersee and Gschwendt), right side (about 10 km) when coming from St. Gilgen. The two tracks here are each 1,300 meters long, that's 4,265 ft, or nearly 1 mile. After paying admission (one ride adult 7.30€, youth 7-15yr 6€, 10 rides family 51€), grab a sled, catch a lift to the top and blaze down the twisting course at a speed you control by the hand throttle. The fun happens, May-Sept 10:00-18:00, July/Aug till 19:00-20:00, but not in bad weather. (Call if you're not sure, tel. 06137/7085 • www.rodelbahnen.at.) If you enjoyed your time here, then you must experience the mother of all Austrian toboggan runs, the 2,200-meter luge at Bad Dürrnberg (p. 46), 20 km south of Salzburg. I dare you!

Good Sleeps, St. Gilgen: The following three digs, listed in order of preference, are centrally located in St. Gilgen, come with breakfast, have a shower/bath and toilet in the room. Note: Room rates do *not* include the town's **bed tax** of 1.60€ per person per night.

$$$ **Gasthof zur Post,** (Mozartplatz 8 • www.gasthofzurpost.at • tel. 06227/2157 • **free Wi-Fi**). Gemütlichkeit at Gasthof zur Post isn't just a term, it's the real deal. Receiving rights to serve beer in 1415, Gasthof zur Post is a historic gem more than 600 years old! And nobody is more proud of the fact than the owners (since 1999) and your cordial hosts: Katharina and Norbert Leitner. Catching the eye of all who enter, the provincial mural spanning the front facade dates from 1618 and depicts scenes of noblemen hunting game. The hotel again entered the history books on August 23, 1784, when W. A. Mozart's sister (Nannerl) held her wedding reception here in the Gaststube, or dining room. With emphasis on homegrown décor, the hotel's fresh rustic interior was built using only timbers and materials from the Salzkammergut. What's more, each bedroom has its own cultured feel with contemporary design elements, and most have a balcony capitalizing on the dreamy views of the lake and Alps. Wine connoisseurs will treasure a trip down the narrow stone steps into the 16th-century vaulted cellar, where Austrian reds and whites are selected to be savored after a busy day of sightseeing and adventure. **Note:** Hotel has elevator, sauna, and recommended restaurant! If your budget allows, opt for the Dbl "Wolfgangsee de luxe" from 214€/night. CC: VC, MC. **To get there:** Gasthof zur Post is situated on Mozartplatz in the heart of St. Gilgen, less than a 5-min walk to/fro the ferry dock and the Salzburg bus stop. **Drivers**, free parking (behind hotel); unload out front then have reception point you the way.

$$ **Hotel-Garni Schernthaner,** (Schwarzenbrunnerstrasse 4 • tel. 06227/2402 • www.hotel-schernthaner.at • **free Wi-Fi**). These traditional Austrian digs, thoughtfully run by the Eisl family, have an indigenous alpine feel in the center of St. Gilgen. Upon checking in at reception (one floor up), you'll be greeted with a warm, genuine welcome by Anneliese, your host. In the evening, community service temporarily beckons her away from the hotel to close the parish church Saint Giles (W. A. Mozart's mother was baptized here in 1720). In the morning, Anneliese neatly places name cards at each table directing guests to their seats from which they can indulge in the breakfast buffet. But you'd better be quick, Hotel Schernthaner only has 17 rooms, all with balcony (higher floor equals better view), and guests are afforded free bicycle use to peddle around majestic Wolfgangsee and beyond. **Note:** Some rooms have a shower, some a bathtub, others have a combination of both. Hotel has elevator and sauna/wellness facilities (for a fee). If staying only 1 or 2 nights, add 3€ per person per night. CC:

VC, MC. **To get there:** Hotel Schernthaner is centrally located in St. Gilgen, less than a 5-min walk to/fro the ferry dock and the Salzburg bus stop. **Drivers**, unload out front then jump upstairs and notify Anneliese whether you'd like to park free outside or pay 3.70€ for a secure garage.

$ **Hostel St. Gilgen,** [HI] (Mondseer Strasse 7 • www.jugendherbergsverband.at • tel. 06227/2365). Located meters from the shoreline and a two-minute walk from the ferry dock (follow lakeside path behind Mozart museum), this 40-room hostel is one of Austria's most popular in the Hostelling International (HI) family—a great way to experience the aquatic activities and splendor of Wolfgangsee for a cut-rate price. **Note:** Bed rate includes sheets and breakfast. CC: VC, MC. All rooms have shower-toilet. Cheaper when staying 3+ nights. Must be a HI member or an extra charge (3.50€/night) will apply. Reception is typically open daily 17:00-19:00 and mornings Mon-Fri 8:00-13:00. Property is closed over the Christmas holidays. Oh, almost forgot, you can't beat their 7€ dinners (usually served at 18:00)—book it (half board) when making your room reservation.

Mondsee, for town introduction, see page 111.

The warmest lake in the Salzkammergut, Mondsee (meaning Moon Lake) can reach a cozy 26-degrees Celsius (79°F) in summer, which probably has a lot to do with why it has become home base for the largest windsurfing and sailing school in the German-speaking world. **Note:** Free Wi-Fi in select spots around town, log-on to FreeWifiMondsee.

Tourist information (Dr. Franz Müller Strasse 3 • www.mondsee.at • tel. 06232/2270 • May Mon-Fri 8:00-18:00—June & Sept Mon-Fri 8:00-18:00, Sat 9:00-12:00 & 13:00-18:00—July-Aug daily 8:00-19:00, Sat-Sun from 9:00—and Oct-April Mon-Fri 8:00-17:00) is located on the town side of the tree-lined road leading to/fro the lake.

Railers, from Salzburg to Mondsee either catch the Hop On Hop Off bus for 25€ (p. 79) or ride bus 140 from the Hauptbahnhof or Mirabellplatz (hourly Mon-Fri, every other hour Sat-Sun, 50-min trip, adult one way 6.70€, day ticket 13.40€, youth 15-18yr 4.70€/9.40€ and 6-14yr 3.40€/6.80€, www.salzburg-verkehr.at) • **from St. Gilgen** to Mondsee take bus 156 (20-min trip, adult one way 3.50€, day ticket 7€, youth 15-18yr 2.50€/4.80€ and 6-14yr 1.80€/3.60€, but plan ahead because bus 156 departs only 3 times per day in summer and much less in winter).

Drivers, the A1 autobahn skirts Mondsee 25 km east of Salzburg—*Ausfahrt* Mondsee (exit 264).

St. Michael's Church (www.pfarre-mondsee.com), a distant relative to the neighboring 8th-century monastery, is glorious to visit. SOM fans will recognize its movie-set interior, and on hot days everyone will worship its air-conditioned feel. St. Michael's can easily be found in the center of town; aim for the twin spires: open generally Mon-Sat 8:00-19:00, and Sunday from 11:00 on account of Holy Mass.

Hallstätter See

Immensely scenic Lake Hallstätter is bendy like a seahorse and, if you didn't know any better, you'd swear you were in Norway. Similar to a Scandinavian fjord, the lake (8.6 km long, 2.2 km wide and 125 m deep) is surrounded by dramatic scenery, gigantic mountains having sheer cliffs that rise up from the cobalt-blue waters. The primary town on this alpine wet dream is **Hallstatt,** a confined but postcard-pretty village bang against a forested mountain, where time seems to have stood still for centuries. Indeed, this community is mega-old! So old, in fact, an entire epoch has been named after it. The term "Hallstatt" refers to the transitional period from the Bronze Age to the Early Iron Age, constituting the lands of west-central Europe to the Balkans, circa 800-400 B.C. Thus Hallstatt, or the "place of salt," is one of the continent's oldest towns. Prehistoric peoples bore deep tunnels into the mountain and mined salt here; boats sent by wealthy traders and monarchs retrieved the "white gold" for a fee. Salt was vital to survival throughout the ages as the mineral was used to preserve foods, i.e. meat—essentially functioning as pre-refrigeration. Due to this unique history and its diverse natural landscape, the artifact-rich village and surrounding area (Hallstatt/Dachstein) has since 1997 taken its place alongside such venerated sites as the Komodo National Park in Indonesia and Uluru National Park (Ayers Rock) in Australia as an esteemed member of UNESCO's World Heritage List.

Hallstatt, situated 85 km southeast of Salzburg and 45 km beyond St. Gilgen, is a remote and petite village (population 900) that doesn't take long to stroll through. Drivers will either park in lot P2 by the salt-mine funicular or in lot P1 if staying the night. Railers will be escorted into town by Stefanie, the boat. **But note** that Hallstatt is dead in the off-season (Nov-March) when many businesses are closed.

In town you'll discover colorfully quaint houses lining the shore; a sleek church spire resembling the tip of a spear defining the skyline; the world's oldest salt mine (since 1200 B.C.); wads of camera-toting tourists in summer; and a peaceful cemetery accommodating Michael's chapel, a.k.a. the Bone House. Yikes! Oh, and it's best to have some bread on hand to feed the ducks and swans, or you may offend tiny hearts.

Note: This year the traditional *Corpus Christi* (Fronleichnam) festival lands on Thursday June 15, 2017, beginning with Mass at 9:00 in the Catholic church followed by a resplendent procession of costumed villagers then boat parade at about 10:30 (lasting 2.5 hours, but double-check times in advance with TI in case of changes). Arrive early if you'd like to reserve a place on one of the sightseeing boats joining the wondrous waterborne spectacle.

Suggestion: Instead of returning via Seestrasse to exit Hallstatt, walk Dr.-F.-Morton-Weg that climbs above and parallels Seestrasse thus more scenic.

HALLSTATT

Map legend:

- 🎋 scenic viewpoint
- ▲ grocery store
- ⓢ post office
- @ free Wi-Fi

MAP NOT TO SCALE
To walk from one end of Hallstatt to the other, i.e. 7 to 7, is 10 min.

1. Funicular railway
2. Museum Hallstatt
3. Protestant church
4. Catholic church
5. Bone House
6. Photo point
7. Scenic boat rides

Ⓐ Grüner Baum
Ⓑ Grüner Anger
Ⓒ Pension Sarstein
Ⓓ Gasthof Zauner
Ⓔ Bräugasthof
Ⓕ Gasthaus Simony

Tourist information (Seestrasse 99 • www.hallstatt.net • tel. 05/950-9530 • **free Wi-Fi** • <u>Mon-Fri 8:30-17:00</u>, Jan-April also Sat 9:00-13:00, May-June also Sat-Sun 9:00-15:00, July-Oct Mon-Fri till 18:00 & Sat-Sun 9:00-16:00) is located in the wood-paneled Sparkasse building next to the 'bus terminal' at the main vehicular entrance to Hallstatt. Daytrippers arriving by bus and Drivers will walk past the TI on the way into town. (Railers, you will arrive into Hallstatt by boat, see below Railers entry for details). Stop by the TI, pick up a map, meet friendly Teresa and her colleague and consume their local wisdom, choose from colorful brochures, consider the WC (.50¢).

Internet: The whole of market square, or Marktplatz, is a **free Wi-Fi** hotspot as well as at the TI building (see previous entry).

Post Office: Mail your postcards at the P.O. (Mon-Fri 8:00-13:00, Wed also 14:00-17:00) centrally located in town at Seestrasse 169, across from Museum Hallsatt.

A **grocery store** ("Nah & Frisch," Mon-Fri 7:30-12:30 & 13:30-18:00 but May-Sept all day without break, Sat 7:30-12:00) is located across the road from the TI. Another option, yet limited, is the **Spar** market (daily 9:00-18:00) in the 'Gemischtwaren Handlung' shop by the market square (Marktplatz).

Laundry: Have a coffee and wash at the small *Waschsalon* (daily 9:00-18:00, 7€/wash, 7€/dry) in the 'Gemischtwaren Handlung am See' shop by the market square (Marktplatz).

Railers: From **Salzburg**, you can reach Hallstatt either by train from the Hauptbahnhof (change in Attnang-Puchheim, total journey 2.5hr, www.oebb.at, small groups purchase the Einfach-Raus-Ticket p. 73) or more scenic catch the regularly scheduled bus 150 from outside the Hauptbahnhof that will shepherd its passengers through the lake district to Bad Ischl (rail station) where you pick up a train to Hallstatt station (total journey 2.5hr). If you're coming from **Vienna**, catch the train from either Westbahnhof or the new Hauptbahnhof and change in Attnang-Puchheim (hourly until last connection around 15:00, total journey 4hr, www.oebb.at). → Upon arriving at **Hallstatt station**, you'll quickly realize you're on the wrong side of the lake—thus a cute boat named Stefanie (pictured) will be there to escort you (for 2.50€) across the lake to Hallstatt. From the Hallstatt boat dock (Landungsplatz) to the tourist information office is a 10-min walk, on the other side of town. (To get there, bounce straight off the dock and swing left around the corner, pass the pointy church [to your left] then the market square [to your right], and continue straight all the way to the end of Seestrasse to the TI.) **Note** that Stefanie's *last* pick up from the train station to Hallstatt is 18:50. Stefanie's first departure from Hallstatt to the train station is 6:50 (but 8:10 on Sun), then regularly throughout the day until its last departure at 18:15 (check times at the dock or with TI in case of changes).

Drivers: Hallstatt is a fair drive from downtown Salzburg, about 85 km (or 90 min), but wonderfully scenic—follow signs to St. Gilgen then Bad Ischl, Bad Goisern, Hallstatt. If you're coming from **Salzburg** on the A1 autobahn (heading east direction Vienna), take the Mondsee exit (No. 264) and drive along the lake to St. Gilgen then Bad Ischl, Bad Goisern, Hallstatt. If you're coming from **Linz/Vienna** on the A1 autobahn (heading west direction Salzburg), take exit No. 224 (Regau) to Gmunden then Bad Ischl, Bad Goisern, Hallstatt. **The road** approaching Hallstatt will funnel into a one-kilometer-long tunnel cutting through the mountain above town. To drive in Hallstatt during the touristed season, April-Oct, is *verboten!* (In the off-season, Nov-March, you can drive in Hallstatt but not park. In this case, drive through the tunnel, turn left and steer straight into town.) → Since cars in Hallstatt are restricted to residents, you must park in one of the numbered pay lots outside town—I recommend **P2**. To get there, continue straight through the tunnel then turn right following signs to lot **P2** (first 15 min free, 15 min to 1hr 3.50€, 1-2hr 6€, 3-6hr 8€, 7-12hr 9€, cash or VC/MC okay), within a 10-min walk of central Hallstatt and a Frisbee toss from the world's oldest salt mines (p. 90). If P2 is full, park in P1. **Note:** If you have a hotel reservation, the parking situation is different, see Good Sleeps—Drivers.

☞ **Churches:** There are two churches in town, Catholic and Protestant. Throughout the centuries the townsfolk have repeatedly changed denominations according to the trend, or who was in power. Today, most of Austria is Catholic, and so is Hallstatt. Consecrated October 15, 1863, the **Protestant church** is situated on the waterfront, adjacent to the market square, and is recognizable by its spear-like spire (pictured). The much older, 14th-century **Catholic church** is the significant structure perched above the village. Here you will discover tremendous views and the...

Bone House, locally Beinhaus, allow 10 min for a visit (ask for English info sheet • May-October daily 10:00-17:00, March-April Wed-Sun 11:30-15:30, otherwise closed • adult 1.50€, youth .50¢). → For a chilling experience visit the house of bones in the cemetery behind the Catholic church, 105 steps above the market square (take lane running alongside mustard-yellow Café Derbl). Dating from the early 18th century, a ghoulish custom permitted graves to be cleared every 10-15 years to conserve what little land Hallstatt had available. Skulls were exhumed, cleaned, then left to bleach in the sun for weeks before being stored in the adjacent chapel (Michaelskapelle, a.k.a. Beinhaus), where oodles of calcium-deficient bones and skulls are on display in neatly stacked rows. Of the 1,200 skulls exhibited, some with teeth missing and grinning jaw bones, more than half have been ornately painted (mostly during the years 1780-1900) with flowery designs, oak leaves (symbolizing glory), laurel wreath (victory), roses (love), black crosses, and the name of the deceased identified on the forehead. Look for the darkest skulls; these are the oldest. The last skull to enrich the cranium collection was as recent as 1995, when the final request of a woman was honored to be placed in the house of bones, at the top of the heap, beneath the cross (identified by the year of her death, 1983). Today, Catholics are allowed (since the 1960s) to choose cremation as a funeral rite, which bodes well for land-restricted Hallstatt. Whether you're pious or not, the Catholic church and its neighboring cemetery are **must-see sites**, and the lake views from here are enchanting!

Museum Hallstatt, center of town Seestrasse 56, allow at least 75 min for a visit (May-Sept daily 10:00-18:00, April & Oct daily 10:00-16:00, and Nov-March Wed-Sun 11:00-15:00 • adult 10€, student 8€, senior 60yr+ 9€, family 20€ • www.museum-hallstatt.at), features 26 rooms taking visitors on "A journey through the ages, 7,000 years of Hallstatt's culture and history": from past epochs to today's village of archeological discoveries. The journey begins with a 5-minute 3D film (pick out your glasses then push button for English), followed by an exhibit of 'human excrement' from the 4th century B.C., and (in room 8) big and little kids alike will have fun with the four-way mirror (pictured).

Salt Mines, locally Salzbergwerk, allow 3 hours for a visit—this includes traveling to/fro mines and 70-min tour (open April 1 thru Nov 26, 2017, closed remainder of year—daily, April thru Sept 24 9:30-*16:30, Sept 25 thru Nov 5 9:30-*15:00, Nov 6-26 9:30-*14:30—*last tour but you must be on the funicular railway at least 30 min before to make it in time • www.salzwelten.at • price (includes round trip on funicular and 70-min German-English tour of salt mine), adult 30€, student/senior 27€, youth 4-15yr 15€ (ages 0-3yr not permitted in mines), family 2+1/2+2/1+1 63€/75€/40€, discount with Salzburg Card and the Salzkammergut Erlebnis Card. The **funicular** railway (called the Salzbergbahn) is located at the south end of town (within a 15-min walk of the market square, Drivers park in lot P2) and is synchronized to run with the opening and closing of the salt mines (tickets to the mines can be purchased at the funicular; note time of last funicular down). **Funicular & hikers**; salt mine only (without funicular) adult 22€, student/senior 20€, family 2+1/2+2/1+1 46€/56€/30€; round trip on funicular (without salt mine) adult 16€, student/senior 14€, family 2+1/2+2/1+1 34€/41€/22€. **Note:** By the funicular top station, step out to the tip of the triangle-shaped **Skywalk** jutting from the mountainside like a slice of cake high above Hallstatt for the **most awesome view in town**. Best on a clear day. Not for those who have a fear of heights, like me. Yikes!

With salt deposits being exploited as early as the 2nd millennium B.C., the Hallstatt mines are recognized (via carbon dating) as the world's oldest that are, astonishingly, still worked commercially today (by some 3 dozen miners who yield roughly 500,000+ cubic meters of salt per annum). Situated high above Hallstatt, deep in the mountain, the salt mines can be reached via one *steep* funicular (cable railway taking 3 min) followed by a 15-min walk past a prehistoric burial ground (to which the fertile findings here of some 4,000 peoples and their advanced tools confirmed the transitional period from the Bronze Age to the Early Iron Age, known as the "Hallstatt" era). Tourists throw on oversized miners' uniforms, march into the cool mountain (temperatures range between 7-10°C/44-50°F), explore subterranean cavities dug by prehistoric peoples, meet the "man preserved in salt" (discovered 1734), slide down two long wooden banisters (stairs also an option), and ride a bench on wheels out of the mountain. (If it's late in the day, don't miss the last funicular down the mountain otherwise plan on a 45-min trek, albeit picturesque and healthful.)

Boat Rides: The Hallstätter See Schifffahrt (ferry) company has been touring the lake's glacial waters since 1862, as well as operating the milk-run between Hallstatt (Markt) and the train station (Bahnhof) since 1881. Today, they have a fleet of four boats and you're welcome aboard. Consider the 50-minute **scenic excursion** from Hallstatt to Obertraun (bottom end of lake) and back, adult 10€, youth 4-14yr receive discount—other excursions available; see the ferry cashier for details or go to: www.hallstattschifffahrt.at. The shortest and easiest lake jaunt is with **Stefanie**, the boat ferrying travelers to/fro the train station on the opposite shore, 2.50€ each way. At Hallstatt train station, note the boat return times then go for a hike. A popular destination is the **suspension bridge** (Hängebrücke) traversing the deepest part of the lake, 125 m (410 ft). The bridge is a short (5-min) walk from the train station; go north, or left when facing the station from Hallstatt. **Note:** If you're interested in renting an electric or muscle-powered (paddle) boat to cruise the lake on your own, you have a few summer choices around town: ask TI or your hotel reception for details.

Best Views & Hikes: Hike above Hallstatt (start from center of town behind museum) following signs leading to the trail **"Welterbe-Rundweg"** to capture stunning vistas from ancient paths, two bridges and a **waterfall** (reach the first bridge in 15 min then trek another 6 min to reach the green bridge at the waterfall), or effortlessly climb the mountain via the funicular railway and step onto the **Skywalk** for the **most awesome view in town** (see Salt Mines). Close and convenient, negotiate the 105 steps rising from the market square (Marktplatz—take lane running alongside mustard-yellow Café Derbl) to the **Catholic church and graveyard**. The scene, deepened by rows of wooden crosses spiked above immaculately tended plots dressed in a breadth of multicolored flowers, is right out of a movie. Another best view, this one pretty as a postcard, takes us to the **"photo point"** in the Römisches part (north end) of town that all the pros go to get that dreamy spread of Hallstatt. (To get there, face the front entrance of the Protestant church [recognizable by its spear-like spire], jog left and continue straight a few minutes on the main lane as it climbs away from the market square and village center to the photo point ahead. You'll know it when you reach the perfect shot—best results in the morning.) On the other side of the lake are more hiking and viewing opportunities. Start by cruising with Stefanie across the lake and trekking to the **suspension bridge** (see previous entry for details). If you time it right when a train is passing by the bridge, you'll feel like you're part of a real-life model train set.

Nature lovers should inquire at the TI for the plethora of unbeatable hiking and cave-exploration opportunities in this World Heritage region of Hallstatt/Dachstein (www.dachstein-salzkammergut.com), especially the over-the-edge adrenaline rush afforded by the "5fingers" viewing platform overlooking Hallstätter See and the lake district included in the Dachstein "Panorama Ticket" (adult 30€, youth 16.50€). Nature junkies should pay extra for the "All-Inclusive" pass (44.50€/24.50€)!

Good Eats: You can typically get a traditional and tasty meal at: • **Gasthof Zauner** (top of market square, specializing in fresh lake fish) • **Bräugasthof** (on the water's edge, near post office, sit inside beneath a white-washed ceiling or outside on the terrace within bread-tossing distance of graceful swans, May-Oct, cash only, pork schnitzel 14€) • Head to the secreted back garden of **Gasthaus Simony** and lounge by the lakeside with waddling ducks, delicious desserts, and voluminous views • Or for more money, reserve a table at the beloved **Seehotel Grüner Baum** (see next page) before sundown to savor the delicious views with the equally delectable cuisine.

Good Sleeps, Hallstatt:

Hallstatt is idyllic, romantic, excellent for recreationists who enjoy hiking, cave exploration, climbing, boating. In peak season (April-Oct), Hallstatt is resplendent in the warmth of summer, multihued flowers and tourists. In the off-season (Nov-March), Hallstatt is dead, dark, and cold. Generally speaking, with the exception of recreationists or travelers on a special getaway (like a honeymoon or restful retreat), one night in Hallstatt will suffice.

Railers, since Hallstatt's train station is across the lake, you'll be arriving into town on Stefanie, the boat (2.50€/person each way).

Drivers, automobiles and Hallstatt are a bad mix. Thus, in 2011, it was approved that only residents be allowed to drive in town during the touristed months (April-Oct). In the off-season (Nov-March), however, Hallstatt is dead and (typically) open to every make and model—but you'll still need to park outside town, as explained below. Because of the driving difficulties hampering Hallstatt, I've listed the skinny on parking to get you to your digs with the least amount of fuss. And it starts with the Grüner Anger (see below), where parking is free and easy for you. Otherwise, continue straight out the one-kilometer-long tunnel cutting through the mountain above town and follow signs straight to the parking garage **P1**, designated for overnight guests. At lot **P1** (just past gas station), press the button for Hotel Ticket/Guest, enter, and park in any available space. Mosey over to the Hotel Info point (Kassa), across lot from parking entrance, and notify the attendant of your hotel reservations. If unattended, press the button to call up the hotel shuttle. A bus or mini van taxi will arrive shortly to take you to your digs. The price to park is 12€/24hr 1-3 days (8€/24hr 4-7 days, 6€/24hr 8+ days), payable at the on-site automat, cash or CC. **Note:** After you've fed the automat for your stay, you're allowed to drive in/out of the lot as often as you'd like. The shuttle service is included in the parking fee, thus it is not required to tip the driver (but if you feel the need to do so then by golly go for it). Before checking out of your digs, arrange with reception to be shuttled back to your vehicle.

$$$$ **Seehotel Grüner Baum,** (Marktplatz 104 • www.gruenerbaum.cc • tel. 06134/82630 • **free Wi-Fi**). This romantic 4-star superior hotel furnished with flat-screen satellite TVs, coffee-and-tea amenities, heated oak-parquet flooring, and free chocolate in the rooms is ideally located on market square bang on the lake boasting sensational views. Flowered balconies in summer decorate the landmark honey-mustard facade of Hallstatt's historic grand Seehotel Grüner Baum, or Lake Hotel Green Tree, while Stefanie cruises past hourly with a new boat load of open-mouthed travelers in disbelief at the beauty of it all. **Note:** These digs fill up fast, thus book earlier rather than later to beat the bunch to your beautiful bed. If your budget allows, treat yourself to a lake-facing room with balcony. Check-in from 15:00, check-out by 11:00. Reception is open 8:00-22:00 but notify staff if arriving after 18:00. Room rate includes breakfast (8:00-10:00) and use of sauna (bathrobe and slippers in room). All major CCs accepted. **To get there: Railers**, the Grüner Baum is meters away after stepping off Stefanie in Hallstatt (bounce straight off the dock and swing left around the corner to your digs next to the church on the left). **Drivers**, follow directions under Good Sleeps, i.e. park in P1 then catch the shuttle to your digs.

$$ **Grüner Anger,** (Lahn 10 • tel. 06134/8397 • anger.hallstatt.net • **free Wi-Fi**). This warmly run Austrian-style inn by Andrea and Gottfried Sulzbacher is a pleasant overnight choice for Drivers, who can park for free out front, and for anyone else seeking local hospitality in the 'green pastures' of Hallstatt, hence Grüner Anger (pronounce A like in Austria), at the south end of town but *without* lake views or an elevator to help carry your bags to the 2nd floor. Virtually a hop, skip and a jump from the tourist information office and the funicular railway lifting visitors up the mountainside to the world's oldest salt mines (p. 90), Grüner Anger also affords its guests the use of free bicycles and delicious 4-course menu options in their recommended restaurant from 13€ (18:00-19:45 but reserve your table before 17:00; check in advance what day restaurant is closed; consider the fresh lake fish grilled to palate-pleasing perfection by chef Andrea). **Note:** Price includes breakfast buffet. Add 2€/person if staying only one night. CC: VC, MC. Check-in 15:00-20:00. Children up to 5yr are free with parents. If visiting the salt mine, ask reception for discount voucher. **To get there: Drivers**, continue straight through the tunnel crossing town and (out the other side) drive a short

distance farther then turn right to Grüner Anger. **Railers**, these digs are a 15-min walk from the boat dock in town, thus you can go by foot or call Grüner Anger with your exact arrival time and Andrea or Gottfried will pick you up if possible (if you show the Stefanie boat captain your reservation he may call Grüner Anger for you).

$$ **Pension Sarstein,** (Gosaumühlstrasse 83 • tel. 06134/8217 • **free Wi-Fi** in common area). Caringly run by English-speaking Isabel and Lederhosen-wearing Klaus, this traditional bed-and-breakfast at the north end of town abuts the scenic shoreline of Hallstätter See affording its guests romantic lake views and a waterfront garden ideal for relaxing in lazy chairs and a gentle swim in the midst of waddling ducks and graceful swans. Rustic rooms with pine-wood furnishings accentuate this peaceful pension that guests awake from deep, revitalizing sleep to the quiet stillness of the morning *and* (often) stiff bath towels from being hung too long on the clothesline. Ha! **Note:** Cash only. Breakfast optional. Add 5€ per person if staying only one night. Trpl/family (4 pers.) possible. These digs fill up fast, reserve well in advance. Request room with lake view and balcony. Since there is no formal reception desk here, it's best to give a general time of arrival when booking. If the outside door is locked upon your arrival, ring buzzer to be let in. Because this is a multi-level property, there are a number of stairs to negotiate, i.e. no elevator! Borrow one their bicycles (free for guests) and increase your sightseeing possibilities, e.g. ride to Obertraun for a day trip (buy picnic goodies at Nah & Frisch on way out of town). Lastly, laundry service is available (i.e. Isabel/Klaus will wash your clothes) for a nominal fee. **To get there: Railers**, these digs are within a 5-min slightly uphill walk from the boat dock. On Stefanie, look for Pension Sarstein ahead on the right as you motor towards Hallstatt. **Drivers**, discuss the parking situation with Isabel—depending on the time of year and availability, you may have the option of parking for free a few hundred meters from the property—otherwise, follow directions under Good Sleeps, i.e. park in P1 then catch the shuttle to your digs.

The Sound of Music
do-it-yourself tour

"The Sound of Music" (SOM), based on a true story, is arguably the most popular musical film of all time. A guidebook to Salzburg simply would not be complete without a tribute to its creation. With more than five years of experience as a SOM tour guide living in Austria, I've written the following step-by-step instructions so you can do the tour yourself, easily and efficiently, leading straight to the locations made famous by this timeless classic. You will save a tidy sum in comparison to paying for a commercial tour at around US$50 per person, essentially recouping the price of this guidebook several times over. Additionally, my tour visits more sights and you're not rushed in doing so. (The commercial tour, for example, does not visit the cemetery or festival halls or Mirabell Gardens and only drives past a number of other sites. Where the commercial tour does earn a portion of its worth is by getting you to the lake district [25 km] outside Salzburg to visit St. Michael's Church at Mondsee, where the wedding scene was filmed. But, if you have wheels, even this value is insignificant.)

So come along, let's start with the basics then set off on our SOM tour.

SOM 101

The Movie: In 1963, a Hollywood scouting team began searching locations in the Salzburg region. Back in California, director Robert Wise was role casting. Mia Farrow auditioned for the role of Maria, Kurt Russell and Richard Dreyfuss tried out for the younger roles. Wise considered Sean Connery, Richard Burton, and even Doris Day for leading roles before ultimately casting a group of relative unknowns. By spring 1964, after three months of exhausting rehearsals, the 250-person cast and crew arrived in Austria with a shooting schedule of six weeks. Everything was on cue, a seemingly watertight program, except for the weather—six weeks turned into a slog of 11! Upon completion, everyone returned stateside to wrap up the interior scenes on a Twentieth Century-Fox sound stage in Los Angeles. By that time, Friedrich (Nicholas Hammond) had grown 6 inches in 6 months thus Lisl had to stand on a box to appear taller. Marta (Debbie Turner) lost her two front teeth but the props department came to the rescue with substitutes.

Finally, to the elation of all involved, "The Sound of Music" was released in March 1965 and theaters everywhere were sold out. Julie Andrews and Christopher Plummer played the starring roles in the Rodgers and Hammerstein production, which in April 1966 won five Oscars—at the 38th Academy Awards, the first to be televised in color—for Best Picture • Best Director (Robert Wise) • Best Sound • Best Film Editing • Best Music (Scoring of Music).

Main Characters: One of my favorite scenes in the movie is when Maria meets Georg for the first time.

Herr von Trapp: "Why do you stare at me that way?"
Maria: "Well, you don't look at all like a sea captain, Sir."
Herr von Trapp: "I'm afraid you don't look very much like a governess."

Maria Augusta Kutschera (played by Julie Andrews) was born on a train en route to Vienna, Austria before midnight January 26, 1905. Maria aspired to be a nun and consequently became a postulant, or candidate seeking admission into a religious order, at Salzburg's esteemed Nonnberg abbey. It was here that she became aware of Georg von Trapp, a titled widower, when in 1926 he requested a home tutor for his third child (second-oldest daughter, Maria) who had become bedridden with rheumatic fever. The Reverend Mother Abbess responded to Herr von Trapp's request by sending him Maria, whom she felt wasn't ready for a sequestered life of chaste and obedience. The following year, on November 26, 1927, Maria and Georg tied the knot. (Note that it was not until 1936 that the von Trapps sang publicly as a family.)

Georg Ritter von Trapp (played by Christopher Plummer) was born on April 4, 1880 in the coastal town of Zara (present-day Zadar), Dalmatia located some 250 rugged kilometers south of Zagreb, the capital of Croatia. Yes, you read it correctly, Croatia! If Georg had been born within the last 95 years, there'd be no Sound of Music and we wouldn't be having this chat. You see, in those days, most of the Balkan Peninsula was aligned with the Austro-Hungarian Empire. Therefore, Georg had the privilege, as did his father, to be a naval officer serving greater Austria (remember, present-day Austria is landlocked with no access to seaports). Georg met his first wife, Agathe Whitehead, in 1910. She bore him seven children. Tragically, Agathe contracted scarlet fever and died in 1922, leaving the children motherless. Interestingly, Agathe was the granddaughter of (Englishman) Robert Whitehead, inventor of the torpedo. Robert had a workshop in the port town of Fiume (present-day Rijeka, Croatia), where Georg was stationed as a submarine commander. Thus Georg met Agathe and got married in Fiume, where their first two children, Rupert and Agathe, were born.

Maria Meets the Children: In actual fact, the seven children born to Agathe and Georg von Trapp were: Rupert (1911-92), Agathe (1913-2010), Maria (1914-2014), Werner (1915-2007), Hedwig (1917-72), Johanna (1919-94) and Martina (1921-51). In the movie, Hollywood immortalized them as:

Liesl, 16: She doesn't need a governess.
 Friedrich, 14: He's impossible.
  Louisa, 13: She's not Brigitta.
   Kurt, 11: He's incorrigible, yet seemingly normal.
  Brigitta, 10: She thinks Maria's dress is the ugliest she's ever seen.
 Marta, 7 on Tuesday and she'd like a pink parasol.
Gretl, 5: She's practically a lady.

And as portrayed in the first part of the movie, the widowed captain's villa was surely a glum place of order and obedience. Before Maria, Georg did indeed call his children with a whistle (because of their large residence and gardens), just as he did to give commands to his sailors on the high seas. According to Maria (Georg's third child), to call Rupert, Georg blew one low note followed by one high note. Agathe's call was one low followed by two high notes, Maria was one low and three highs, and so on. When Georg required all the children, he blew a series of highs and lows ending with a low trill, but they never had to march or stand at attention. But after Maria's arrival from the convent, she loosened things up, introducing laughter and song to the household.

The Anschluss, America, and Movie History: In the early morning hours of Saturday March 12, 1938, Hitler's armies marched into Austria and declared the Anschluss, or annexation of the republic to the new German empire. Many Austrians dreamed of the day when both nations, Germany and Austria, would unite to form the greater Reich. There were many others, however, who desired no such idealistic fusion of the two nations and were content with their peaceful lives, i.e. the Trapp family.

Georg von Trapp, a reserved man possessing immense pride and wisdom, envisioned the harsh realities that lay ahead with the Nazis' tight grip on his beloved Austria. The regime ordered Georg out of retirement to serve the then German War Navy, or Kriegsmarine. This was, to say the least, not Georg's cup of proverbial tea. But Hitler's call to duty was a masked blessing for the von Trapps, prompting Georg to speak to each member of his family about their future. He asked, 'What would become of us if we were to remain in the country?' In essence, either stay and say "Heil Hitler" or pack up and *get out!* With only the possessions in their rucksacks, the Trapp family pretended to go on a hiking trip to Italy and slipped through the Nazi web by train. And just like that, in a matter of hours, they had left everything behind: their personal items, valuables, mansion of a house, becoming refugees without a country. (Note: Pictured is Bahnhof Aigen, the station from which the family boarded the train to Italy. Logistically it was an easy affair, the station literally sits behind the von Trapp estate.)

The family remained in Italy for about five weeks before heading to England, where they sailed 11 days to New York in September 1938. Dashing from country to country like fugitives was no easy task for the von Trapps, who had since swelled to nine children and Maria was pregnant with another on the way. (In 1929, Maria gave birth to Rosmarie, then Eleonore in 1931, and Johannes—president of the Trapp Family Lodge—in 1939).

Although the von Trapps didn't speak English and had few dollars, life in America promised a new beginning far from Nazi tyranny. Moreover, they were now a family of singers who could possibly strike it rich. Alas, six months later their visitor's visa expired without option for renewal. "When the Lord closes a door, somewhere he opens a window." Then, a stroke of luck, instead of having to return to Hitler's Austria, the von Trapps were invited to perform concerts in Scandinavia.

The family toured Denmark and Sweden and Norway and then it happened: September 1, 1939, Hitler smashed his armies across the Polish frontier, kick-starting World War II. All borders in Europe were sealed shut and foreigners, even those with concerts planned, were asked to go back to wherever they came from. For the von Trapps, this was a possible death sentence.

Again, good luck fell upon the Trapp family as if God had personally dropped a miracle in their lap. Mr. Wagner, their manager in America, sent word that he arranged a new U.S. visa in sync with performances for a multi-state tour. In addition to the message, he sent money for a return voyage on the passenger ship SS Bergensfjord. Georg and Maria readily packed up their 10 children and, once again, cruised across the Atlantic Ocean.

On October 7, 1939, the SS Bergensfjord docked safely in Brooklyn. However, New York is not a city without drama, and Germanic peoples landing on American soil immediately after the Nazi boot stepped into Poland was, understandably, a sensitive issue with the immigration authorities. As a result, they were detained at Ellis Island while their paperwork was checked, and re-checked. While the *von Trapps waited behind bars, they once again pondered their future. Meanwhile, stories circulated of immigrants being detained for weeks on end before being shipped back to Europe, or elsewhere. One family even had to take refuge on a ship for months while it cruised between ports because no country would accept them.

> *To view official government records of the passenger list and certificate of arrival, go to: http://www.archives.gov/boston/exhibits/von-trapp.html

During their fourth day of confinement, the von Trapps received a final decision from the authorities. A guard appeared at their cell and told them they were *free* to leave. The jail door swung open and outside awaited the great land of opportunity. The sprung jailbirds toured America and became reasonably well-known as the "Trapp Family Singers" (performing regularly in the US, as well as in 30 other countries, until 1956).

In 1942, the von Trapps scraped $1,000 together to purchase an old farmhouse (they called Cor Unum, Latin for "One Heart") on 600 acres in Stowe, Vermont, where the countryside reminded them of Austria. In 1950, they incorporated Cor Unum into the Trapp Family Lodge (www.trappfamily.com), which today comprises some 2,500 acres and 200 rooms, suites and guest chalets. Sadly, Georg never saw this dream unfold. Herr von Trapp, an extraordinary man whose surname would become as synonymous with Salzburg as Mozart, passed away May 1947. (Maria departed us on March 28, 1987 and the two are buried together in the family cemetery at the lodge.)

Two years after Georg's passing, Maria penned the family's enterprising journey, "The Story of the Trapp Family Singers." Not believing it would ever amount to anything, Maria sold all the rights for $9,000. From the book sprang a two-part German film production in the 1950s called "Die Trapp Familie." The Germans subsequently sold the rights to the Americans, who (Rodgers and Hammerstein) made it into a long-running, hugely successful Broadway show. Twentieth Century Fox film studios bought the rights for $1.25 million and the rest is history. Interestingly, the movie aired for the first time on Austrian television around the year 2003, and many Austrians outside of Salzburgland have never heard of the von Trapp family.

THE TOUR

To wander Salzburg and behold its age-old sites is amazing. There's hardly a better way to spend a day in Europe, especially if the weather is nice. To complement this superlative plan, I have composed two do-it-yourself SOM tours: Walking, and Driving. **The Walking Tour**, as the name suggests, is easily achieved on foot and embraces all the Old Town attractions seen in the movie. (Note that I'll point out the **toilets** en route starting immediately with those at University Platz.) **The Driving Tour**, for those of you with wheels, can venture outside of Salzburg and marvel at the remainder of the sights as well as the must-see lake district (Salzkammergut p. 79).

Whether you only do one or both DIY tours, at the end of the day, the result is the same in this fairy-tale land of Salzburg: Your sightseeing discoveries, the same as those made by the Hollywood film scouts in 1963, will be the treasured memories of a memorable time. And these are for you to keep, forever.

Suggestion: Before you set off on the tour, why not see the movie so the sights and sounds are fresh in your head? If you're staying at one of my recommended, SOM-friendly accommodations—such as YoHo (p. 66), JUFA (p. 63), Gabi's Apartments (p. 63), Hotel Goldgasse (p. 64)—then you're good to go. If you're *not* staying at one of the aforesaid accommodations, no problem, you're welcome to join the hostelers at

YoHo in watching their daily free SOM screening at 20:00, or stop by the JUFA hostel-hotel for their SOM screening at 20:00 (ask reception to start movie). Lastly, if you have time, watch the movie again post-tour. No matter how many times you've already seen the film, you'll see it with fresh eyes after you learn and experience first-hand the gripping history and sensational sights that have helped make this movie an enduring classic. For even more SOM flavor, consider an evening at **The Sound of Salzburg Dinner Show** (p. 54), the **Marionette Theater** (p. 54), or see the musical that has come home to the Salzburg **Landestheater** (Provincial Theater, see TI or staff at your accommodations for latest performance dates).

Drivers, depending on your plans and where you're coming from, it may be better for you to do the Driving Tour first to avoid extra parking hassles in Salzburg.

Railers, you're not completely left out in the cold when it comes to the Driving Tour; you can do most of it (everything except the lake district) on your own by bike. (To rent a bike, flip to page 9 or ask TI for latest rental locations.) Start early and don't forget to pack a picnic. Although touring by bike can be tiring, it's more comprehensive, healthier, and much cheaper than the commercial tours on offer for about 44€ per person. That said, if riding a bike isn't your thing, arrange a bus tour via the TI or your accommodations. Or, if you're part of a small group, consider renting a car (which you will need to plan in advance, but with a car you'll have the option of visiting other exciting destinations, e.g. Berchtesgaden (p. 73), Werfen (p. 75), Hallstatt (p. 86).

(DIY SOM) WALKING TOUR, University Platz to Mirabell—90 min.

Let's start our Walking Tour in the middle of Old Town on a square called University Platz, which doubles as a green market and is situated behind the rich-yellow facade of Mozart's birthplace. One way to get there is to go to Getreidegasse (pedestrian shopping street) and stand at No. 9 facing Mozart's birthplace (p. 22). Adjacent (left) is a shop-lined passage, walk through this to…

❶ **University Platz** (GPS: N47 47.969 E13 02.614). This is a great place to start our tour for two reasons: **(1)** availability of picnic items (Mon-Fri early till around 18:00, Sat till 14:00)—vendors offer everything from fruits and vegetables to meats and cheeses to grilled sausages (Würste) and various kinds of pretzels (around 3€ ea.), e.g. chocolate, cinnamon-sugar, pizza. **(2)** Remember the scene when Maria juggled the tomatoes and Gretl dropped hers? Filmed right here. **Note:** The golden facade you see is the back of ❹ Mozart's birthplace. Also note, the plaque above the *restaurant Zipfer reads: "In this house lived W. A. Mozart's sister Nannerl (widowed baroness von Berchtold zu Sonnenburg) from October 28, 1801 until her death October 29, 1829." (*If you cannot find the restaurant, face the back of Mozart's birthplace and the Zipfer is over your right shoulder.)

2017 edition   Walking

☞ To reach the next site, take the lane (Wiener-Philharmoniker-Gas
jacent to the restaurant Zipfer. (Note that you'll immediately pass pay t
.50¢, on the right. The men's room, *Herren*, is downstairs.) The lane v
Max-Reinhardt-Platz, the southern end of the elongated…

self-guided walk — Sound of Music

- ❶ University Platz
- ❷ Festival Halls
- ❸ Toscanini Hof
- ❹ St. Peter's Cemetery
- ❺ Untersberg Mtn.
- ❻ Abbey, Nonnberg
- ❼ Residenz Fountain
- ❽ Mozart Steg
- ❾ Mirabell Gardens
- Ⓐ Mozart's Birthplace
- Ⓑ Horse trough
- Ⓒ Mönchsberg Lift
- Ⓓ Kapitelplatz
- Ⓔ Cathedral Sq. (Domplatz)
- Ⓕ Hotel Sacher
- Ⓖ Mozart's Residence
- Ⓗ Marionette Theater

❷ **Festival Halls,** locally Festspielhäuser. This enormous 17th-century structure, formerly the archbishop's stables and riding school, extends the entire length of the block and houses Salzburg's three principal theaters. It was upon the stage of the middle theater that the Hollywood von Trapps sang their farewell songs before escaping to the cemetery. True to life, the von Trapps did sing here and win the group contest at the Salzburg Festival, as portrayed in the movie, but in 1936, not 1938 (and without Georg as part of the ensemble). Maria and the children may have had angelic voices but

...ever meant to sing publicly. Without their blessing, the von Trapps were entered ...o the 1936 contest by an influential acquaintance at the last minute. Georg was not happy, and the family was frantic, as this passage in Maria's book, *The Story of the Trapp Family Singers* (p. 120-21 in my 1967 paperback edition), reveals: "My husband was aghast. He loved our music, he adored our singing; but to see his family on a stage—that was simply beyond the comprehension of an Imperial Austrian Navy officer and Baron." (Georg sternly protested the entry, but it was too late to withdraw. The moment had arrived.) "We stumbled onto the stage, stepping on our own and everybody else's feet ... In a daze we sang our three numbers, and none of us can remember today which ones they were. A gentleman down in the audience tried hard to look mildly interested but perfectly detached. Poor Georg! Our only wish, when we were off stage again, was to evaporate immediately, but we had to stick it out and wait for the awarding of prizes. As if in a fog, we saw the judges return from their conference. Silence settled over the vast crowd, and from afar we could hear the announcement: 'The first prize is awarded to the Trapp Family from Salzburg.' I remember that I didn't understand the meaning of these words, because I applauded wildly with the other people, looking blank. Upon instruction we had to go on stage once more and receive our prize, a diploma signed by the Governor of Salzburg. ...When my eyes searched around for my husband, his seat was empty. He had left in despair. Success or no success—the whole thing was a nightmare to him. It pained him bitterly to see his family on a stage, and only the solemn family resolution never, never to do such a thing again put his troubled mind at ease."

Ironically, less than two years later, it was his family's singing ability that liberated them from Nazi subjugation. Georg, needless to say, learned to be a great fan of the "Trapp Family Singers." If time allows, I recommend you visit the halls via the one-hour, multilanguage tour. (For more on the Festival Halls, including tour times, see page 20.) **Optional:** At the other end of the halls you'll find the ❷ horse trough (GPS: N47 47.964 E13 02.439), erected in 1695 as a princely bath for the archbishop's prized horses, briefly seen during the "Do-Re-Mi" curtain-wearing sequence (just before the tomato-juggling scene at University Platz). What's more, a few minutes farther along are the elevators accessing the ❸ Mönchsberg (Monks' Ridge) observation terrace, where they also sang "Do-Re-Mi" (see Mönchsberg Lift p. 38).

☞ Next stop, Toscanini Hof. Continue straight, in the direction you were walking, and bounce through the underpass.

❸ **Toscanini Hof:** In this secluded courtyard, named after one of Italy's great conductors, Arturo Toscanini (1867-1957), Herr Zeller, Hitler's Nazi boss of Salzburg, pulled up in his Mercedes looking for Georg (you'll fleetingly see the two giant-sized doors to your right). Herr Zeller hurriedly got out of his ride and goose-stepped into the right *corner to enter the staging area. Inside, Max and the children were rehearsing for the upcoming folk festival. They informed the Nazi tyrant that Georg and Maria were still on their honeymoon. ***Note:** Beyond the atmospheric Felsenkeller bar-club are doors that (when open) really do lead to the staging area. Also note, pictured on the wall left of the two giant-sized doors is the middle theater, or Felsenreitschule.

☞ From the Toscanini Hof, jog through the passage (look to security pylon on left after you walked in). Continue straight through the first courtyard (College of St. Benedict) and into the next one (St. Peter's monastery) toward the fortress. Stop at the forward arched passage (right corner).

To your right is St. Peter's Stiftskeller, Europe's oldest restaurant (p. 56). Return here for dinner? When ready, skip through the passage into…

❹ St. Peter's Cemetery,

(daily 6:30-18:00, April-Sept till 19:00), the oldest active graveyard in Austria, is more than a 1,000 years of age. It is here the Trapp family hid during the escape scene. (Watch out for Rolf!)

Veer right and climb the graveled path to the catacombs (Katakomben). Stand before them but don't go in.

From here, you can see that even if one of the gated vaults framing the cemetery were open, there'd be nowhere to hide. In reality, Hollywood hid the von Trapps in a studio but this cemetery inspired the director, Robert Wise.

Face the catacombs then shuffle left two wrought-iron vaults (LII) and you'll see (on the ground, middle right) the name Canonicus Franciscus Wasner—this priestly man is the real Max Detweiler. He was not the conceited sponge the movie portrays. Father Wasner, whom the von Trapps first met on Easter 1935, was the family's spiritual advisor and musical conductor. It is absolutely essential when reviewing the history of the von Trapp family that Father Wasner be included, from winning the Salzburg Festival group contest in 1936 to their escape to Italy, to life in America and finally at Cor Unum (their homestead in Stowe, Vermont). Without Father Wasner, it is very possible the story would not exist. And here he rests before you, in Austria's most glorious graveyard. **Note:** For more on the cemetery, including a do-it-yourself tour of the catacombs, flip to pages 18 & 36.

☞ When finished visiting the cemetery, face Father Wasner then go left along the graveled path, paralleling the vaults, and straight out the gate. Climb the cobbled lane (Festungsgasse) past the cable railway (Festungsbahn) and Stieglkeller (which, by the way, has a recommended beer garden p. 57). The view will develop into a wonder!

> **Readers participating** in my DIY tour of *Salzburg, Mozartplatz to Mirabell*, begin reading from here:

At the top the lane splits direction. Go left; this leads to the abbey (3 min). Eventually you'll come to an archway; above it is St. Erentraud, first abbess, 712 A.D.—hence she's holding a representation of the abbey—soon I'll show you her burial place in the crypt of the abbey church.

Go through the archway; follow the road as it bends right. Continue a bit farther and stop at the wooden benches beneath the huge maple tree. Spectacular view, no? Hopefully it's a clear day.

With your back to the wrought-iron gate (No. 4), gaze outwards to the forested hill in the valley with the canary-yellow structure nestling in the trees—this is the so-called Monats Schlössl (Month Villa), which belongs to Schloss Hellbrunn (where the "gazebo" is located) and can be seen on the Driving Tour. Now, move your eyes right and check out Untersberg mountain, resembling a colossal wave at Waimea Bay.

❺ **Untersberg,** (for more on Untersberg, including riding the cable car to its summit, see page 44). Soaring (1,865m/6,117ft) above Salzburg's southern suburbs is perhaps Austria's most intriguing mountain: Untersberg. It is upon this landmass in the opening scene of the movie that Maria says she was singing. Maria explained passionately to the Reverend Mother Abbess that Untersberg is her mountain, and as a child she used to climb a tree and peer into the convent's garden (obviously with megapowerful binoculars) to watch the sisters at work. Moreover, you'll see the uniquely shaped Untersberg numerous times in the movie with its lengthy plateau and V-shaped crevice. (Crevice not seen from this angle. In fact, only about half of Untersberg is in Austria and the V-shaped crevice marks the Bavarian frontier.) For example, when Maria is singing in the opening scene amongst the birch trees you'll see the V-shaped crevice in the background. (From that angle she's actually in Bavaria, which contradicts her narrative to the Reverend Mother.) Also, you'll boldly see Untersberg when Georg and Maria are squabbling after the children fall in the lake. However, the most classic time is the final scene, when the von Trapps are escaping over the Alps into Switzerland—you can't help but notice Untersberg in the background vibrantly framed in Cinema Scope. Actually, Maria and the gang are climbing the mountainside adjacent to Hitler's Eagle's Nest. In essence, they are escaping into Nazi Southern Command. Oops!

Let's get back to the opening scene. When Maria hears the bells chiming while on Untersberg, we now know (from our view point) that not only did Maria have bionic hearing and the vision of a superhero, but she also must have been an Olympic athlete in training to even contemplate reaching the convent in time. No wonder she was late!

☞ Turn around and enter through the wrought-iron gate (at No. 4) the nuns were twice seen behind talking to visitors.

❻ **Abbey, Nonnberg:** Dating from the 8th century A.D., the abbey on the Mountain of Nuns, or Nonnberg, is the oldest known convent in the German-speaking world. Together with St. Peter's monastery, this Benedictine abbey represents the foundation of Christianity in Salzburg. Nonnberg abbey, true to life, is where Maria really assumed her postulancy; where she and Georg really got married (in the abbey church) on November 26, 1927 (he was 47, she was 22); and where Hollywood filmed three parts of the movie: **(1)** when Maria left the convent to meet the captain while singing "I Have Confidence"; **(2)** when the children were looking for Maria after she went missing; **(3)** and during the escape scene, when the Nazis demanded entry to search for the family of nine who seemingly vanished. (It's amazing how sneaky-fast the von Trapps were, going from the festival halls up to the abbey and back to the cemetery in just seconds.)

Note: Because the convent is off-limits to the public, the movie crew was only given permission to film externally in and around the abbey church, which is where you are now. In front of you, the rose-marble portal leading into the church dates from 1497. Step inside and angle left through the pillars to see the Romanesque wall paintings (circa 1150 A.D.) that still survive from an earlier church that stood here before it was ultimately destroyed by fire. If it's dark beyond the glass, this means .50¢ is required for illumination. If the lights are on and the nuns are *singing in their secluded choir above, you've timed it just right. When ready, walk to the front right of the church and if the wrought-iron door is open descend into the crypt (the burial place of St. Erentraud, Nonnberg's first abbess). *Note: For a heavenly highlight, time your abbey visit with the angelic voices of the nuns, whose number here total around two dozen and who typically sing for 10 minutes Mon-Fri from 15:45, and again for 30 minutes at 17:15.

> **Readers participating** in my DIY tour of Salzburg, head back the same way you came and "Mosey through the gate into St. Peter's Cemetery" p. 18.

☞ (Let's resume our walking tour:) Exit the church grounds and head back towards the cemetery the same way you came, passing the cable railway. Instead of returning through the cemetery gate, go right and follow the cobblestones down into **Ⓓ** Kapitelplatz—this is the asphalt plaza populated by souvenir stands and a huge chessboard. Continue straight through the arches into **Ⓔ** Domplatz, or Cathedral Square (**toilets** within archway, left side); bypass the cathedral (to your right) and exit through the next set of arches. This vast graveled square is Residenzplatz, home of…

❼ Residenz Fountain: Smack-dab in the center of Residenzplatz with its water-spouting horses is the fancifully fluid Residenz fountain. Erected in 1658, it is said to be the most beautiful Baroque fountain north of the Alps. You'll recognize it from the scene when Maria splashes water in the horse's face while singing "I Have Confidence" (she splashed the horse facing the "Hypo" bank, blue logo), and you'll see the fountain again immediately after the wedding scene when Nazi flags are hanging off the Residenz building (with its three stories of windows) and German soldiers marching through the square. Can you imagine the older locals who unknowingly went into town that morning to do some shopping? They almost certainly would have collapsed at the mere sight of the Wehrmacht troops and their high-kicking jackboots. *Déja-vu!* (**Note:** The fountain is covered for winter, typically from early Nov. until the end of March.)

Time to throw on your specially tailored 'play clothes'

☞ Beyond the fountain, in the next square, you'll see a statue of Mozart—walk past him and angle downhill toward the river. Cross with the traffic light and step onto the footbridge. This is the...

❽ Mozart Steg: On this iron footbridge, built in 1903 and named after the legendary Wolfgang Amadeus, the opening scenes of the "Do-Re-Mi" curtain-wearing sequence were filmed. When you're about two-thirds of the way across, turn around for a stunning view. (The film crew capitalized on the view by positioning themselves off the bridge half way to the forward traffic light.) Once you've reached the end of the bridge, you'll remember the kids enthusiastically bopping from railing to railing and frolicking along the lush riverbank.

> **Readers participating** in my DIY tour of Salzburg, return to Mozartplatz and continue from there, p. 14.

☞ To reach the next and last site on our walking tour, cross at the forward traffic light and go left. Continue straight some distance to the next intersection. Stop here.

To your left is the main bridge into Old Town and to your right the Hotel Stein. (Return here with time and visit the Stein Terrasse p. 47 for an eye-popping view.)

Keep trekking forward (on right side of street). Ahead on the left, the flowered balconies and flapping flags belong to the ❻ Hotel Sacher Salzburg (p. 69), where Julie Andrews and director Robert Wise stayed during filming.

Continue straight. Weave your way past the people waiting for their bus (at Theatergasse) and stop on the corner. The building over your right shoulder is ❼ the Mozart Residence (p. 40), where the family moved to in 1773. The Hotel Bristol across the street (at your 1 o'clock) is where Christopher Plummer and the children stayed.

What you need to do now is rambo the triple-wide street in front of you to the other side, where the bus shelters are. Once it's completely clear of oncoming traffic and perfectly safe, go!

Great job. We're going to continue straight, but if you were to go left toward the traffic light then right around the corner, the first building you'd reach is the ❽ Marionette Theater (p. 54). It was these puppets that inspired the Lonely Goatherd sequence in the movie.

Continue straight ahead and pass between the two sets of Greek-inspired statues marking the entrance into the marvelous...

> EDITOR'S NOTE: Please review us on the Web. As a small business, we get pumped about the little things. That's why positive support and word-of-mouth from our readers means the world to us. It let's us know how we're doing, thus we'd greatly appreciate it if you could share your experience about this book by typing a brief review on *Amazon*. If you've enjoyed a particular Salzburg site because of our attention to it, please mention Harriman in your *TripAdvisor* comment. ☺

❾ Mirabell Gardens, a jewel of landscape design, where diehard SOMers go

bonkers and I tend to lose guests. Thus, I will end our walking tour here so you can enjoy the splendor at your own speed. But first, I'll explain a few things before bidding adieu.

Maria and the children skipped all through these gardens, as I'm sure you will, too. First, you probably recognized those Greek statues as the scene when Maria and the kids synchronized an arm-raising get-together.

Go to the fountain in front of you where you saw them crisscrossing one another.

Notice the string of linden trees to the left. On hot days they provide cool sanctuary. Head over to them and continue along the tree-lined path until the dirt changes to pavement. Stop here.

In front of you (right) should be a wrought-iron fence enclosing the rose garden.

At this junction, all points are within striking distance:

To your **left** is the ivy arcade the kids ran through.

To your **right,** where the path arcs into the grass, you'll capture a postcard-perfect view (with the splendor of the gardens and the majestic skyline of Old Town all at your photographic disposal).

Straight ahead is the Pegasus (winged horse) fountain they ran around (climb the 15 steps to its left and cross the wooden bridge to find the dwarf they patted—first on left, having glasses, mouth open, holding hat), and beyond the fountain are the "Do-Re-Mi" steps (from where the above picture was taken). The flanking unicorns are great to pose on. Have fun!

Note: In winter, the gardens are half closed—you can see the sites but not fully experience them. For more info on the gardens, flip to page 24. For info on the Do-Re-Mi scene in the alpine meadow, see "SOM fans" on page 77.

(DIY SOM) DRIVING TOUR,
Anif to Moon Lake—2 hours

There are five sites in this section [**10-14**], four are in Salzburg and the fifth is in the lake district (Salzkammergut p. 79). A suggested amount of time to visit is written for each site. The route is fairly simple to navigate and the countryside is delightful to behold, especially in the lake district. **Note:** Choice picnic spots include Schloss Hellbrunn (second stop) and anywhere in the lake district (last stop). Regarding the latter destination, if the weather's nice, bring your bathing suit.

Drivers, I've written simplified directions from site to site for you follow.

Railers, don't think you're excluded from the driving tour, you can, in fact, see 4 out of the 5 sites in this section (everything except Mondsee [**14**] in the lake district) on your own by *bike. (To rent a bike, flip to page 9 or ask TI for other rental locations.) Your route, though, will be different to that of Drivers. (*__Note:__ If riding a bike isn't your thing, arrange a bus tour via the TI or your accommodations. Or, if you're a small group, consider renting a car.) **To reach the 5th site** (Mondsee) in the lake district from Salzburg, catch bus 140 from the Hauptbahnhof or Mirabellplatz (hourly Mon-Fri, every other hour Sat-Sun, 50-min trip, adult one way 6.70€, day ticket 13.40€, youth 15-18yr 4.70€/9.40€ and 6-14yr 3.40€/6.80€, www.salzburg-verkehr.at). **Suggestion,** (May thru Sept 24, 2017): After breakfast, ride bus 150 from Salzburg to St. Gilgen on Wolfgangsee (p. 80, buy day ticket from driver), spend the day here (e.g. ride boat across lake to Sheep Mountain and back), then catch the last bus 156 from St. Gilgen (at 18:05) to Mondsee (20-min trip)—there's much less to see and do in Mondsee (p. 85 & 111) thus a visit won't take long—but don't miss the last bus 140 departing Mondsee (at 21:35) back to Salzburg. **Note:** Double check times and prices in advance with staff at your accommodations or TI in case of any changes.

Cyclists, pick up a city map from the TI and get yourself to Freisaalweg, a graveled recreational path southeast of the fortress. This will turn into Hellbrunner Allee, which runs past Schloss Frohnburg [**12**] and concludes at Schloss Hellbrunn [**11**]. From here, ride through Anif to reach the Water Castle [**10**] before backtracking to Schloss Leopoldskron [**13**]. (Consider cycling to the Trapp Villa [**I**] at the end of this tour.) Start early and pack a picnic. Although touring by bike can be taxing, it's more comprehensive, healthier, and much cheaper than the commercial tours on offer for about 44€ per person.

☞ Let's begin our driving tour at the Water Castle (GPS: N47 44.768 E13 04.049), located in the southern suburb of Anif. If you're coming from the city, have the TI or staff at your accommodations point the way. If you're coming from outer Salzburg, exit the A10 autobahn at Salzburg-Süd and follow signs to Salzburg/Anif. At the first set of lights turn right, direction Hallein. Coming up on the left, just past the margarine-colored Hotel zum Schloßwirt (first big structure on left), is a short cobbled driveway before a gated entrance. Park momentarily in the driveway facing the...

⑩ Anif Water Castle, (1 min suggested). Built in the 17th century as a residence for the bishops of Chiemsee, this neo-Gothic water castle (sitting behind the massive willow tree) is briefly featured from the air in the opening scenes of the movie. Besides its SOM fame, the castle can also be seen near the end of the 1974 movie thriller "The Odessa File" starring Jon Voight. Since the castle is privately owned, tours are *not* possible. From the gate, capture a *photo. However, make it snappy, notice the golden plaques on either gatepost—they're informing you in three languages to 'beat it'! ***Note:** If you'd like to capture a similar castle photo that I pictured here, continue straight in the direction you were traveling and after a few hundred meters you'll see a bus stop on the left (large H painted onto pavement), where you need to stop momentarily. (Use the road on the right to turn around.) Be quick, keep an eye out for approaching buses, and elevate yourself to snap a pretty picture over the wall.

☞ To reach Schloss Hellbrunn, go back to the traffic light and drive straight through the intersection into the spick-and-span village of Anif. On the other side of town is the Salzburg Zoo (right), and a few hundred meters farther is the Salzburg city-limits sign, make the next right at the end of the golden wall.

Soon you'll pass a small parking area within the walls to your right; continue straight past the second parking area (right) and at the third parking area (right) find a space and cut the engine. (Take a ticket: first 30 min are free, up to 2hr/2€, 3hr/2.80€, max 3.60€.) Walk through the palace's pointy back gate (nice photo opportunity to the front facade) then go left and the gazebo will be to your immediate right. From here, consider a stroll through the gardens. Unpack your picnic? **Note:** Salzburg Card holders receive free admission into the Schloss, trick fountains, and zoo p. 41-42.

⓫ Schloss Hellbrunn, (10 min to half a day suggested). Decades ago, the gazebo was relocated here from the private gardens of Schloss Leopoldskron. Now accessible to the public, more than 300,000 fans visit the gazebo annually to relive the harmonious scene "Sixteen Going on Seventeen" performed by Rolf (Dan Truhitte) and Liesl (Charmian Carr, who at the time was 21 going on 22). You may have noticed the gazebo looks smaller; that's because this one was only used for external shots and a second, bigger prop was used on the set in Los Angeles. If you're jiggling the door handle to get in to dance on the benches, you'll be disappointed to know that it's always kept locked since previous, equally enthusiastic visitors have been carted off with sprained ankles and broken limbs. Case in point, Charmian Carr slipped and fell while rehearsing the scene and her foot went through a glass window pane. Crew members wrapped a bandage around her ankle and said keep going, "The show must go on." **Note:** No part of the movie was filmed at this location. When facing the gazebo, *free* **toilets** are behind you, the zoo is left at the end of the tree-lined path, and the green shield to your right explains a little more. For the history of Schloss Hellbrunn, flip to page 41.

☞ Turn left out of the parking lot, return to the main road, go right and continue in the direction of Salzburg. After 1 km start looking to your right for Schloss Frohnburg—this is the estate enclosed within golden walls, across the meadow, behind a row of trees. (Don't confuse it with the golden estate with white trim in front of you.) Alas, there's nowhere to pull over, so drive slow and have your camera handy. What's more, a brief but magnificent view to the fortress will open up in front of you. (**Cyclists**, you'll get a much closer look at Frohnburg because the graveled bike path, Hellbrunner Allee, passes directly in front of the estate.)

⓬ Schloss Frohnburg: You'll recognize this estate in the movie as the front of the von Trapp villa. Remember when Maria approached the villa while singing "I Have Confidence" and swinging around those obviously *empty* bags before peering through the gate? You may also remember when the family silently pushed their vehicle out the gate, only to find Herr Zeller and his Nazi boyfriends there to greet them. (The Gestapo were tipped off by the family's butler.) And when Georg ripped down a long Nazi flag hanging from the front facade after returning home from his honeymoon. Although it's difficult to recognize, these were not the only scenes filmed here. Schloss Frohnburg was also used (in conjunction with Schloss Leopoldskron, our next stop) as the back of the house (backside of Frohnburg cannot be seen from the road). In fact, if you don't see the lake, the scene was filmed at Schloss Frohnburg. For example, when Rolf throws pebbles at Liesl's window, and when Georg (who is facing the lake) tells the kids to get their dinner, they hustle past him and into the back of Frohnburg. **Note:** Most all interior scenes of the von Trapp villa (and abbey) were shot on a Twentieth Century-Fox film set in Century City, Los Angeles. Historically, Schloss Frohnburg dates from the 17th century and was used as a country manor by the archbishops. Today, the estate accommodates students and study rooms for the Mozarteum (www.moz.ac.at/en), or Salzburg University of Music, Theater and Visual Arts.

☞ At the upcoming intersection turn right, then make the first left (Fürstenallee). At the junction ahead, go left (this is still Fürstenallee). Continue to the second set of lights and turn left (Sinnhubstrasse). On the right you'll have an enormous view of the fortress. Lower your eyes and you'll see a lone cottage in the meadow. This formerly belonged to the town executioner. Perhaps nobody wanted to hang out with him. (Pause for laugh.) The last person to wear the noose in Salzburg was in the early 1800s on the knoll behind the cottage.

Continue straight; the road will narrow into an Einbahnstrasse, or one-way street. At the second traffic light turn left onto an even narrower road (Leopoldskronstrasse).

At the forthcoming junction go left, following the sign Schloss Leopoldskron. Pass the Freibad Leopoldskron (community pool) and make the subsequent right into Firmianstrasse. Since this is a one-way road, watch out for cars heading your way and immediately pull into the *lot and park (but before you get out of the car, grab some bread for the ducks and swans). *Note: The lot is reserved for customers of Marchhart's Thai-Fish-Steak restaurant but it's closed Sun-Mon and doesn't open until 17:00 Tue-Sat.

Mosey some 200 meters on Firmianstrasse (pass mini golf on right) to the concrete vehicle barriers and lakeside path. Continue on said path another 180 meters along the lake until you reach the oak tree growing out of the water, GPS: N47 47.180 E13 02.205.

From either side of the tree you're rewarded with a memorable picture of the fortress framed behind the palace (like the pictured inset). If you happen to be at the lake when a tour group arrives, notice how the guide stops the group well short of this best-picture spot. Time is money, ya know.

⓭ **Schloss Leopoldskron,** (20 min suggested, mostly because of walk). Originally built in 1736 for Prince-Archbishop Leopold Firmian, this stunning Rococo structure represented the back of the von Trapp villa (facade facing lake). No doubt you'll remember what scenes were filmed here. My favorite is just after the kids fell in the lake, when Georg interrogates Maria over children in trees and tailored curtains. After bitter squabbling, Maria exclaimed: "I am not finished yet, Captain!" Flustered, Georg replied: "Oh, yes you are, Captain!"

For the actors and crew, though, filming the boat scene wasn't as smooth as it appeared on screen. You see, little 5-year-old Gretl couldn't swim, so it was planned for Maria to sit with the little one and when they fell overboard Maria would immediately carry her to shore. Simple, right? Well, when they all stood up, Maria lost her balance and fell backwards off the boat. Gretl, on cue, fell forward and instantly sank (head to the bottom, one of her legs straight up in the air)! The scene cuts to an open-mouthed Georg then back to the kids, but only six are visible (and Maria is behind the boat not in the picture). The scene once again cuts to Georg, at which time a crew member jumped in to save Gretl from drowning (obviously edited from the film). When the scene cuts back to the kids, Louisa is cheerfully carrying Gretl to safety. Tragedy averted!

And after all these years, Gretl (Kym Karath) says she's "still not fond of the water after that experience." And who would be, it took *four* takes to get the scene: fall in the lake, dry off, repeat. And that water was "freezing" cold, according to Liesl (Charmian Carr), who recalled her frigid feelings some four decades later as if they were yesterday.

Although this location was used exclusively for its lake scenes—the exterior of Leopoldskron palace is never seen in the film (the exterior that you do see is actually Schloss Frohnburg)— Boris Leven (production designer) was inspired by the palace's sumptuous mirrored Venetian room thus he recreated it in Los Angeles for the grand ballroom scene.

Today, Schloss Leopoldskron houses the Salzburg Global Seminar, an international conference center (www.salzburgglobal.org), as well as the highly rated Hotel Schloss Leopoldskron (www.schloss-leopoldskron.com).

In winter, the lake freezes over and throngs of locals keenly use it as a giant ice rink. In summer, the lake is a popular place to go for a stroll, jog, or to kick back and cast a line (widely caught fish are carp and pike).

☞ To our next and last venue, roughly a 45-minute drive, will deliver us from Salzburg to Mondsee (Moon Lake) in the wonderfully scenic Salzkammergut, or lake district. Thus I recommend you supplement this section with the Salzkammergut chapter, p. 79.

1) From the parking lot, pull briefly onto Firmianstrasse, turn right so you're once again on Leopoldskronstrasse, then make a quick left onto Leopoldskroner Allee (as you make the turn the gated entrance into Schloss Leopoldskron will be to your right).

2) At the fork ahead go right, passing the executioner's cottage again. (Notice the palatial digs on your right—this is the Altenheim, or old folks' home.)

3) Turn left at the traffic light and follow the road right around the bend then yield left at the junction (onto Erzabt-Klotz-Strasse).

4) At the next set of lights turn left (Petersbrunnstrasse), where the abbey's red onion-domed steeple will present itself divinely. Go straight through the forward lights and cross the river.

5) Before the next traffic light go right following the sign to St. Gilgen. At the second traffic circle ahead turn left. Follow this busy road 1.5 km (about 1 mile) and you'll come to the big intersection of Linzer Bundesstrasse—<u>turn right</u>.

6) You'll only be on Linzer Bundesstrasse for half a kilometer—after crossing the railway bridge follow the sign right to St. Gilgen. This road (Minnesheimstrasse) will snake its way above Salzburg and eventually straighten out, escorting you through some of Austria's most striking countryside.

7) After 15 km (just after the town of Hof) you'll reach the inviting waters of Fuschlsee (p. 79), the beginning of the Salzkammergut.

8) Keep driving towards St. Gilgen, located another 12 km on the shore of the next lake, Wolfgangsee. The moment you see the lake (on downhill left curve), pull over at the rest area (on right through narrow road entry). From here you can capture a similar image as the one briefly featured from the air in the opening shots of the movie. The lake is called Wolfgangsee and the town beneath you is St. Gilgen (p. 80). Another SOM sight is the pointy mountain in front of you with a structure planted at its summit. Maria and the children were seen steaming up the side of this mountain during the "Do-Re-Mi" curtain-wearing sequence on the Sheep Mountain Railway (p. 83).

9) Exit the rest area and descend towards St. Gilgen. At the bottom, go around the turning circle direction Mondsee. You're now on Austria's "Romantic Road."

10) Along the route you'll pass the privately owned Schloss Hüttenstein, an enchanting mustard-yellow castle perched upon a forested hill. Behind the Schloss is Krottensee, an idyllic lake named Turtle. Below the castle is Schlossmayrhof, a lovely farmhouse bed-and-breakfast run by the Zopf family, www.schlossmayrhof.at, tel. 06227/2380).

11) Soon you'll reach the blue waters of Moon Lake, locally Mondsee. As you get closer to the town of Mondsee, situated on the distant shore, you'll spot what you came for: the twin steeples of St. Michael's Church.

12) Upon arriving in Mondsee veer right following the sign to Mondsee-Süd, then ahead make the first left. Your best place to park is in the lot across from the gas station, GPS: N47 51.177 E13 20.919. (If full, park adjacent to the lake. If you do park at the lake, ignore step 13 and walk the tree-lined road straight into town, to the church.)

13) After parking, walk the lane right of the gas station, following the green sign pointing Zentrum. Take this into town; you're aiming for the twin-steepled church. The asphalt lane will connect with a graveled path skirting an extensive field. Take this path to the tree-lined road on the opposite side and go left into town.

⓮ Mondsee: (The strudel stop, 30 min to a few hours suggested. If the weather is nice, consider a swim, Mondsee is the warmest lake in the Salzkammergut, reaching 26-degrees Celsius, or 79°F, in summer.) Translating to Moon Lake, Mondsee has to be romantic! The main town of concern here, and the reason for busloads of tourists, is the lake's namesake: Mondsee. Even though the Romans settled the town nearly 2,000 years ago and monks officially established it in 748 A.D., Mondsee didn't make any real headlines until 1965, when the movie "The Sound of Music" premiered. It was in the town's Baroque church (St. Michael's) that Hollywood married Georg and Maria von Trapp.

When film scouts arrived in Salzburg in 1963, one of their target locations was a church for the wedding scene. However, most churches weren't hip to the idea; only a few would allow filming. Of their limited choices, film scouts chose this one. The following year the cast and crew arrived to shoot the scene. St. Michael's Church was wonderfully ornamented; extras filled the pews while an organ played and the nuns sang "How do you solve a problem like Maria...." We all remember the scene when Maria elegantly paced the nave in her long, flowing white gown to meet her beloved sea captain waiting patiently by the altar. **Note:** St. Michael's is generally open Mon-Sat 8:00-19:00, and Sunday from 12:00 on account of Holy Mass. Public **toilets** are located nearby at the side of the Rathaus, or town hall, which is directly opposite Café Braun (mauve-colored facade). Across from St. Michael's you can find **scrumptious strudel** served with vanilla ice cream at Café Braun, locally known as the best. (According to the owner, Frau Braun, the SOM film crew used the second floor of her building as a rehearsal/dressing room.) After strudel, stroll along the tree-lined road to the lakeside promenade. It's time well spent.

That's a wrap, folks!
I hope you enjoyed the tour.
So long, farewell, auf Wiederseh'n, good*bye*...

To get back to Salzburg (25 km), the A1 autobahn is conveniently located on the north side of Mondsee. But **note** that vehicles traveling on the Austrian autobahn system are required to have a "Vignette," or toll sticker (p. 115).

©Villa Trapp Foundation

Postscript,
❶ **Trapp Villa:** You've seen all the SOM movie locations made famous by Hollywood, but what about the *real* von Trapp villa? Dating from 1863, this historic property was not used in the filming of the movie (for reasons explained below) but today it is open for travelers to tour as well as those seeking a unique overnight experience.

Idyllically set within an 8 acre forested reserve (that is the city's largest privately owned park) in the Salzburg suburb of Aigen, the 14-room von Trapp villa is significant because it is here the story truly began in 1926 when a determined 21-year-old Catholic girl from the convent arrived to care for the captain's sick daughter.

Georg and the children had moved here in 1923, where the family remained until Hitler's fascist army marched into Salzburg 15 years later. After the von Trapps fled Austria, the Nazis seized the villa. Heinrich Himmler, head of all Nazi police forces, was especially fond of the property and resided here when in town on "business." At this time the villa's leafy quaintness was sacrificed to a cordon of armed guards and barbed wire. Postwar, a religious order, the Missionaries of the Precious Blood, purchased the villa and kept it secluded from the community. Until now! The missionaries leased the property to a hospitality group that opened it to the public as **Villa Trapp** (bed-and-breakfast-style accommodations • tel. 0662/630-860 • www.villa-trapp.com).

Not only will you have the opportunity to sleep in the family's former bedrooms, but you'll also have the possibility to enjoy a specially prepared SOM dinner in the family dining room (where the children promptly gathered for meals on whistle command) and to get married in the house chapel (presently set in Georg and Maria's former bedroom—note that the location of the original chapel, where Father Wasner gave Easter Mass in 1935 when he first met the Trapp family and discovered their exceptional singing ability, is now the breakfast room). Although no actual furnishings from the von Trapp household remain, the villa is indeed in original condition—including the parquet flooring and the tall bending staircase whose wooden hand-railing repeatedly entertained the seven youngsters as a thrilling slide when their father wasn't looking—and outfitted with period furniture and fixtures as well as photos of the von Trapps and some family items.

Tour Villa Trapp: Although the von Trapp villa is a private residence reserved for the exclusivity of its overnight guests, it is also open once per day to sightseers seeking to tour the property (typically 12 noon, reserve in advance, tour duration 45 min • adult 15€, youth to 14yr 7€, for sale at ticket agents or Villa Trapp • tel. 0662/630-860 • www.villa-trapp.com).

To get there, Villa Trapp is located at Traunstrasse 34 in the suburb of Aigen, 3 km southeast of Salzburg's Old Town. **By taxi** from Old Town is roughly 15€. **Railers** (if you're carrying a Salzburg Card I suggest you travel by bus—see "By bus" below, otherwise) from Salzburg's central station, there's a regularly scheduled train (departing every 30 min Mon-Sat, hourly on Sun) to Bahnhof Aigen (from where the von Trapps originally "escaped" the Nazis in 1938), 9-min trip then 9-min walk. From Aigen station bounce down the steps, through the underpass to the other side of the tracks, and up the steps. Veer right, go straight a few meters then right around the corner and follow the whitewashed wall all the way to the intersecting street and right around to the front gate of Villa Trapp nestling in the trees. **By bus** from the city, hop on #7 direction Salzburg Süd and get off at Bahnhof Aigen (train station from where the von Trapps originally "escaped" the Nazis in 1938), 10-min ride (bus departs Hanuschplatz and Mozartsteg every 10 min, and every 20 min after 19:00 Mon-Sat and all day Sun). From Bahnhof Aigen, it's less than a 10-min walk—jog across the street, down the steps, through the underpass to the other side of the train tracks, and up the steps. Veer right, go straight a few meters then right around the corner and follow the whitewashed wall all the way to the intersecting street and right around to the front gate of Villa Trapp nestling in the trees. **Drivers,** free parking on property. **If you're heading** west direction Salzburg on the A1 autobahn, exit at Salzburg Nord. Drive towards Salzburg. Continue on this busy avenue (Salzburger Strasse turning to Vogelweiderstrasse) all the way to the end. At the traffic light, turn left. Ahead, under 1 km, veer right onto a one-way section of road (Ignaz-Härtl-Str, after gas station) then go right at the forward junction. Drive this heavily trafficked road 1.5 km (about 1 mile) to the end and turn left (direction Schloss Hellbrunn, Zoo). This will put you onto Aigner Strasse, leading to Aigen. Continue straight and at the second traffic light (Blumaustrasse), turn left. Drive beneath the train tracks (on which the von Trapps originally "escaped" the Nazis from nearby Aigen station in 1938), follow the road right around and make the second right into Traunstrasse. At the other end of this residential street, beyond the whitewashed wall, is Villa Trapp (right) nestling in the trees. **If you're coming from** the A10 autobahn, exit at Salzburg-Süd and drive towards Salzburg. After about 4 km turn right (immediately past the Park+Ride) direction Aigen. Continue straight and cross the river. Go left on the upcoming traffic circle, putting you onto Aigner Strasse leading to Aigen. Continue straight—you'll soon drive beneath the train tracks on which the von Trapps originally "escaped" the Nazis from nearby Aigen station in 1938—about 3 km ahead at the 4th traffic-lighted intersection turn right (Blumaustrasse). Drive beneath the train tracks again, follow the road right around and make the second right into Traunstrasse. At the other end of this residential street, beyond the whitewashed wall, is Villa Trapp (right) nestling in the trees.

Continued from St. Sebastian's church cemetery, p. 41:

Mozart, Constanze Weber (b. Jan. 6, 1763 — d. March 6, 1842). Here lies the wife of the great Wolfgang Amadeus. Mozart met his spouse through the opera singer Aloysia Weber, Constanze's sister, whom he was dating at the time! Wolfgang's father, Leopold Mozart, loathed Constanze. In a letter to his father, Wolfgang affectionately described Constanze in a plea to inspire a family-like relationship between the two: *"She is not ugly, but at the same time, far from beautiful. Her beauty consists of two little black eyes and a nice figure. She isn't witty, but has enough common sense to make her a good wife and mother.... She understands house-keeping and has the kindest heart in the world. I love her and she loves me...."* The plea fell on deaf ears and the two parties never reconciled their differences. Ironically, Constanze is buried next to Leopold Mozart. Not only does the placement of these two bitter adversaries side by side drive one's curiosity, but Leopold must be turning in his grave since Constanze's headstone (pictured in the middle) hugely dwarfs his (on the right).

Mozart, Leopold (b. Nov. 14, 1719 — d. May 28, 1787). Respected composer, violinist, and father of the eminent Wolfgang Amadeus. Leopold was born in Augsburg, Germany, to middle-class parents, Johann Georg Mozart, a bookbinder, and Anna Maria, a homemaker. Leopold left Augsburg at the age of 17 to attend college in Salzburg. It is here that he lived for the rest of his life, becoming a court composer for the prince archbishop. Having a secure job, Leopold married his true love, Anna Maria Pertl, in 1747. She gave birth seven times while living in their modest third-floor apartment at Getreidegasse 9—only two survived infancy: Maria Anna (Nannerl) and Wolfgang Amadeus. While Nannerl showed signs of a promising career as a musician, Wolfgang left no doubt that he was a musical genius. Leopold was so proud of his son that he sacrificed his own career as a composer to coach young Amadeus. But as Wolfgang grew older, his desire for individuality and independence put him at odds with his domineering father. Alas, the two grew apart after the passing of Wolfgang's mother (in Paris in 1778) and his marriage to Constanze Weber. During this traumatic period, Leopold knew he needed his son more than ever. Fortunately, in 1785, he was able to travel to Vienna, where Wolfgang had moved, to see him one last time. Leopold is buried in St. Sebastian's church cemetery, Salzburg—next to Constanze Weber (see previous entry).

Continued from Mozartplatz, p. 12:

Mozart, Wolfgang Amadeus (b. Jan. 27, 1756 — d. Dec. 5, 1791). Regarded as one of the greatest composers of all time, Mozart worked in all musical genres of his era, producing an extraordinary amount of compositions considering his short life. By the time Mozart died at age 35, he had composed 27 piano concertos, 23 string quartets, 17 piano sonatas, more than 50 symphonies, and six major operas, notably "The Marriage of Figaro" (1786), "Don Giovanni" (1787), and "The Magic Flute" (1791). Mozart died in Vienna, in 1791, weeks before his 36th birthday. A monument (pictured) has been erected in St. Marx Cemetery, Vienna, on the approximate spot where he is believed to be buried. The cemetery is located in the suburb of St. Marx, 3 km southeast of central Vienna. A visit is recommended. Unique is the fact that the cemetery was closed to burials in 1874; therefore the graveyard appears as it did in the 19th century, presenting an age-old setting of sunken headstones, worn markings, and spiders tending to their intricate webs. These coordinates (GPS: N48 11.031 E16 24.200) will lead you to the cemetery gate. Toilets are on the right after entering through the gate. To reach Mozart, climb main gravel path straight and before Jesus follow the "Mozart Grab" sign left. **Note:** Mozart is the figure depicted on Austria's 1€ coin.

Continued from Drivers/Parking, p. 8:

Parking Dial: Before hitting the road, make sure you have a nifty parking dial: a small, 24-hour (blue) cardboard disk that is manually rotated and called a Parkscheibe, or often Parkuhr, in Austria. With the dial properly displayed on your dashboard you will be permitted to park for free in designated areas.

There should be a dial in the glove box (or in the side-door panel) of your rental car. If your car did not come with a dial, and you haven't yet left the rental agency, go back in and ask for one. If it's too late, you can purchase a dial cheaply at a gas station or magazine shop. When applicable, a diagram of the dial will be featured on local parking signs along with a maximum time limit, like 1 Std. (short for Stunde meaning "hour"). Rotate the dial to the time you pulled into the space (Ankunftszeit, or arrival time) and put it on the dashboard. This way the parking inspector can see when you arrived and if you've overstayed your welcome.

Vignette; Drivers: The maximum speed limit on the Austrian autobahn is 130 kilometers per hour (kph), but to drive on this efficient motorway you are required to have what's called a "Vignette," or toll sticker affixed to the windshield of your vehicle. The Vignette color this year (2017) is turquoise. If it is not this color, it's *not* valid! But even if it is the correct color, it still may not be valid. This is because the Vignette is sold in three (time-constrained) categories: 10 days 8.90€, two months 25.90€, and one year 86.40€. You can obtain this little decal at most any gas station approaching the border (and some gas stations within Austria). **Note:** Affix the Vignette to the inside corner of your windshield or behind the rear-view mirror. (Your rental car may already have a toll sticker from the previous renter; you're in luck if it's still valid.) If you happen to get pulled over without a valid Vignette, the fine is around 240€, on the spot! Lastly, the law requires that you have an international driving permit to drive in Austria (which you can typically pick up for around $15 from your local auto club).

116 ©Brett Harriman   BrettHarriman.com

Continued from Drivers/Parking, p. 8:
The following examples of **traffic signs** can be commonly seen throughout Austria on its extensive network of roadways.

	Do not enter
	Closed to all vehicles
	One-way street
	No parking
	No parking or stopping
	Autobahn
	Short term parking (Kurzparkzone)
	Tow-away zone (Abschleppzone)
	Traffic circle ahead
	No left turn
	Sharp curve ahead
	Curves ahead
	Crossroad with non-priority road ahead
	No passing
	Road narrows ahead
	Height restricted to 2.9 meters
	Intersection ahead
	Slippery when wet
	Priority road ahead
	Priority road
	Yield
	Uneven road ahead
	Dead end
	Train Xing with barrier ahead
	Train Xing without barrier ahead
	Pedestrian zone
	School bus zone
	Drive slow — residential zone
	Pedestrian crossing
	Horn use not allowed

TRAFFIC SIGNS

meet the author
brett harriman

Brett Harriman grew up in the seaside town of Dana Point, California, and was fortunate enough to have parents who dragged their kids with them everywhere they went, including on overseas vacations. Thus, the travel bug kicked in early.

Brett's writings are inspired by his love of travel, to which he has driven across America, trekked around Australia, and explored Europe extensively. Brett lived in Australia for a decade and in Europe for five years, where he was an official tour guide for the U.S. Armed Forces in Germany. In that role, Brett led more than 10,000 servicemen and women and their families through many historically rich cities, towns, villages and Alpine hamlets.

Brett continues to spend some three months every year in Europe leading tours and updating his guidebooks (trekking across cities and towns knocking on doors and asking a zillion questions, inspecting hotel rooms and looking under mattresses, double checking prices and opening times and transportation schedules, sampling schnitzel and beer and strudel...).

In 2011, for all his hard work, Brett was selected by the president of Oktoberfest to represent the USA during the world-famous festival in Munich, Germany.

When he is not in Europe sleuthing out the latest travel information or on tour, Brett spends his time in Pahrump (55 miles west of Las Vegas), Nevada, where his parents have retired and he finds serene sanctuary to compile and compose his travel book series, tour packages, and publishing business.

Brett Harriman toasting Oktoberfest in Munich, Germany, September 2013

THE END

Join Brett Harriman in Europe
Pick a tour, pack your bags

Belgium Beer & Battlefields tour — July-August 2017

Germany & Austria Highlights tour — September 5-14, 2017

Oktoberfest in Munich, Germany — Sept. 16 thru Oct. 3, 2017

BrettHarriman.com

Complement this guide with other Harriman books and resources

Every year our brand recognition increases across the world together with our array of destination guides and tour programs.

If you're headed to Germany, Austria or Belgium, let us educate you with local knowledge and history so you can make informed decisions that save time, as well as money, while leading to new adventures and acquaintances abroad.

To minimize the advent of stale news and maximize the value of your dollar, we strive to set the gold standard when conducting our research.

So come along, and travel like a local — *your journey begins now!*

Coming soon

Coming soon

Harriman novel

Free on our site

Printed in Great Britain
by Amazon